CALIFORNIA

WOMEN ON THE MOVE

*A series of Books on the American West and Midwest
by Women who Traveled and Settled there
between 1835 and 1877*

Mrs Frank Leslie

MRS. FRANK LESLIE, *Miriam*

CALIFORNIA

A PLEASURE TRIP FROM

GOTHAM TO THE GOLDEN GATE
APRIL, MAY, JUNE, 1877

(1877)

FACSIMILE
With an Introduction by
MADELEINE B. STERN

NIEUWKOOP * B. DE GRAAF
1972

Facsimile of the edition New York, 1877.
ISBN 90 6004 304 9
LC 72-86546

INTRODUCTION

Mrs. Frank Leslie took her *Pleasure Trip from Gotham to the Golden Gate* in 1877 — a crucial period in the history of westward expansion in the United States. The journey fell almost midway between 1860, when the trans-Missouri West was wilderness and much of the land belonged to Indian tribes roaming the plains and subsisting on buffalo, and 1890, when the earth had been tunneled by miners, the Indians were undergoing the process of "civilization," the buffalo were all but extinct, and the frontier no longer existed.[1]

A prime factor in this dramatic metamorphosis was the railroad which linked the Atlantic and Pacific coasts.[2] On May 10, 1869, at Promontory Point, Utah, the meeting of the Union Pacific and the Central Pacific lines had been celebrated by a nation still recovering from the tragedy of civil war. It had been an historic rendezvous, for it heralded at once the exhilarating expansion of the country and the end to its frontier. Upon miles of track the coach-wheel brought miners and cattlemen, farmers and immigrants to settle the American West. During the spectacular 'seventies the Age of the Pioneer gave way to the Age of Steel.

At this significant moment, the Leslie journey was undertaken and its events recorded by a woman who produced in her graphic vignettes of western life — its Indians, scouts and miners — a colorful source for Western Americana. But Mrs. Leslie's *California* is distinguished from most travel books of the American West because the journey she describes was neither rugged nor austere but lavish and luxurious. She viewed the West from the vantage point not of a pioneer woman but of a

1. Allan Nevins and Henry Steele Commager, *The Pocket History of the United States* (New York [1951]), pp. 309-310.

2. Louis B. Wright, *Life on the American Frontier* (New York [1971]), pp. 206-209.

flamboyant *grande dame,* and in writing her history she achieved not merely a solid contribution to American travel literature but a fresh and original, if at times disdainful, version of western life during a time of startling change.

Her own background motivated her point of view and many of the events in her remarkable career culminated in the journey she narrated. Her book is in a sense a mirror of herself. To appreciate it to the full, the reader must therefore acquaint himself with the extraordinary life and dazzling personality of its author.[3]

Between 1836, when she was born in New Orleans, and 1914, when she died in New York, Mrs. Frank Leslie, under a variety of names, lived many lives. As Miriam Florence Follin, illegitimate daughter of Charles Follin (a descendant of French Huguenots) and of Susan Danforth (daughter of a Revolutionary soldier) she spent her early years in the colorful Vieux Carré of New Orleans, Queen City of the Mississippi. There she was educated by her father to develop into a *grande dame* and to this end she was tutored privately in French and Spanish, Italian, German and Latin. The copper-haired gray-eyed Miriam proved an apt pupil in most philological mysteries, especially in the idiom of romance.

At the age of eighteen, after the family had removed to New York, she experienced a short, forced and unsavory union with a jeweler's clerk who for a brief period gave her the name of Mrs. David Charles Peacock. This marriage, which ended in separation, was to play an extremely important part in the history of *California: A Pleasure Trip from Gotham to the Golden Gate.* Its sensational details were placed on record in a Judgment Roll in New York's Supreme Court — a Judgment

3. Madeleine B. Stern, *Purple Passage: The Life of Mrs. Frank Leslie* (Norman, Okla., [1953], reprinted Norman, Okla., [1971]), *passim.* Throughout, all biographical details are based upon this, the only full-length life of Mrs. Leslie.

Roll which, many years later, would be aired in an attempt to ruin the author of certain derogatory statements in that seemingly innocuous travel book.

Long before that time the charming and beautiful Miriam played other roles under other intriguing names. She took to the road as "Minnie Montez," stage sister of the legendary adventuress, Lola Montez. That association also had connections with Mrs. Leslie's interest in the West for it had been in the mining settlement of Grass Valley, California, that the actress Lola Montez had met Miriam Follin's half-brother Noel Follin. Noel's letters from California undoubtedly aroused in his young half-sister an early interest in the background of the American West. His own interest had been aroused in the spectacular Lola, whom he accompanied on a theatrical tour to Australia. On board ship Noel Follin either fell or was thrown overboard. In her remorse at this tragedy Lola Montez journeyed east, offered her services to the Follin family, and took young Miriam under her histrionic wing.

Such dramatic skills as she mastered sped her on the way to becoming the embodiment of grace. By the time Miriam was twenty-one she conquered the impressive scholar and celebrated archeologist, Ephraim George Squier, to whom she was married in 1857. She remained Mrs. E.G. Squier for fifteen tumultuous years in the course of which she translated Alexandre Dumas' *Demi-Monde*, attended Lincoln's first inaugural ball, and whetted her taste for travel in journeys to Europe and Peru. During that period she also met the publishing magnate who would introduce her to life on Publishers' Row and to the fascinations of the American West. He would also become, after her divorce from Squier, her third husband.

Frank Leslie, with his lively eyes and ruddy, bearded face, was a man of energy, vigor and dynamic magnetism. His *Illustrated Newspaper* had made him a power on Publishers' Row. Into its folio pages he poured just enough text to float his pictures instead of just enough pictures to adorn his text.

Having gauged the public taste with skillful precision, he catered to it promptly, providing avid readers with graphic renditions of the murders and executions, the wars and prize fights that titillated their appetite. In time he would provide them with pictures of a West opened up by the iron horse.

Meanwhile, with a host of other weeklies and monthlies, almanacs and illustrated books appearing over his imprint, the name of Frank Leslie was becoming a household word. The well-known archeologist, E.G. Squier, joined the editorial staff of what was swiftly developing into a publishing empire, and in 1863 his wife became editor of *Frank Leslie's Lady's Magazine*. To her various skills Miriam now added the arts of flowery prose writing and editorial acumen. From her editorial corner she watched the House of Leslie expand until it employed from three to four hundred assistants including seventy wood engravers and boasted an aggregate circulation of some half a million copies per week.[4]

To her study of the arts of publishing Miriam joined an equally intense study of the arts of the publisher. It was inevitable that, after a sensational divorce from the now unbalanced E.G. Squier, she should acquire yet another name — Mrs. Frank Leslie. On July 13, 1874, the thirty-eight-year-old editor of a woman's magazine was married to the suave and elegant fifty-three-year-old magnate of Publishers' Row. One month later, E.G. Squier was committed to an asylum for the insane, a circumstance that would also assume some part in the history of Mrs. Frank Leslie's *California*.

Luxuriously, prodigally, against an ornate background in

4. Madeleine B. Stern, *Imprints on History: Book Publishers and American Frontiers* (Bloomington, Ind., 1956), pp. 221-232. Frank Leslie's method of producing his pictures marked an innovation in the art of illustration. Dividing the woodblock into small sections so that a number of engravers could work on the same picture at the same time before the wooden squares were screwed together, he completed large double-page engravings in a single night instead of in two weeks.

New York or at their summer seat in Saratoga Springs, the Leslies lived out their life together. The hospitable host and radiant hostess entertained lavishly and among the notables who graced their table were General Ulysses S. Grant and a variety of United States Senators; Don Carlos, pretender to the throne of Spain; Dom Pedro, Emperor of Brazil; and Joaquin Miller, the Poet of the Sierras, who could tell many a racy tale of Indians, mining camp and pony express.

In 1869, after the completion of the transcontinental railroad, Frank Leslie had sent a staff artist to record the journey for his *Illustrated Newspaper*. Now, in 1877, a year after the United States Centennial celebration, the Leslies decided to make the journey themselves. To their fascination with the country's developing network of railroads — which offered their services free in return for Leslie publicity — was added their intense interest in the West. To enrich the columns of Leslie's weekly with descriptions and illustrations of frontier landscapes and western towns, Frank Leslie assembled his traveling entourage. As for Mrs. Frank Leslie, she would provide the public with a record of the journey in a book that reflected the allure both of her own extraordinary personality and of the American West during the exuberant 'seventies.

On April 10, 1877, the party of twelve editors, journalists and artists assembled at New York's Grand Central Station. Besides the Leslies (and Miriam's Skye terrier Follette) the travelers included their friends the Hackleys, the writers Edwin A. Curley and Bracebridge Hemyng, the artists Miss Georgiana A. Davis, Water R. Yeager and Harry Ogden, the photographer W.B. Austin, the business manager Hamilton S. Wicks, and W.K. Rice, son of the Governor of Massachusetts. They watched while champagne baskets and hampers were loaded onto the sumptuous "Palace" car that had been renamed the "Frank Leslie." Amid cheers and waving handkerchiefs, whistles and the exploding of signal torpedoes, the train pulled out of the station and one of the most lavish nineteenth-century transcontinental journeys began. The two-month Leslie excursion would cost $15,000 despite the fact that the railroad service was free. Its details would be recorded in a lengthy succession of articles that would run in *Frank Leslie's Illustrated Newspaper* between April 1877 and May 1878.[5]

In her own special way Miriam Leslie would capture the highlights of the spectacular extravaganza known as the Leslie Transcontinental Excursion. Her perceptive observations would be filtered through the crucible of her own personality. She would produce no dry-as-dust run-of-the-mill baedeker, but a book filled with personalized comments on miners and Indians, tycoons and magnates, on the moral climate of San Francisco and the "Prunes, Prisms, and Propriety" to which she was exposed. Despite her often flowery style, despite an occasional looking down the nose at western crudities, she would reflect the social consciousness of a responsible woman in a position of some power as she aired a genuine indignation at social injustices toward the Orientals of California. "Let the nineteenth century answer," she would write, taking notes from the vantage point of a hotel on wheels, watching the kaleidoscopic parade of America flash by. Her book would be the product not of the hardworking pioneer woman settler but of the exalted woman visitor from the East. As such it would present a study in sharp contrast to the earlier record of such a traveler as Eliza

5. The start of the journey was described in *Frank Leslie's Illustrated Newspaper* (April 28, 1877), pp. 140-141. The series "Across the Continent" ran in *Frank Leslie's Illustrated Newspaper* between July 7, 1877 and May 25, 1878, with some western features running later. Some of those articles were reprinted in Richard Reinhardt, *Out West on the Overland Train* (Palo Alto, Calif., [1967]). See also Robert Taft, "The Pictorial Record of the Old West, XI. The Leslie Excursions of 1869 and 1877," *The Kansas Historical Quarterly* (May 1950), reprinted in Robert Taft, *Artists and Illustrators of the Old West: 1850-1900* (New York, 1953). Quotations are from Mrs. Leslie's *California*.

Farnham[6] and it would offer a view of western life that few other women could have duplicated.

"The nineteenth century," Mrs. Leslie wrote, "flies upon the coach-wheel." To this now all but obsolete method of transportation she gave particular attention and her notes on railroad travel in 1877 have an extraordinary fascination. In Chicago the Wagner Palace Car with its curtained couches and divans, its salon and ornamental panels, was exchanged for a Pullman Palace Car named the "President" which had cost $35,000 to build and had recently been exhibited at the Centennial Exposition. Its kitchen boasted a mammoth roaster and a charcoal broiler; its refrigerator and larder were contained in boxes beneath the car. Fish was caught en route, trout and antelope were foraged for by the conductor. The Leslie party enjoyed Delmonican repasts as they sped by at twenty miles an hour while the coyote howled outside. Subsequently other trains would be described by the author – the Pacific Railroad, "the road of the world," a private Palace car that was "a perfect little *bijou*," a train on a narrow-gauge road, an emigrant car, a Pullman accommodating an editorial party from Nebraska "on board with a small press, on which they printed the daily journal of their travels." As the Leslie party moved farther west, a stand of arms was carried in the baggage car for protection against highwaymen. Astutely Mrs. Leslie saw connections between the coming of the railroad and the introduction of tokens of "civilization." As she would remark to a Mormon Elder, "the railway has come and brought a whole train of French milliners and fashion plates," imports which, in the eyes of the high-styled Mrs. Leslie, must result in the elevation and enlightenment of women and hence in the eventual decline of polygamy.

Long before her encounters with the Mormons, Mrs. Frank

6. Eliza Farnham, *California, In-Doors and Out* (New York, 1856, reprinted Nieuwkoop, Netherlands, 1972).

Leslie took careful notes on a West that sat for its portrait while the nineteenth century ran upon the coach-wheel. The wooden pavements of Chicago — "a city of magnificent beginnings" — gave way to the bluffs of Omaha with its bearded emigrants in alligator boots, its border ruffians and gambling sharps, its miners and Indians. The dramatis personae was enlarged at Fremont, where loose-limbed Westerners and tourists in linen dusters joined the gallery of mounting portraits. Through the Platte Valley they sped, on to Cheyenne — "the Magic City of the Plains" — where the party alighted. Scouts in sealskin caps and fringed buckskin, Mexicans, teamsters, miners en route to the Black Hills, crowded the streets of this "Town of a Day," this "straggling settlement of wooden houses." At McDaniel's Theatre — its "bar gorgeous with frescoed views of Vesuvius and the Bay of Naples," its stage wings adorned with statues of the Venus de Medici and "another undressed lady of colossal proportions," the redoubtable Mrs. Leslie observed the injunction printed in bold letters above the bar: "Gents, be liberal."

Miriam drew her prose vignettes of frontier life as rolling prairie gave way to low bluffs, canyons and buttes to the grand sweep of mountains. The backdrop shifted. Herds of cattle and wild horses dotted the landscape, log houses and sagebrush, canvas-topped wagons and cinnamon bears, a stream of Mormons and Chinese laborers along the railroad. While she held her aristocratic nose at repulsive-looking braves in striped blankets, she was enthralled by moonlight on the white alkali patches of the desert. On the planked sidewalks of Carson City, Indians lounged in their calico rags and red paint. After the snows of the Sierras, the valley of the Sacramento lay before her. The background and characters of a continent captured in her notebook, Miriam Leslie had arrived at the City of the Golden Gate.

San Francisco unfolded its colors and contrasts to the perceptive editorial eye of the *grande dame* from Gotham. The

Leslie party was ensconced in the suite at the Palace Hotel recently occupied by Dom Pedro, Emperor of Brazil. Warren Leland, prince of landlords, welcomed them to the fabulous seven-storied caravansery of the West with its tiers of balconies, its palms and banana trees, its fountains and Doric columns. From this ornate and plush background they emerged for their encounter with San Francisco in the spectacular 'seventies. There, Mrs. Leslie observed, "the climate, like the society, like the morals, and like the social habits . . . is a little mixed." As she walked the streets of the city on the Pacific she saw a sideshow of fortune-telling monkeys and howling dervishes, prestidigitators and patent medicine dealers. Shop windows were resplendent with oriental carpets and Chinese brocades. From the wooden wharves and jetties she could note the flags of many nations flying from the masts of their ships. The Russian fleet, lying in harbor, would shortly sail at proclamation of the Russo-Turkish War. San Francisco was cosmopolis to this completely cosmopolitan visitor who "saw very elegant toilets, and very fine jewels, both in carriages and upon pedestrians to whom we had no letters of introduction."

To most of the city's bigwigs the Leslies did have introductions. Mayor Bryant drove them about behind his elegant four-in-hand. The Nevada Senator William Sharon, now a California Croesus, invited them to his country estate at Belmont — a palace filled with all the luxuries known to man save one: "We did not, in all that mansion, see a book, or a bookcase, or any spot where one might fitly have been placed, or expected to be placed! " Coleman, owner of the whole of the San Rafael valley, invited them for the day and Ex-Governor Stanford was their host at dinner in "the most magnificent house on this Continent."

From the Barbary Coast to the county jail, from Woodward's Gardens to the Mission Dolores, the visitors wandered. Chinatown, seen under the guidance of a detective, was especially interesting to Mrs. Leslie, who attended Scene 102 of Act 53 at the Royal Chinese Theatre, made her own obeisances at a Joss House, and wandered through a honeycomb of rooms in an opium den. "The cry of 'cheap labor,' " she would write, "so furiously raised against the Chinese, principally by the classes to whom any labor is abhorrent, is as unfounded as it is malicious. A good man-cook in a family gets $35.00 per month, and a waiter $25.00. . . . Whether we like him or not, the Chinaman in California has become a fixed fact, and one not to be done away with except by giving the lie to our own Institutions."

At the suggestion of "Lucky" Baldwin, another California tycoon, the Leslies visited his ranch at Santa Anita, near Los Angeles. The "semi-tropical air" of Los Angeles impressed Miriam immediately. Its shops, "most of them open to the street," its abundance of fruits and flowers that made one feel as if "promenading the hall of an Agricultural Fair," its Mexican women in mantillas, its Spanish and Chinese were all grist for the mill of the note-taking woman editor from Publishers' Row, who commented: "Los Angeles has, within ten years, become a 'live' American city, and might in one sense date its existence from about that time, although in another claiming a century's growth. At any rate, like some other creatures of an uncertain age, Los Angeles is more charming on acquaintance than at first sight." Of apparently certain age was the so-called oldest woman in the world, Eulalia Pérez, whom Mrs. Leslie interviewed in Spanish. Claiming to be one hundred forty, with grandchildren of eighty, Eulalia made the astute and flattering comment that her interviewer need not have "married a man with white hair."

A tour of the Yosemite completed the California extravaganza. On the way, Miriam enlarged her studies in contrasts with a night at Cold Spring Station, a settlement consisting of two houses and a watering trough. In a three-room cabin — half posting house and half grocery shop — the party passed a memorable night in the course of which Mrs. Leslie concocted a meal and slept on the supper table, pillowing her coiffured head on a bag of salt. She had brought not only her fashion but her

XVI

fortitude to the West.

Having observed much of the high life and some of the low life of California, Miriam was prepared to return home with her husband, her friends and her notes. The journey back was marked by sojourns at two unusual cities which called into play all of her descriptive powers. Indeed, her delineations proved so graphic that their documentary value is matched only by their biographical interest.

Virginia City, Nevada, was a mining town that had sprung up in the wake of the Comstock Lode. Although its C Street presented to the passer-by a succession of saloons, opium dens and brothels, the town was proud of its history and its mines, its International Hotel and its newspaper, the *Territorial Enterprise,* on whose staff Mark Twain had worked. Frank Leslie, who was almost as interested in silver mining as in railroads, explored the depths of Virginia's Bonanza Mine while his wife explored the shabby streets perched halfway up the Nevada Mountains. Her conclusions, shortly to be published in the penultimate chapter of her book, were devastating:

> To call a place dreary, desolate, homeless, uncomfortable, and wicked is a good deal, but to call it God-forsaken is a good deal more, and in a tolerably large experience of this world's wonders, we never found a place better deserving the title than Virginia City.

The remainder of Chapter XXXII would substantiate her generalizations. Virginia's architectural style, she observed, might perhaps be inferred "from the fact that about two years ago the whole town burned down one night, and was rebuilt as good as ever in six days." "Every other house," she continued, "was a drinking or gambling saloon, and we passed a great many brilliantly lighted windows, where sat audacious looking women who freely chatted with passers-by or entertained guests within." An evening stroll was possible only with a police escort. In sum: "Virginia City boasts of forty-nine gambling saloons and one church, open the day we were there for a funeral, an event of frequent occurrence in the lawless little city. The population is largely masculine, very few women, except of the worst class, and as few children." Mrs. Leslie was apparently unaware that one member of Virginia City's masculine population was Rollin M. Daggett, the fighting editor of the town's *Territorial Enterprise,* who had not merely a chauvinistic pride in the city of the Comstock Lode, but close connections with her second husband E.G. Squier.

Eager to forget Virginia's assay office and wooden shacks, its prostitutes and gamblers, the erstwhile Mrs. Squier turned her attention to another city whose laws interested her more closely than the lawlessness of the Bonanza town. Although the Leslie party had visited Salt Lake City, Utah, on the westward trip, they were sufficiently curious about Mormonism to make a repeat stop on the homeward journey. The Mormon doctrine and practice of polygamy especially interested the oft-wed Mrs. Leslie. Indeed its beneficent economic effects were borne out as the party approached the "verdant fields" and neat cottages, the schoolhouses and co—operative store of a Mormon settlement. As Mrs. Leslie succinctly phrased it, "Certainly, polygamy is very wrong, but roses are better than sage-brush, and potatoes and peas preferable as diet to buffalo grass." Whenever opportunity offered she seized the occasion to inter-view Mormons on the intriguing and debatable subject. From Salt Lake's photographer and editor, banker, merchant and Elders she elicited opinions. Miss Snow, widow of the Mormon leader Joseph Smith and at present temporarily "sealed" to Brigham Young, announced, "We consider ourselves among the finest women in the world, and aim to compete with our sisters elsewhere in every pursuit and every branch of education." When the persistent interviewer inquired "if the various wives of one husband got along amicably among themselves, . . . she decisively replied: 'Perfectly so, their religion inculcates it; and besides, their work is so large, and their aims so high, that they have no time and no capacity for petty jealousies.' "

Having observed President Brigham Young's background – his residence the Lion House, the Beehive House that housed a dozen of his wives, the schoolhouse for his seventy children, the Mormon Tabernacle, Mrs. Leslie approached with alacrity the Mormon leader himself, for none was better equipped to discuss the "peculiar institution of Utah." Under her skillful questioning, the interview which began perfunctorily gathered momentum. "Do you suppose, Mr. President, that I came all the way to Salt Lake City to hear that it was a fine day? " " 'I am sure you need not, my dear,' was the ready response of this cavalier of seventy-six years, 'for it must be fine weather wherever you are!' The conversation established after this method went upon velvet."

Seated on the sacred sofa, Mrs. Frank Leslie quickly captivated the Mormon President who, looking like a well-fed Senator, allowed himself to be drawn out on Mormon history and Mormon doctrine, Mormon wives and Mormon husbands, domestic relations and the eugenics of Mormonism. The children, he informed her, were trained from infancy to respect the concepts of polygamy. But who, she demanded, trained the mothers? "What religion can make a woman happy in seeing the husband whom she loves devoted to another wife, and one with equal claims with herself. Any woman, I should think, would spend all her strength, use every effort of mind, body and soul, to attract and retain his love, admiration and attention. Isn't it so, Mr. President? " With an "inquisitorial glance" at his astute and seductive interviewer, Mr. President replied: "You look like just the woman to do that sort of thing, but fortunately, perhaps, there are not many of that mind among us." "Do Mormon husbands feel no preferences? " she persisted. "Well, perhaps," Brigham Young replied, "human nature is frail, but our religion teaches us to control and conceal those preferences as much as possible, and we do – we do."

With so quotable an interview trapped in her notebook,

Mrs. Leslie headed east. On June 7, the party returned to New York — and to the crisis of 1877. The expenses of the transcontinental excursion, coupled with large personal debts, the over-expansion of the Frank Leslie Publishing House on the one hand and the decline in circulation of its publications on the other — all had contributed to a disastrous financial situation. Leslie faced it by making a temporary assignment of his property for the benefit of his creditors and by serving as general manager of the establishment he had founded.

Meanwhile, the series of illustrated articles headed "Across the Continent" continued to appear in *Frank Leslie's Illustrated Newspaper* and Mrs. Frank Leslie polished up her own notes of the journey. In December 1877, *California: A Pleasure Trip from Gotham to the Golden Gate* was issued by G.W. Carleton & Co. of New York, publishers of the popular humor of "Josh Billings" and "Artemus Ward," as well as of numerous other best-sellers. Carleton's device — the Arabic symbol for "books" which, upside down, seemed to spell his initials — was imprinted now on Mrs. Leslie's contribution to the literature of travel.[7]

The reviews must have gratified her. They were widely distributed, appearing in *The Evening Post* and the *New York Herald,* the *Providence Journal* and, of course, *Frank Leslie's Lady's Journal.* According to *The Sun,* "the author brought, to unusual opportunities of social study, the taste and insight of a cultivated woman, and a happy faculty of description," while another review went so far as to assert, "Had Madame de Sévigné been able to perform a journey from New York to San Francisco . . . she would have written some such a work as Mrs. Leslie's." The consensus was that she had written "a charming account of a charming trip," a "pleasantly written" history.[8]

7. Stern, *Imprints on History, op.cit.,* pp. 191-205.

8. For reviews, see *The Evening Post* (December 27, 1877), p. 1; *Frank Leslie's Lady's Journal* (January 5 and January 19, 1878), pp. 130 and 162; *New York Herald* (January 27, 1878), p. 6; *Providence Journal* (December 31, 1877), p. 1; *The Sun* (April 7, 1878), p. 2.

It was not until July 14, 1878 that the charm and pleasantness of Mrs. Leslie's *California* were ruthlessly challenged. Virginia City's *Territorial Enterprise* of that date devoted its entire mammoth-sized front page to an article entitled: OUR FEMALE SLANDERER. MRS. FRANK LESLIE'S BOOK SCANDALIZING THE FAMILIES OF VIRGINIA CITY — THE HISTORY OF THE AUTHORESS — A LIFE DRAMA OF CRIME AND LICENTIOUSNESS — STARTLING DEVELOPMENTS. A twenty-four-page pamphlet of the same date entitled TERRITORIAL ENTERPRISE EXTRA. CONTAINING A FULL ACCOUNT OF "FRANK LESLIE" AND WIFE reprinted the vicious exposé in handy format.[9] Miriam Leslie's derogatory remarks about Virginia City, which would shortly be substantiated by Mrs. M.M. Mathews in her *Ten Years in Nevada*,[10] had instigated a detailed and baneful series of revelations. From Miriam's illegitimate birth to the episodes with David Peacock and Lola Montez, from her extra-marital activities to her divorce from E.G. Squier, the sordid details of her "strange, eventful history" were maliciously aired. Based largely upon the Peacock Judgment Roll which had been supplied by E.G. Squier, the *Territorial Enterprise Extra* formed a defamatory indictment far more damaging than the remarks that had provoked it. Leslie's efforts to buy up every copy were not entirely successful, and the violent excoriation with its Virginia City imprint provides today not only a sought-for piece of Western Americana but a fascinating insight into Mrs. Frank

9. *Daily Territorial Enterprise* (Virginia, Nevada, July 14, 1878), p. 1; reprinted as *Territorial Enterprise Extra. Containing A Full Account of "Frank Leslie" and Wife* (Virginia City, Nevada, 1878). See also Madeleine B. Stern, "Mrs. Leslie Goes West," *The Book Club of California Quarterly News Letter* (Fall 1959), pp. 77-80.

10. Mrs. M.M. Mathews, *Ten Years in Nevada* (Buffalo, 1880), p. 193: "Many of the men support more women than the law allows them. They live after the Salt Lake style . . . .. Here they marry but one, and the unmarried ones are always dressed the richest."

Leslie's early life and her *Pleasure Trip from Gotham to the Golden Gate.*

She would survive both the fulminating indictment and other disasters that followed it. Indeed the events of her later life were as dramatic as those of her salad days. After Frank Leslie's death in 1880, Miriam inherited not only the Publishing House but its debts and opportunities. She paid the former and developed the latter by capitalizing upon an event of national importance. President Garfield's assassination in 1881, his lingering illness and death provided material for a journalistic coup that re-established the bankrupt publishing empire. By issuing three illustrated papers in a single week to fill the public demand for graphic reports of the brutal tragedy, Miriam Leslie – who changed her name legally to "Frank Leslie" – made money and history. Her tour de force was an achievement unparalleled in the newspaper world. As head of the House which phoenix-like had risen from the ashes, she herself became an almost legendary figure on Publishers' Row. Reorganizing every department of her business, she was acclaimed an "Empress of Journalism," a "commercial Joan of Arc."

Meanwhile her private life kept pace with her public career, as the "Empress of Journalism" enacted the role of *femme fatale.* A French marquis, a Russian prince and a Spanish grandee slipped eventually in and out of her net. In 1891, when she was fifty-five, she married Oscar Wilde's brother, William Charles Kingsbury Wilde – her last matrimonial adventure which, like the first two, was to end in divorce. By the time she died in 1914 after the outbreak of the First World War, she left a fortune of nearly two million dollars to the cause of woman suffrage – a windfall that doubled the impetus of the movement in America. The woman who all her life had lived woman's rights helped carry the cause to certain victory after her death.

Before her dramatic departure from the earthly scene, Miriam made two return trips to the California she had described in 1877. In 1892 the first annual convention of the International League of Press Clubs was held in the City of the Golden Gate. Willie Wilde and his wife, "Frank Leslie," were members of the party that left Grand Central and journeyed by rail to the West. In the course of her speech on "Reminiscences of a Woman's Work in Journalism," delivered at the League's Open Session, Miriam spoke of her deep desire to revisit San Francisco since it had been after her return from that city fifteen years before that she had met "the great crisis of her life." Once again, in 1910, after she had adopted yet another name — that of Baroness de Bazus, which she claimed as a family title — the *grande dame* returned to San Francisco. The city had weathered fire and earthquake and had changed as markedly as the author of *California: A Pleasure Trip from Gotham to the Golden Gate.* Now in her seventies, Miriam was a guest of the Pacific Coast's women's press association. For the benefit of a reporter at the old Palace Hotel she once again relived the exuberant days of the Leslie Transcontinental Excursion of thirty-three years before.

Both the excursion and the book that recorded it deserve a niche in American travel literature. Mrs. Frank Leslie was the author of several other books — largely inconsequential commentaries on social life that bear no comparison with her major work on California. As the account of a high-style journey to the West at a significant moment in American history, the record is a valuable one. Its vivid and graphic sketches of railroad travel and western settlements enrich our knowledge of the American background during the 1870's. The viewpoint of the sophisticated woman from the East heightens the interest of her observations. The work adds to our knowledge both of the West and of Mrs. Frank Leslie, and so it is invested with documentary and biographical importance.

The book which incited such a violent reaction after its publication has now become scarce and sought after. Nearly one hundred years after its original appearance it is at last reprinted. The twentieth century may thus be reminded of a nineteenth century that ran grandiosely on the coach-wheel to a California gaudy with contrasts, and of the fascinations of the woman who recorded the journey and painted a scene that she herself adorned.

CALIFORNIA.

A

PLEASURE TRIP

FROM

NEW YORK TO SAN FRANCISCO.

Crossing Dale Creek Bridge—130 Feet High.

CALIFORNIA

A

PLEASURE TRIP

FROM

GOTHAM TO THE GOLDEN GATE.

(APRIL, MAY, JUNE, 1877.)

BY

MRS. FRANK LESLIE.

PROFUSELY ILLUSTRATED.

NEW YORK:

G. W. Carleton & Co., Publishers.

LONDON: S. LOW, SON & CO.

MDCCCLXXVII.

Trow's
Printing and Bookbinding Company,
205-213 East 12th St.,
NEW YORK.

PREFATORY, TO THE READER.

D EAR five hundred friends already mine, and five hundred hundred more, who will, as I fondly dream, become mine through these pages, let me disarm criticism beforehand by assuring you that nobody could point out a fault or a shortcoming in this little book, which I do not know all about and deplore most modestly beforehand. In fact I have my doubts as to calling it a book at all, that title implying a purpose, and deliberateness, and method, which are not of my circle, although regarded by me with respectful admiration. No, let us rather say, that this work of mine is a vehicle, through which, with feminine longing for sympathy, I convey to you my pleasures, annoyances, and experiences in the journey it narrates; or, if you like better, it is a casket, enshrining the memory of many a pleasant hour made bright and indelible by your companionship, your kindness, your attention and hospitality.

The world is so *exigeant*, and Time the Effacer is so ruthless, that one loves sometimes to "materialize" those pleasant, or more than pleasant recollections, and so put them not only beyond the risk of loss from one's own memory, but in such form that they can be communicated anew to those who originally shared them.

Take then my embodied recollections, dear friends, and each of you find among them the one memory distinctively your own, and believe that round that central point all the rest are constellated; and for you, O critics! if you will indeed attempt to bind a butterfly upon the wheel, or anatomize the vapory visions of a woman's memory, remember that in all courtesy you should deal gently and generously with a work proclaiming itself from the outset not so much a book as a long gossipy letter to one's friends, and an amiable attempt to convey to the rest of the world some of the delight it commemorates, and if you do not find a great deal in it, dear critic, remember that to competently judge a woman's letter or a woman's book, one must have learned to read between the lines and find there the pith and meaning of the whole.

M. FLORENCE LESLIE.

NEW YORK, November, 1877.

LIST OF ILLUSTRATIONS.

CONTENTS.

―――――

STREET IN THE CHINESE QUARTER, SAN FRANCISCO.   Page 144.

FROM GOTHAM TO FRISCO

CHAPTER I.

THE BEGINNING.

DOES anybody like the beginning of anything? To our mind the well-known French proverb about the first step bears a deeper meaning than is usually attributed to it, and is intended not so much as an encouragement to doubters as for a Hafiz-like warning against the folly of ever beginning anything after the inevitable annoyance of beginning one's life. The beginning of a dinner, of a ball, of a play, of a day, of an acquaintance, of a book, of a pair of boots, does anybody like any of these? Even the beginning of a love, can it compare with its earliest noontide? And as for the beginning of an end, whether of lives or empires, who can doubt that Ariadne's death-blow fell when Perseus cast his first wistful glance toward the open sea, and that Moscow was a feller stroke to the great Emperor than St. Helena.

So let us hasten over the beginning of our journey toward the Golden Gate, artfully promising for those who shall patiently begin and continue as we began and continued, richer and fairer things are reserved in the end.

Briefly, then, we state that, passing from the chilly

gloom of an April night of this present year of grace
into the terminus of the N. Y. Central R. R., twelve
somewhat wearied, somewhat nervous, very expectant
persons, accompanied by the friends to whom William
Vanderbilt Rex had issued an ukase permitting them
to pass the dismal gates which ordinarily divide,
rigidly as that of death, the outward-bound passenger
from those he loves and leaves, found prepared for
them a special and magnificent car, named by Mr.
Wagner for the Chief of our party, took possession,
went through the round of leave-takings, from the
tremulous silent embrace and last, deep look, to the
cheery, careless hand pressure and gay parting word,
heard the conductor's warning cry of "Time's up," and
were off, amid the reverberating roar of the fusilade
arranged by Mr. Wagner as a parting compliment to
his friends, and the hearty cheers of the escorting party
left upon the platform.

A few tears quietly brushed away, some clearing of
suddenly husky throats, and the travelers begin to
look about them at the quarters already representing
home and home comforts to wearied minds and bodies.
And here let us suggest, that added inducements to
timid and conservative tourists could be held forth by
changing the name of such a cosmos as this car of ours
from "palace" or "drawing-room" to "home" cars, or
some equivalent title, for who that has wintered in
Italy would be tempted to accept a palace as his
perpetual residence, and who would desire to sit for a
week in a drawing-room, clad in body and mind as be-
fits the ceremonious reception of the world, with one's

mask well tied on, and one's skeleton safely locked
away !

So the charming little residence in which we found
ourselves shall be called a home, and very soon assumed the pleasant aspect suggested by the word, as
the bouquets, shawls, rugs, sofa-cushions, and various
personalities of the three ladies of the party were developed and arranged upon or around a table in the
central division of the car, which was to represent the
general *salon*, our end being partitioned off by curtains
to serve as bowers for such of the party as had given
hostages to society in the shape of husband or wife;
while the other end, also screened by curtains, became
a pleasant Bohemia where the artists, *littérateurs* and
photographers of the party sleep and work.

Bed seems a good place to everybody at an early
hour in this beginning evening, for bed is one of the
few exceptions to the great rule laid down in our first
sentences, and to a weary traveler it is pleasanter to lie
down at night than to rise up in the morning; unless,
indeed, at the Yosemite, and that is not yet.

So we watch with interest the lowering of the ornamental panels behind which are stowed capital mat-
tresses, gay blankets, sufficient pillows and snowy
linen, admire the deft dexterity of the pleasant official
who, with these, converts our sofas into cozy, curtained
couches, and presently retire to find within their shades
the sweet sleep which never comes too soon or stays
too late.

The conductor has warned us we shall find our
breakfast at Rochester about half - past ten in the

morning, and although the gay Bohemians at the other
end of the car have seized an earlier opportunity of
breaking their fast, we, the graver portion of the
party, decorously restrain our unwonted appetites until
the appointed hour and place, when we are rewarded
by so enjoyable a meal that, whether it were the late-
ness of the hour, the merit of the viands, or the
unusual fatigue and excitement which gave it zest,
deserves and shall receive a red-letter mark in these
annals.

At Rochester our car is switched off and connected
with a train bound for Niagara, and presently the Suspension Bridge and mighty Cataract are in view. Of
course we pause to visit the Falls, for some of our
party have never seen them, and the rest are but too
happy to see them as often as possible. Passing
quickly through the poor little town, whose closed
hotels and desolate shops look forlorn and hopeless in
this dull season, we reach the Park, and presently stand
beside the mighty mass of moving waters, whose slow,
resistless sweep, " not hasting or resting," calm in the
magnitude of their power, relentless as death to those
who affront them, careless as Destiny of those who do
not venture within their grasp, solemn as eternity,
terrible and beautiful as life; so the vast waters pour
their ceaseless flood century after century, while generations of mortals stand beside them, gaze, wonder,
make their idle comments, and pass away to die and
be forgotten, while still the mighty flood sweeps on
and down changeless and immortal.

It is finally conceded that the best effects of color

are to be obtained at Prospect Point, close beside the American Fall; there one may admire the profound blue-green, like the finest turquoise, of the deep and narrow stream; the clear, cold beryl tint of the Fall itself, and the snow-white steam and vapor and spray lighting up the whole.

Just to the right of the Fall, at its foot, lay a great, rounded hill of ice, the accumulation of the Winter's frozen spray, and close beside this hill runs down, at an angle of thirty-three degrees, the steep plane of the inclined railway. We took passage in its queer cars, arranged like a series of carpeted stairs, and were wheeled down at terrific speed to a point where an admirable upward view of the Cataract was to be obtained, but as the snow still lingering on the ground was of a melting and penetrating mood, we did not linger long, but, crossing over the Suspension Bridge to the Canada side, the familiar view of the Horseshoe Fall came in sight, and we looked down into the blue depths of the channel, two hundred and four feet at this point, according to our driver.

Upon the Canada side it is quite easy to distinguish the voices of the two Falls—the deep, thunderous roar of the Horseshoe Fall, and the more rippling and silvery voice of the American; and after one has passed the wonder and excitement of a first visit to this great marvel of Nature in listening silently and alone to this vast antiphony of the two wonderful voices, and in contemplating the mighty march of the unhastening, unresting flood, now sliding along a solid mass of sapphire waters, just flecked here and there with foam, and anon hurled into the abyss below, whence the voice of its torment for ever ascends, while in the dense cloud of glittering white vapor above, one may fancy the wailing spirit of the flood to shroud herself from mortal gaze.

No wonder that Niagara is, or should be, the despair of painters : they may give its height and width and form, even its coloring, but they cannot even suggest that slow majesty of motion, that wonderful harmony of sound.

Returning to our Wagner home we cast fond and searching looks toward the hampers provided for our refreshment by attentive friends, and from them are presently produced a chicken, some ham, beef, and various accessories ; the table is spread and our artist dispatched in search of bread. I say *our* artist, for, although several are with us, H—— is ours, *par excellence*, not only because he has grown up beneath the eye of our Chief, but from his thoroughly sympathetic nature, combining the ability of a man with the winning qualities of a boy ; the *enfant gâté* of our office—the *enfant terrible*, occasionally, of our party.

The bread is produced, but where are the plates ? Echo answers, where ! but paper is voted an excellent substitute, and, at least, we are rich in knives and forks, for did not our Chief himself visit the Meriden Britannia Co., on the day of our departure, and, with his own hands bear home the shining parcel, now hopefully, and now despairingly, sought for in bags, valises, baskets, even in shawl-straps and pockets, and finally decided to be in a trunk on its way to San Francisco.

And here let me pause to say a word to my long-suffering sex bound upon voyaging, near or far: do not consent to share bag or valise with any man unless you wish to find collars, cuffs, and ruffles crushed into a corner beneath a pair of boots, your tooth-brush saturated with liquid blacking, and the contents of your powder-box distributed throughout the whole, ready to fly out at any moment, proving that even your complexion is not a right that anybody is bound to respect!

The merry pic-nic was just concluded when the conductor appeared, loaded with plates, knives, forks, etc., and it was speedily voted that the repast already taken was but a lunch, and all found appetite, after an amazingly short interval, for a dinner fit, as some enthusiastically declared, for the Gods on Mount Olympus.

On the Ice under Niagara Falls.   Page 21.

CHAPTER II.

THE TAGUS AND LAKE ERIE.

ONE would not wish to be unpatriotic, but certainly the approach to the City of Toledo, Ohio, does not compare favorably with that of its namesake upon the golden-sanded Tagus. Mile after mile of ragged woodland, mile after mile of roughly cleared fields dotted with charred stumps, mile after mile of saw-mills and lumber-yards, brought us finally to the town, over which hung a cloud of dull brown smoke, with great buildings looming out of it, which we were informed were the largest grain elevators in the United States, built upon piles on the shores of the lake, or rather of the estuary leading to it.

This mode of building seems nearly as popular in Toledo as in Amsterdam, and so large a portion of the environs of the city seems wading out into the adjacent swamps and marshes that one looks for malaria and similar evils, as a matter of course, but is informed by the inhabitants that their excellent system of drainage obviates the trouble entirely. As we walked through the town, which, although only about twenty years old, boasts 55,000 inhabitants, we were struck by the air of alertness and busy prosperity everywhere visible, even at the uncomfortably early hour of our promenade, and while our companions noted with approval the blocks of handsome warehouses and shops in the main street we pondered pensively on the apothegm: "It is the early bird that gets the worm"; with its appropriate retort: "And serves the worm right for being out at such an hour!" The morning wore on, however, and in due time we presented ourselves at the establishment of the *Toledo Blade.* The building is fine and imposing, so also is its editor-in-chief, Dr. Miller; and after an interchange of courtesies and compliments we were indulged with a sight of that wonderful sword with its Toledo blade, presented by his Supreme and Royal Highness, King Alfonso, of Spain, through his Royal Commissioners to the Centennial Exposition, to the representative journal of America, all of which information and much more, we found inscribed in stately and graceful periods of the purest Castilian in the testimonial accompanying the sword, which was ceremoniously unfolded from a gorgeous Spanish flag whose brilliant red and yellow seemed gairish and tawdry within-doors, although so rich and imposing when draped above a balcony filled with dark-eyed Senoritas, and waved by the perfume-laden breezes of its native land.

The sword itself seems in size and weight better fitted for the hand of Orlando, or Charlemagne, or Cœur de Lion, than any less stalwart champion, but the hilt was magnificently incrusted with gold and silver, and the blade was proved to possess the marvelous suppleness and tenacity traditionally belonging to its family, and although we insisted that Dr. Miller should not run the remotest chance of accident by putting it to the test of bending the tip to touch the hilt, we are firm in the faith that it could have been triumphantly achieved.

Leaving Toledo at one o'clock, we sped into Indiana and gained our first impression of prairie, or, as Westerners like to call it, per-air-ry, country, and, while here, record a conclusion arrived at after seeing whatever lies between the Atlantic and Pacific, that the prairie, like the Red man, requires to be seen in a state of savage nature to be at all interesting, and that neither is to be thus seen without considerable risk of life to the spectator. Cultivated Indians are loathsome, cultivated prairies are stupid; and the scenery of northern Indiana is cultivated prairie. We dined at Elkhart, and found a bit of an oasis in the shape of a host, whose cultivation and refinement pleasantly prepared us for an interview with his wife, whose appearance and manners would have graced any Fifth Avenue drawing-room. She kindly invited us into her private apartments, which proved models of taste and elegance, although the house itself was neither better nor worse than the average Western railway refectory, The table was served by young women, and among them one of so striking and Juno-like an aspect that "our artist" sacrificed his dinner to the pleasure of sketching her, while she willingly abandoned her usual duties to serve as model.

Toward night, we catch a glimpse of Lake Michigan and its foam-crested waves dashing against the stone wall which restrains their incursions upon the city, and could fancy that we saw the broad Atlantic stretching before us, instead of merely an inland lake. And now we are in Chicago, and at the Grand Pacific Hotel, and, after eagerly devoting a few minutes to a basin of fair water, which none but travelers can appreciate, assemble in the supper-room, a superb hall—light, bright, and marvelous in frescoing and gilding. As for the meal itself, a week of such sumptuous fare would be enough to derange one's digestion for life.

Tired Nature's sweet restorer was sought with wonderful unanimity at an early hour, and the next morning, having breakfasted as admirably as we had supped, we made ready to explore the wonders of Chicago ; for, like most other Americans, we knew less of our own country than of many others, and we determined to correct our ignorance without delay.

We found the fashionable avenues, Wabash, Calmut, Prairie and Michigan, wide, straight, and interesting as drives, from the number and diversity of handsome private dwellings, generally detached, and built in all varieties of styles and ornamentation ; even the frame buildings are costly and ornate, and the brick richly decorated with brown-stone copings and carvings. A favorite material, also, is a soft, creamy, yellow stone, similar to that so popular in Paris, and, possibly, the association, recalling the good-natured satire that good Chicagoeans, when they die, go to Paris, may have added to the pleasing effect.

The wooden pavements of the streets, although smoother to drive upon than stone, are the cause of a great deal of dust ; and there still exists a difference of opinion between street and sidewalk, as to level, necessitating a system of steps, descending from the latter to the former, a little startling to evening promenaders. This, however, is in course of alteration, as the entire level of the city is being raised several feet since the fire, and a great many streets of fine warehouses and shops have been erected on the new basis.

There are very few trees, except along Dearborne Street, and the northerly part of Michigan Avenue, where the great fire did not reach, and where the houses are nearly all of wood and detached. On Prairie Avenue we were shown a stately and magnificent mansion of brown-stone, standing in the midst of spacious grounds, and fronting on the avenue from the lake. Our driver informed us that "Mr. Pullman was five years a-building it," and we gratefully hoped that the aggregate comfort conferred on the traveling public during those five years, by hotel and palace cars, had been built and cemented in those brown-stone walls. The piercing wind from the lake, which is at once a blessing and a nuisance to Chicago, tempering the heat in mid-summer, but a little disagreeable in April, especially when laden with clouds of dust, made us glad to turn our backs and return to the more sheltered portions of the city. State Street reminded us of Broadway, although with more uniformly fine and solid blocks of buildings, nearly all of yellow brown-stone. Clark Street is its rival ; property-holders in each street vieing with each other since the fire, in the attempt to make their own street the centre of importance. The same rivalry exists between the avenues of private residences, and from this laudable ambition, probably, arises the reported fact that every rich man in Chicago is involved in debt.

In State Street we paused at the Corn Exchange, a fine building, *per se*, but evidently seldom profaned by the use of the scrubbing-brush or broom. The sales for the day were just over, and the brokers and dealers swarming out of the door, and in the lobbies, with the noise and hilarity of schoolboys just released from their lessons. We went into the hall where the sales are made—a fine, large chamber, with a clicking of telegraphic machines on every side, and piles of corn, torn papers and rubbish, inches high in places. From a careful study of the bulletins posted on tall, black frames, here and there, we gathered that "Liverpool wheat was dejected, and corn stiff," and in unsympathetic glee took our leave of the Corn Exchange, and went our way to Feild, Leiter & Co., the Stewarts of Chicago. We found a large, but not imposing establishment, presenting rather an excess of thread and needle and small ware counters, but having a novel and excellent system of checks. The first salesman of whom one makes a purchase, noting it upon a blank memorandum which the buyer takes to the next counter, has the purchase recorded, and so on, until payment of the whole is made at the last counter; thus saving much time, noisy shouting of "Cash!" and the annoyance of awaiting the arrival of the erratic imps generally answering to that cognomen.

Our next visit was to the Academy of Fine Arts, which we found up-stairs in a big stone building, devoted, as it seemed, to almost everything else under the sun, and satisfied to squeeze the Fine Arts away in a corner as an after-thought. The establishment is rather languishing, as its patrons, a few of the wealthy men of Chicago, have lately felt unable to do very much for its support, and we all know that the higher and more esthetic needs of human nature are the first to be pinched by a deficiency in the supplies.

The Academy possesses but two rooms, in which students in oils, water-colors, crayons, still-life and portraits are jumbled promiscuously together. There is no life-school proper, although a few were drawing and painting from the model—only the head, however—and most of the drawing is from the flat.

From these rooms we visited a few studios, finding the majority of them not much in advance of the Academy. In one, however, we encountered a lady whose olive-tinted skin and dark eyes proclaimed her of the Latin race. She was working industriously at a pastel head of a beautiful young girl, and with the vigorous and rapid touch of a sure and experienced artist. The imperfect English and marked coldness of the few words our remarks elicited induced us to address her in Italian, and the advance was met by a vivid upward flash of the dark eyes, that wonderful brightening of the skin so much more striking in an olive complexion than the pink blush of the Saxon, and the breathless reply: "No, I am Parisian; perhaps Madame speaks French?" We replied in the affirmative, and then came such a torrent of words instead of the icy monosyllables of the first few moments, and in five minutes we listened to a dissertation on Art in

Chicago, Art in Paris, Art all over the world, in fact; and then a brief outline of the artist's own personal history, a delicate probing of our own, and finally such handshakings, such tender adieux, and such reluctance to part company at the ultimate confines of the Academy of Fine Arts, that one felt, with a pitying sympathy, how starved the poor exiled soul must have become in its expatriation, when the accents of its native tongue, even from stranger's lips, could raise such a whirlwind of excitement and delight.

Next we visited another studio, also that of a lady, but this time a landscape-painter; the artist herself was absent, but the honors were done by the quaintest little object in life, whom we found encased in an immense pinafore, perched upon a high stool and working away for dear life upon a brilliantly colored picture. He announced himself as twelve years old, although that number of years seemed altogether too liberal an allowance, and stated that the spirit of an artist burned in his bosom, and he was one of Madame's pupils. His idea of art seemed to be the getting over the largest amount possible of canvas in the least possible time, and his faith in his preceptress in this line was unbounded. After a brief inspection of the other treasures of the studio, we took leave of our Michael Angelo in embryo, wishing him, a little sadly, the realization of all his brilliant dreams. He responded confidently, and we left him scrambling up to his perch again, to resume work upon the big, bright picture.

The next afternoon we started for a survey of the

north end of the city, Dearborn Avenue, the Water
Works, and Lincoln Park. The Water Works are new
and beautiful, and eccentric in architecture, like most
of the town, and with a wild excess of tower and but-
tress and queer little points and pinnacles everywhere,
cheerfully relieving the solemn gray of the rough-
hewn granite blocks of the main edifice. From this
point we drove along the lake shore upon a road artificially filled in upon swamp land. The lake itself
wore a sombre hue, yellowish-gray in color, and rather
tea-like in effect, but the waves dashed in very
respectable surf upon the sea-wall and the little jetties
thrown out here and there.

It was Sunday afternoon, and the respectable *bour-
geoisie* and family men of Chicago were out with wives
and olive - branches, in wagons of every pattern and
degree, in spite of the piercing wind and blinding dust.
The more aristocratic part of the population was not
visible, and one wondered whether the New England
element in Chicago is strong enough to render Sunday
driving unpopular, or whether the *élite* preferred
staying at home to dream of the *Champs Elysées.*

The Shore Road led us into the Park, just now in
the same embryotic condition New Yorkers can recall
as prevalent some dozen years ago in Central Park, and
let us hope as glorious a result is in store for the
former as well as the latter creation. There is the
beginning here of a zoological collection, already quite
rich in birds.

On our way home we saw the large frame house
which, oddly enough, was the only one left standing in

"THE THOUSAND MILE TREE."

that district, while the flames destroyed everything about it. We saw also the Roman Catholic Cathedral, a superb white marble building, with the padded doors so common on the European continent.

Relics of the fire meet one at every turn; lots piled up with blackened brick and stone and dismal rubbish, and sometimes the picturesque shell of a ruin. We were shown the small block of dwelling-houses used as a hotel after the fire, when every hotel in Chicago was burned.

Aldene Square, probably called square because it is round, is a charming little park, containing drives, trees, flowers, fountains, etc., and nearly surrounded by a series of houses, various in size and construction, but of equal elegance, and all built by a single man.

To sum up the impression produced by a careful study of Chicago, it is a city of magnificent beginnings, a thing of promise. Few American cities can boast so many noticeably handsome dwellings, or such massive blocks of stone along the business streets, but the crudity of youth is as inextricably mingled with the promise of maturity as in a big-boned boy of eighteen, or a blushing girl of thirteen, from whom one parts with resignation for a time, looking pleasurably forward to renewed intercourse a few years later.

We remarked, that physicians' names, instead of appearing on the door-plates, as with us, were lettered in black or gold on the glass light above the front door, and along with the number, a great facility, one would imagine, for those seeking medical services after nightfall, but, *per contra*, the names of streets are mysteriously printed just above, instead of upon, the glass of the gas-lights.

We sit down to our last meal at the Grand Pacific Hotel, cast a final admiring glance at its cheerful parlors, wide corridors, superb dining-hall, murmur a grateful acknowledgment of the faultless *cuisine* and perfect system of attendance, which render this hotel one of the most comfortable houses in the country, and then, not without a certain excitement, prepare to resume our journey, now about to develop more characteristic features, since where breathes the man who has not been in Chicago? while only a select few of the sons of Adam have personally compared the crisp waves of the Atlantic with the grander and more rhythmic swell of the Pacific.

GRAND PACIFIC HOTEL, CHICAGO.

CHAPTER III.

ON arriving at the station, we find that we have exchanged our beloved Wagner Home for the famous Pullman Hotel Car, exhibited at the Centennial Exposition, and built at a cost of $35,000. We are greeted on entering, by two superb pyramids of flowers, one from Mr. Potter Palmer, and the other with compliments of the Pullman Car Co.; then new-found Chicago friends arrive in rapid succession, to wish us God-speed, and, in the midst of a cheerful bustle and excitement, we are off, and able to look about us at our new home. First, we are impressed with the smooth and delightful motion, and are told it is owing to a new invention, in the shape of paper wheels applied to this car, and incredible though the information sounds, meekly accept it, and proceed to explore the internal resources of our kingdom. We find everything closely resembling our late home, except that one end of the car is partitioned off and fitted up as a kitchen, storeroom, scullery—reminding one, in their compactness and variety, of the little Parisian *cuisines*, where every inch of space is utilized, and where such a modicum of wood and charcoal produces such marvelous results.

Our *chef*, of ebon color, and proportions suggesting a liberal sampling of the good things he prepares, wears the regulation snow-white apron and cap, and gives us cordial welcome and information; showing us, among other things, that his refrigerator and larder are boxes adroitly arranged beneath the car, secured by lock and key, and accessible at every station. At six the tables are laid for two each, with dainty linen, and the finest of glass and china, and we presently sit down to dinner. Our repast is Delmonican in its nature and style, consisting of soup, fish, *entrées*, roast meat and vegetables, followed by the conventional dessert and the essential spoonful of black coffee.

We are not a late party that night, retiring at ten, and in the morning are startled by an announcement from the "Sultana," a tall, willowy woman, with dark, almond-shaped eyes, who affects brilliant tints, and lounges among her cushions and wraps of crimson and gold, with a grace peculiarly her own, and with a luxuriance so Eastern, as to have won for her the *sobriquet* of Sultana. We are startled by the announcement that her rest had been disturbed by the howling of wolves! The young lady who does the romantic for our party turns pale with envy, especially when the brakeman, appealed to as authority, admits that there is a small coyote wolf about the prairies, even so far East, which might possibly have been heard. All day, until sunset, we sweep along over rolling prairie lands of a rich, tawny yellow, with here and there a tiny town, and here and there a lonely settler's cabin, with a little winding footpath stretching up to it.

At Dixon, the train stopped for the passengers' supper, and we stole away for a little exercise and solitude. A storm was imminent, the distant thunder muttered ominously, the lightning came in pulses, and from the far, dusky reaches of the prairie, blew a wind stronger and freer, yet softer, than other winds, with a fragrance sweeter than flowers on its breath. Some strange, wild influence in the scene sent a new sensation tingling through one's blood. All sorts of poetic fancies and inspirations seemed hovering close above one's head, when a dash of rain recalled the realism of life, and sent us hastening back to the car, where all the lamps were lighted and the tables laid for dinner.

"What a dismal scene!" exclaimed some one, looking out of the window.

"We are very fortunate to be snugly ensconced, with plenty of lights and dinner in prospect," replied the Sultana, drawing her cashmere about her shoulders.

By breakfast-time the scenery had changed, the rolling prairie giving place to a succession of low bluffs—steep, hilly, brown, and infinitely wild; then came a quiet little lake, dotted over with wild ducks; more hills growing green in the hollows; swamp-willows budding redly; herds of grazing cattle and wild, shaggy horses; until, at last, we roll into a long, flat, straggling town, and are told it is Council Bluffs.

"And why Council Bluffs?" we suavely inquire of the wise man who gives us this information.

"Because, on these bluffs the Indians assembled in council; also because, beneath the shadow of the Bluffs in 1853, a little company of enterprising spirits held a council as to the propriety of building the City of Omaha, upon the opposite shores of the Missouri; also because the Conductor counsels us to re-enter the car, as the train is about to start; also—— "

" Enough! enough! your last reason is conclusive." And a few minutes later we are rolling over the magnificent bridge, said to be one of the finest in the world, and almost a thousand feet in length. The stream — weak coffee as to complexion, pea-soup as to consistence — rolls sluggishly between its iron piers. As for the bridge itself, its cost, its construction, its ingenuity, is it not written in all the guide-books, all the travels, all the diaries of all the *voyageurs?* and to these various sources the statistical reader is referred for information.

Arrived in Omaha, the true beginning, perhaps, of our California trip, we took a carriage, and set forth to view the town. We found it big, lazy, and apathetic; the streets dirty and ill-paved; the clocks without hands to point out the useless time; the shops, whose signs mostly bore German names, deserted of customers, while principals and clerks lounged together in the doorways, listless and idle. This depressing state of affairs is, presumably, temporary, for we were told that, two years ago, Omaha was one of the most thriving and busy cities of the West, claiming for itself, indeed, a place as first commercial emporium of that vast section; and, certainly, its position at the terminus of the three great Eastern roads, and the beginning of the one great Western one, would naturally entitle it to that pre-eminence, when aided by the enterprise and the dollars of such men as have, in twenty years, built a great city from a wayside settlement.

Doubtless, when the hard times, which seem to affect everybody and everything, from the baby's Christmas toys to the statesman's visions of international commerce, are over, Omaha will shake off the lethargy depressing her at present, and rise to the position her citizens fondly claim for her. We saw some tasteful private residences, with conservatories and stables; the High School building, which might justly be called a palace of learning; the military headquarters, and barracks of the armory of the State; the Grand Central Hotel, a large and imposing edifice, admirably conducted; and also the less imposing, but more remarkable house erected by the brilliant and erratic George Francis Train, who, arriving at Omaha one day, was told there was no accommodation to be had for his party.

"No rooms to be had!" exclaimed he. "Then I'll build me a hotel!"—and he did, within six weeks.

Returning to the station, we found the platform crowded with the strangest and most motley groups of people it has ever been our fortune to encounter. Men in alligator boots, and loose overcoats made of blankets and wagon rugs, with wild, unkempt hair and beards, and bright, resolute eyes, almost all well-looking, but wild and strange as denizens of another world.

The women looked tired and sad, almost all of them, and were queerly dressed, in gowns that must have been old on their grandmothers, and with handkerchiefs tied over their heads in place of hats; the children were bundled up anyhow, in garments of nondescript purpose and size, but were generally chubby, neat

and gay, as they frolicked in and out among the boxes,
baskets, bundles, bedding, babies'-chairs, etc., piled
waist high on various parts of the platform. Mingling
with them, and making some inquiries, we found that
these were emigrants, bound for the Black Hills, by
rail to Cheyenne and Sioux City, and after that by
wagon trains. A family of French attracted attention
by the air of innate refinement and fitness which seems
to attach to every grade of society in *la belle France*,
and we chatted with them for some moments. A great
many families claimed German nationality, and Ireland,
England and Scotland were represented, as well as our
own country. One bright little creature — perhaps
three years of age—was quite insulted at being called
a baby, and exclaimed, indignantly :

"No, no, me not baby !"

"What are you, then ? A young lady ?" we inquired.

"No, me 'ittle woman. Me helps mammy sweep,"
replied the mite ; and apologizing for our blunder, we
handed her some silver for candy, which she accepted
with alacrity ; and as we watchéd her setting off on her
shopping expedition, a neat, pretty old lady, perched
upon a big bundle, said, with much conscious pride :

"That's my grandchild, ma'am."

We congratulated her, and passed on, to visit the
emigrant lodging-house and outfitting-shop adjoining
the station. The shop, although large, was crowded
and the air insufferably close ; long counters ran across
the room, and upon them, and upon lines stretched
above, lay or hung, every variety of equipment desirable
for pioneer life—clothes, blankets, mats, tins, hats

shoes, babies' rattles, impartially mixed and exhibited, while some attention to the æsthetic needs of humanity was shown, in various stuffed heads of moose and deer, with quails perched upon their antlers.

In the eating-room we "assisted," by inspection, at a good, substantial, homely dinner, neatly served at twenty-five cents a plate, and a placard informed the guests that children occupying seats at table would be charged full price; a precautionary measure not unreasonable, as it seemed to us, in view of the swarms of innocents who had certainly never encountered a Herod!

Lodging is the same price as dinner, and the superintendent of this part of the house triumphantly informed us that the sheets were changed every night.

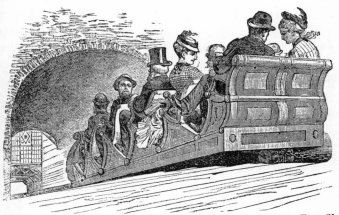

On the Inclined Railway to the Foot of Niagara Falls. Page 21.

CHAPTER IV.

THE UNMENTIONABLE PLACE.

AFTER passing North Bend, we came upon an Indian camp belonging to a portion of the Omahaw tribe. The lodges — five or six in number — were of white skin, and picturesque in shape; their occupants gathered around a small camp-fire—the men, tall, straight, dark and dignified, wrapped in toga-like blankets; the women, dirty and degraded, with their pappooses bundled on their backs, the queer, little dark faces peeping out like prairie dogs from their burrows. Further on we met a second band—half a dozen men on horseback—carrying their lodges bundled up and driving a little herd of shaggy Indian ponies. It was a wonderfully new picture for us, the great plains rolling away on either side in apparently illimitable extent, clad in their richest shades of russet and tawny gold in the distance, and the tender grass and moist black earth close at hand, a wild mass of thunder-clouds crowding up from the south, and the low-hanging trail of smoke from our engine sweeping away north-ward like a troop of spirits, and this little, lonely band of Omahaws riding slowly away into the storm, casting uneasy glances backward at the flying train. A second picture to place beside that of Niagara in memory's gallery, a second proof that the foremost of human artists is, after all, but the feeblest copyist of the Artist whose name is Wonderful.

The old emigrant trail here runs southward beside the track, and we had the luck to pass two real emigrant wagons : one, white-topped and rather neat-looking, had halted for the night, with the horses picketed out to graze, and the camp-fire lighted; while the other, dark, weather-beaten and forlorn, was doggedly making its way forward.

Our train stopped for supper at Grand Island, a considerable place, and, like most Western places, confidently expecting to be larger when the time arrived. We dismounted to look at our first specimens of buffalo grass, a short, dry, tufted herbage, said to be the especial dainty of not only buffalo, but of all grazing creatures, who leave all other food for it, and unhesitatingly as a gourmand accepts fresh truffles. In front of the station was a little inclosure with a most spasmodic fountain, beside which we lingered for some moments and then returned with alacrity to our Pullman Home.

Very early in the next morning we were awakened by the stopping of the train, for the gentle and constant motion had already become as essential to our repose as that of his ship to the sailor. The conductor presently appeared to warn us that the detention was likely to be one of several hours, as an accident had happened to the freight train some five miles in advance, and the track was both encumbered and injured. The prospect was not cheering, as the rain fell in torrents, and the prairie, sodden and gray in the chill morning light, had lost all the beauty of its sunset garb, presenting one flat, dull expanse, innocent of house, tree, shrub, moving creature, or any point of interest —a perfect picture of desolation.

The several hours of the conductor extended to eight, and required all the attractive powers of the Sultana, all the condensed result of her husband's journalistic and statistical studies, all the young lady's romantic fervor about the plains, and all the fun of the Bohemians, to fill them pleasantly. However, " All things come round to him who will but wait," and to us came at last the delightful jerk of the train, as the iron horse straightened his traces and, with a shriek of exultation, started again upon his journey.

Arrived at the scene of disaster, we could not wonder at the length of the detention, for a herd of cattle, attempting to try conclusions with a steam engine, had been forced to retreat, leaving six of their number on the field of battle ; and so inextricably had the poor creatures become wedged in the complicated machinery of the locomotive, that it was hard to decide where the one ended and where the other began, or which had suffered most in the encounter. The cars lay scattered along the track, all more or less wrecked, and the engine, completely dislodged from the rails, lay beside them, a mass of ruin. During our long delay a wrecker train had been engaged in laying a new section of track, and over this we slowly passed, resuming presently our usual rate of speed, which, however, rarely exceeds twenty-two or three miles an hour, that being conceded as the rate best adapted to economy, safety and comfort.

in long distances, and certainly resulting in a smoothness and ease delightfully contrasting with the rush, rattle and jar of the Lightning Express.

Soon after this we passed through our first snowshed, very like a covered bridge or wooden tunnel in effect, and were informed that the U. P. R. R. had been obliged to construct hundreds of miles of these, and stone fences at different points of the road, to obviate the drifting of snow banks, capable of not only detaining, but of burying, a train.

And now, not without some little excitement, we arrived at Cheyenne, as it is styled upon the maps, the Magic City of the Plains, the City on Wheels, the Town of a Day, as romancists call it, or in yet more vigorous vernacular, H—ll on Wheels, which latter is, perhaps, its most popular name among its own inhabitants. In view of this reputation, our conductor strongly advised against any night exploration, at least by the ladies of the party, of the streets and shops of Cheyenne, stating that the town swarmed with miners *en route* for, or returning from, the Black Hills, many of them desperadoes, and all utterly reckless in the use of the bowie-knife and pistol; or, at the very least, in the practice of language quite unfit for ears polite, although well adapted to a place which they themselves had dubbed with so suggestive a name. This opposition, was, of course, decisive; and the three ladies, as one man, declared fear was a word unknown in their vocabulary, that purchases essential to their comfort were to be made, and that exercise was absolutely necessary to their health. Under such stress of argument the masculine mind gave way perforce, and not only the sworn beau of the party, but most of the other gentlemen, indorsed the movement and volunteered to act as escort, producing, loading, and flourishing such an arsenal of weapons as they did so that their valiant charges huddled together, far more affrighted at their friends than their enemies, and piteously imploring that the firearms should be safely hidden until needed ; the order was obeyed, and at about half-past nine P. M. the exploring party set forth.

Cheyenne proved itself a fresh and vigorous experience of a true frontier town—streets dark and suggestive of all sorts of fierce experiences connected with the swarms of swarthy, rough-clad men, who lounged at every corner and filled every shop, yet never offered to molest the visitors by word, act or look, although evidently "taking stock" and remarking upon their unfamiliar appearance. Our first visit was to an ammunition shop to lay in supplies for a pistol presented to "our" artist upon his journey, that first pistol which is to every young man now - a - days what the *toga virilis* was to the Roman youth. In this establishment we had an opportunity of examining the outfit deemed requisite for a visit to the Black Hills, in the shape of horribly keen and deadly knives, and firearms of every size and variety. In fact, it was decided by the experts of the party that in this one shop was condensed a larger assortment, and more complete arsenal, of deadly weapons than is to be found in any New York establishment.

From this warehouse of death we passed to more

cheerful scenes, and noticing, by the way, the curious effect in the dark streets of the transparencies hung out as signs by many of the shops. The druggist's and jeweler's impressed us as by far the best stocked we had seen since leaving home, unless in Chicago. Especially we expressed surprise at the value and beauty of the diamonds and other jewels exposed for sale, and were informed that these found a ready market, not only among the successful miners, who, returning from the Black Hills, are tempted to an immediate enjoyment of their new fortunes, but by the herdsmen, who bring immense quantities of cattle to Cheyenne, *en route* for the East, and, having made a large and successful sale, are very apt to invest part of the proceeds in gifts to wife or sweetheart—a custom too laudable to be confined to Cheyenne.

Much was confided to us of the history, past, present and future, of this peripatetic and Hadean city, and also many assertions as to the unusual salubrity of the atmosphere and its virtues in all chest diseases; for it stands almost at the highest point of the long ascent we had been climbing ever since crossing the Mississippi, and is, to be statistical, 6,041 feet above the sea level. Certainly there is a fine tingling touch as this rarified air reaches our lungs, and no doubt a residence in it might be beneficial; the *per contra* being the doubt as to whether we lived at all with the atmosphere so full of glistening blades and whistling bullets as report rather than our experience describes.

It is as well, perhaps, here to put on record the result of certain subsequent investigations of ours in

Cheyenne, after our return from Denver. Between the two visits we had diligently read some interesting guide-books, which set forth the City built in a Day —so called because most of the houses were trundled hither on wheels from Julesburg as the terminus of the railway advanced—as a moral, decorous, and highly desirable abode; so the second arrival being in the morning, we spent half the day in searching for the City of the Guide-books, as we propose redubbing this child of many names, and found, as we had fore- seen, nothing more than the typical frontier town we had glanced at by gaslight; a straggling settlement of wooden houses, minus good streets, and not a private residence worthy the name; the streets crowded with every variety of wild, rough frontiersmen — miners, teamsters, drovers, Mexicans, scouts, ferocious to look upon, but lamb-like in demeanor toward quiet strangers, stepping courteously aside to let us pass, respectful toward women, of whom, by-the-way, there was scarcely one to be seen in the streets of Cheyenne, and even when openly, perhaps rudely, stared at, refraining from returning the incivility. We saw an emigrant train of several wagons starting for the Black Hills, one of the wagons being drawn by eight mules, whose driver managed them by a single rein. A scout in a full suit of fringed buckskin was lounging about—a hand- some man with long, dark curls falling from beneath his seal-skin cap, who treated our open and admiring curiosity with true aboriginal indifference. Another galloped by dressed in a blue cloak over a purple jacket, high cavalry boots, and a sombrero, beneath

STARTING FOR THE BLACK HILLS FROM CHEYENNE. Page 48.

which his hair flew wildly back as he dashed past, guiding his horse from the neck in true Mexican fashion.

As an instance of the peaceful order now reigning in the City on Wheels, we may mention that the night before our arrival a murder had been committed by which a wife and children were left desolate; a subscription was going the rounds for their relief, and had already reached one hundred and fifty dollars; another man had been garroted and relieved of seventy dollars, and a large shop robbed of a considerable amount. Our conductor, named Jim Cohoon, in telling of these things, casually mentioned that a few years ago, while fishing in a small creek near Cheyenne, with his two brothers, they had been attacked by Indians, riddled with arrows, scalped, and left for dead. The two brothers were indeed so, but he, with seven arrows in his body and without his scalp, had managed to crawl three miles for help, and had entirely recovered. He was a fine, handsome-looking young fellow, and so arranged his hair that the injury he had received was not apparent. With some diffidence he exhibited his head to the gentlemen of the party, who explained to us that the scalping was not, as we had supposed, on the crown of the head, but considerably below, at the back, and was heart-shaped.

The public buildings of the City of the Guide-book were: A good brick hotel, five churches, a court-house and jail, a City Hall and schoolhouse, two theatres, and such a number of establishments openly proclaiming themselves concert and gambling saloons, that we ceased to count them, and proposed instead to visit them.

Obtaining permission and escort, we first turned our steps to McDaniel's Theatre, conspicuously advertised as offering a "Great Moral Show," but whether permanently or for that evening only was not mentioned. Passing through a bar gorgeous with frescoed views of Vesuvius and the Bay of Naples, and remarkable for its cleanliness, we found ourselves in the parquette, so to speak, of the theatre—a large room fitted up with chairs and tables, for the use of convivial parties, and served by pretty waiter girls. The stage was narrow, the drop-curtain exceedingly gorgeous, and statues of the Venus de Medici, and another undressed lady of colossal proportions, *posed* strikingly at either wing. At each side of the hall are tiers of boxes, so called, reached by long narrow flights of stairs from the parquette ; these boxes are closed in, and have each a window, through which the inmates must project head and shoulders if curious to witness the performance on the stage ; but, as they contain tables and chairs, it is possible that a glass of wine or lager and social intercourse may be more the object than spectacular entertainment.

At the head of the stairs is a small bar bearing the notice : "No drinks retailed here"; and above, there is printed in large letters : "Gents, be liberal."

Returning through the bar, we passed into the gambling saloon—a large room, exquisitely clean and orderly, with a bar at the end, and long tables at each side, arranged for Rouge et Noir, Roulette, Keno, and our national game of Biblical memory. Behind each was

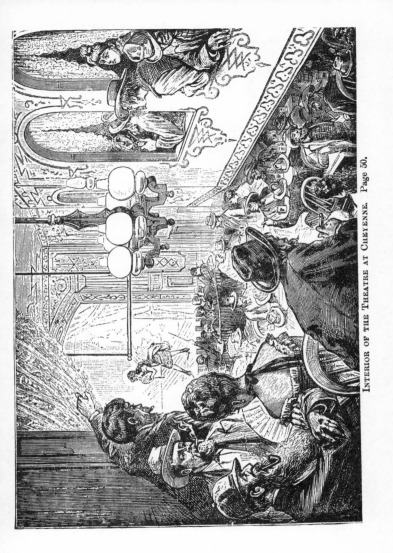

INTERIOR OF THE THEATRE AT CHEYENNE. Page 50.

hung upon the wall a neat placard bearing the rules of the game, price of checks, etc., and, conspicuous by their tasteful frames, the various licenses, costing, as the proprietor pathetically informed us, $600 for every three months. Over the door of this room was printed, in fancy letters, the word "Welcome!" reminding one drolly of the Sunday-school Festivals and similar occasions when such inscriptions are usually met with. But if McDaniel's Theatre and gambling saloon is a whited sepulchre, let us do it the justice to say that it is very white indeed, and nearly the cleanest place, materially speaking, that we were ever in.

From there we went to the Opera House, owned by the same proprietor, and closely resembling the theatre, except in being more nicely furnished and without a bar or gambling saloon. It boasts a band of eight pieces, and a troupe of twenty-five performers.

A little fatigued with our search for the "far-off, the unattainable, the dim," in the City of the Guide-book, we returned to our car, and found the Sultana, unlike her Eastern prototypes, making herself useful as well as ornamental, by the aid of the contents of a little work-box, with whose shining implements she deftly repaired "the rent the envious nail" had made on our last stroll. The sight was homelike and tasteful, and a wholesome antidote to the Great Moral Show we had been witnessing; although inspiring some passing thought of envy and doubt in the mind of one more used to wield the pen than the needle, and just then forced by the pitiless logic of events to confess that although the pen may be mightier than the sword, there are moments in life when the needle is mightier than either.

This chapter closes with a transcript of one of the signs of the Magic City of the Plains, which transcript is offered to the study of archæologists and hieroglyphists :

GAMBLING BOOTHS IN THE EARLY YEARS OF THE RAILROADS.

CHAPTER V

THE GARDEN OF THE GODS.

GOING to sleep in Cheyenne we awoke in Denver, our car having been attached during the night to a train upon the Denver Pacific R. R. south from Cheyenne to Denver. We breakfasted, and were still occupied in that pleasing duty when friends old and new appeared, intent upon hospitality, *ciceroneship*, and the giving and receiving of news. Carriages were in waiting, and with little delay we set out to view the city. It lies broadly and generously upon a great plain, sloping toward the South Platte, with the grand sweep of the Rocky Mountain chain almost surrounding it ; suggesting by its lofty and snow-capped summits Alpine scenery in a softer and more genial climate than that of chilly Switzerland. A large number of handsome houses have already been built on the western side of the city, facing the mountain-view, and one foresees that when Denver shall be forty, instead of twenty, years old, this will become the fashionable and charming quarter ; and, by the way, can any one explain what point of the eternal fitness of things is involved in the western side of so many cities being the aristocratic one ? In Denver it will be the Rocky Mountains, but in London, in New York, in Boston, there are no Rocky Mountains, and—but this subject is too wide for further handling just here — so we return to our muttons in the shape of rows upon rows of cottonwood trees transplanted from their native groves to the streets of Denver, and kept alive by the system of irrigating ditches beside the street, here seen for the first time, but a noticeable feature in our travels farther west. The streets themselves, as well as the roads leading out of town, are as fine as the drives in Central Park— solid, hard, and never muddy, with the advantage of being perfectly natural; the soil being an apparently indigenous Macadam. The style of building is different from that of the East, it being the fashion to construct bed, dressing and bath-rooms on the ground floor, as well as parlor, library, and dining - room; verandas are popular, and nearly every house has a little garden in front.

The shops are spacious, well stocked, and city like, and there is the usual number of churches, school-houses, city halls, etc., indispensable to a thriving, growing, American city.

We spent the evening pleasantly at the residence of a member of the Colorado Legislature and a prominent citizen of Denver, who had kindly invited a number of the dignitaries of the State to meet us; and these gentle-men, almost without exception, impressed us not only as men of strength, purpose, and ability, but conspicu-ous for that genial heartiness of manner, and the gentle kindness of feeling which make the Western gentleman a new and charming type of his class. Without trench ing too far on private grounds, one may venture perhaps, to say, that never was this genial manner and fine feeling better exemplified than in the Governor of the Centennial State; while his young wife has been gifted with a grand dignity of manner and appearance well befitting her position, and blending gracefully with gentleness and refinement.

The following morning we started with our hosts of the previous evening for a visit to Colorado Springs and its adjacent wonders. Leaving our own car in Denver, we took passage upon the narrow-gauge railway called the Denver and Rio Grande R. R., running south from that city, and immediately began the steady upward grade by which it climbs the "divide" between the South Platte and Arkansas rivers. We soon began to see snow upon the track, and the temperature of the outer air had sensibly changed. At the highest point lies Summit Lake, a narrow little stream of water, lying in the shadow of a great sugar-loaf mountain, with a background of purple foot hills and the snows of Pike's Peak, which dominate all this region, and are the central point of nearly every view. The waters of this little lake run impartially north and south, and in descending from its level we soon bade good-by to the snow, and welcomed the buffalo grass and cactus plants telling of a higher temperature. We were now in the region of buttes, and saw ourselves surrounded on every side by their weird, fantastic forms—turrets, winged castles, needle-like shafts, heaped piles that might have been the home of ghoul or sprite of the desert, and detached columns of red sandstone capped with cold gray rock of every height and proportion, from a toadstool to a Corinthian pillar.

Colorado Springs, presumably so called because the Springs are five miles away, is not without its attractions. There are five roads leading away from it; Pike's Peak looks condescendingly down on it. The air is said to be excellent for asthmatics, who therefore abound here, and its morals are guarded by the sternest of liquor laws, which is met by the following humorous device. A visitor consumed by illegal thirst is shown into a small, bare room, at one end of which is a closed window, with a shelf inside like a ticket - office, but having revolving properties. The applicant approaches this window, beside which there is a slit in the wall, and passing through this latter ten or twenty-five cents, as the case may be, sighs audibly: "How I wish I had a glass of ale," or, "If I only had some whisky I should feel better," and presto! the window shelf is turned by some mysterious hand, and presently on it rests a mug of foaming ale or a modicum of spirits; the window is then hermetically closed, and law and order reigns supreme.

Manitou Springs, five miles farther on, is a different style of place, for now we are fairly in the region of the beautiful and strange, and at every moment the exclamations of one or other of the party summoned attention to a new point of interest, while the unsatisfied gaze was never ready to turn from the last.

At Colorado and Manitou Springs are the cottages of two of our most cherished American female authors, Helen Hunt, "H. H.," and Grace Greenwood; the former cozy and attractive, with a huge bay window, brilliant with flowers, attesting the taste of the owner, whom one

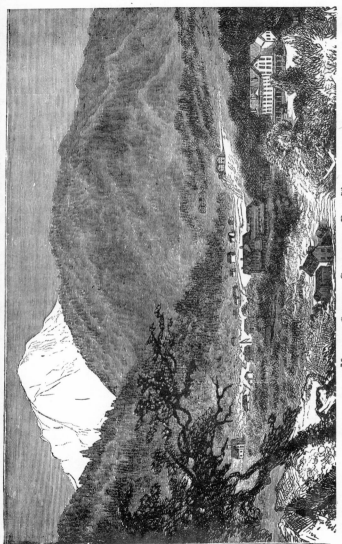

MANITOU SPRINGS, COLORADO. Page 56.

is glad to know has no longer the right to utter those lonely and longing notes whose music found echo in so many hearts. Grace Greenwood's home is also characteristic and tasteful, with some branching antlers above the door, like a forester's house in Tyrol. Here, too, are the residences of some English gentlemen, where nature and art blend promiscuously in rustic bridges across wild mountain fissures, summer-houses perched upon needle-like aeries, and masses of brilliant flowers contrasting with the savage strength of rock and evergreen. At some little distance from here we heard of the daughter and sons of the late Canon Kingsley making a home in the heart of the wilderness, and, as may be fancied, finding a piquant delight in the vivid contrast of the most artificial grade of English life, and the utter naturalness of the American desert, which may yet be taught to blossom like the rose.

There are some fine hotels at Manitou, and several Mineral Springs of varying degrees of unsavoriness, as at Saratoga. The one near Grace Greenwood's cottage flows into a stone basin by the wayside, and bubbles joyously over with a musical invitation to the thirsty visitor not justified by the flavor of its alkaline waters.

From here we drive up the Ute Pass, a cañon popular with those peaceful savages, perhaps for its beauty, more probably for its directness. The narrow roadway climbs up between high walls of red sandstone, zigzagging its way beneath the shadow of stupendous cliffs, with a lovely little stream foaming and brawling far below, leaping down now and again into two lovely cascades, whose voice is the only sound in these eternal

solitudes.   Clumps of dark evergreen, cedar, and fir are
fringed with the tender green of budding willows, and
the tourist might look for hours in quiet delight at mountain torrent and snowy waterfall and contrasting foliage
but for the stupendous and oppressive grandeur of the
heaven-piercing crags above, the dizzy abyss below, the
glimpses of distant mountain peaks, and an undefined
sense of might and majesty everywhere, which makes the
beholder feel that humanity is but a mere impertinent
intrusion upon the scene—a pygmy, whom the slightest
movement of nature might crush in the midst of its
impertinent admiration.

No finer effect, no more impressive scene, is to be
found among Alps or Andes, and so, by-and-by, the
restless world will know, and the Ute Pass will grow
as vulgar as Chamouni.

Returning to Manitou, we branch off into a new
direction, to visit the Garden of the Gods, whose happy,
if not especially appropriate, name has lured us on
through days of expectation, now to be rewarded with a
fullness seldom vouchsafed to grand and indefinite
hope.   The hard, red road along which our fleet little
horses spatter so gayly, winds suddenly into a wooded
hollow, a "park," as the Westerners call it, and we
presently pause before a stupendous gateway, formed
of two great parallel masses of sandstone—smooth,
shining, and glowing in the sun with a vividness of
color grandly shown out by the dazzling white of the
quartz ridge, which lies like an outer wall of marble
just outside all this dull red gold.   These colossal
gates rise to a height of three hundred and fifty feet,

and leave an entrance of two hundred feet in width, through which some gorgeous Pharaonic procession may be imagined passing, with chariots and horsemen and barbaric fanfare of brazen instruments, and captive kings, whom some grim enchanter will presently transform into the grotesque figures crowding the scene beyond. But the Pharaonic pageant fades, and gazing through the gateway and across the garden of these strange gods we see Pike's Peak in the far distance, its snow-clad crest glowing like burnished silver against the pure blue of the sky, and close at hand the sharp spires and minarets of the "Cathedral Rocks," while a little further on sits the "Nun," who has strayed out for some open air devotions. The garden contains about fifty acres of land, its floor of finely disintegrated red sandstone partially covered with thickly tufted buffalo grass, and silvery gray sage brush, while the hanging slopes and gentle rises are dotted with evergreen trees whose sombre green adds the shadow needed to sustain this riot of color and warmth and glow, which fairly makes the blood tingle in its excess; for surely never was sky so blue as that which bent above the Garden of the Gods, never was sunshine so yellow, never were snow-clad peaks and quartz cliffs so dazzlingly white, never red sandstone, whether of old or new formation, so richly red and glowing. "A scene for an artist!" exclaimed a *littérateur*, and an artist at his elbow exclaimed, in quiet scorn: "When the Creator wants this painted I suppose he'll make an artist on purpose to do it. He certainly hasn't yet!" But still one longs to plant Gustave Doré in the midst of that fantastic scene, whose greatest wonder is the vague, half formed ideas, similes, suggestions it awakens in every sensitive mind, and which persons try to communicate to each other, only to find once more how inadequate is human language to represent the human thought.

Our guide, well up in the office, glibly catalogued this and that formation : this was the "Seal" and that the " Scotch Giant," the " Camel," the " Frog," the "Lion"; and pointed out how the strata of the detached rocks followed the same inclination, and ran parallel with the gentle slope of the ground ; but having meekly received as much information as our shallow brain would contain, we drew back within ourselves to gaze in silent, ignorant delight, at these petrified forms of wonder — representatives left behind, as it were, by some unremembered age and race · foretaste, perhaps, of wonders yet to come, when our age and race shall be the unremembered ones ! From dreams like these we are recalled by the Chief's cheerful voice, and again we pass the beautiful gate and enter once more the familiar cold gray of the landscape of the plains, where even the sky is less blue and the sunshine less golden. Twisting our necks for one last glimpse, we photograph on our brain in a never-to-be-forgotten picture, the grand gateway, with its gorgeous color sharply drawn against the vivid blue, the great, snow - clad peak in the far distance, and the hooded Nun who seems bending forward to look after us as we are very reluctantly borne away.

Our next point is Glen Eyrie, a formation similar to, but much less wonderful than, the Garden of the Gods.

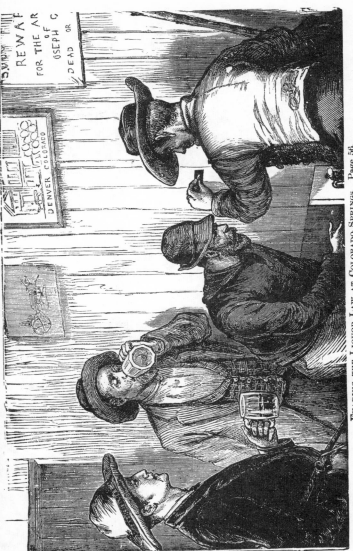

EVADING THE LIQUOR LAW AT COLORADO SPRINGS. Page 56.

Like that, it is entered between two gigantic portals, curiously composite in color of garnet, green, crimson and purple, upon the outer face, while the inner displays every shade of a warm, yellow green   Inside are some grand red sandstone buttes, towering like sentinels, a wilderness of cottonwood and fir trees, a pretty running stream, and fine distant views of the snow-clad mountains and purple-tinted foot-hills.   This glen is the property of General Palmer, and in its midst stands the handsome villa built to welcome his young bride, under whose direction the house was pulled to pieces several times in the building before it became the ideal home of which every bride may dream, but very few so fortunately possess.

The return from this region of enchantment to common-place Colorado Springs was over the flattest, grayest, most mountainous of prairie country, and in the teeth of such a wind as is only possible upon the plains, where neither tree, nor shrub, nor hillock breaks its force.   The chill and exhaustion after a morning of such excitement proved too much for flesh too weak to obey the willing spirit, and by the time we reached the Crawford House, where a good dinner awaited us, the writer was seriously ill, and spent a bad half of an hour while the others dined.   But yet, this experience is among the most precious of all that Western tour, for it gave us a treasure rarer than all the gold of the Black Hills—it gave us a friend.

Having already seen and admired her as our hostess of the preceding evening, we had quietly noted in her beautiful house the selection of pictures, engravings, books, and *objects d'art*, which proclaimed their mistress a person of high literary culture, artistic taste, and extended travel; we had marked with admiration the fine manners, the tone of the best society, the ease, cordiality, and *aplomb* which made every one of her guests the object of special attention, while never neglecting the rest; but now, beneath the touchstone of sickness and suffering we saw developed traits of tenderness, unselfishness, of combined wisdom and gentleness befitting a Sister of Mercy rather than a woman of society; and as her gentle touch, kindly eyes and assuring voice smoothed away the pain and terror and weariness just now so overpowering, a sentiment sprang into being whose life will only end with our own, and all the rest of life will be stronger and better for that hour in which an angel stirred the waters and love rose from their depths.

And now the dinner is concluded, the invalid on her feet again, and we are at the station, but are there informed that the wind is so high that it is not deemed prudent to start the train upon this narrow gauge road. We pass an hour and a half in great anxiety, as we have calculated our day's excursion so as to return just in time to connect our car with the outward-bound train at Denver, and we are now afraid of losing it; but presently arrives a telegram with the cheering assurance that the train shall be detained until our arrival, which comfortable arrangement is carried out, not too greatly to the discomfiture, let us charitably hope, of the punctual passengers already on the ground, and obliged to await our arrival—another exemplification, by the way, of the adage quoted at Toledo, "Served the bird right for being out so early!"

And so we leave Colorado, enchanted with what we have seen, yet reluctant as the child who perforce must leave the feast while any dainties remain untouched; for we have heard of Grey's Peak, that mighty Dome of the Continent, with its wonderful views of the great Arkansas Cañon, from whose height one may gaze dizzily down at the river, two thousand feet below, silently flowing between mile after mile of sheer precipice. We have heard of the mountain of the Holy Cross, where the sacred emblem has been set by God's own hand upon the face of an all-but—inaccessible mountain, the eternal snows that designate its form shining clear and white from the gray rock in which it is set, and visible at a distance of eighty miles. We have heard of wild passes not yet fully explored, which may lead to wonders greater than any of these; of possible gold mines not yet opened; of traditional hoards made by the red masters of these hills, who, conquered, yet unsubdued, have died and made no sign; of all of these and more we hear, and yet, hurried by relentless Time and Steam, we turn our backs and depart, murmuring with Scherezade: "The best remains behind!"

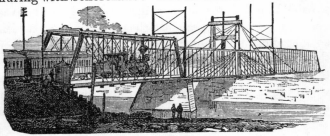

CROSSING THE MISSISSIPPI.

CHAPTER VI.

CATHEDRALS, CASTLES, CITIES, NOT BUILT BY HANDS.

NEXT day about noon we once more start upon our Westward journey, pass through numberless snow-sheds and over a country more utterly desolate than anything we have yet seen, and reminding us forcibly of the Peruvian deserts; the only point of advantage being the thick mat of buffalo grass which, unpromising as it looks, is, we are informed, the favorite food of all cattle, and retaining its sweetness even when apparently utterly dry and withered. To add to the discomfort of the scene, a blinding snow storm came on about dark, so that we were glad to draw down the shades, have the lamps lighted earlier than usual, and with dinner, cards, conversation and music pass as pleasant and cheery an evening as if the howl of the coyote did not mingle with the shriek of the wind and the fierce lashing of the snow against our windows.

Late in the afternoon of the next day the storm subsided, and the clouds rolling away like the vast curtains of Nature's grandest theatre, displayed a scene so magnificent, so novel, and so utterly changed from that we had shut out the night before, that we seemed to have passed through that snow storm from one world into another. We had entered the region of the Uintah Mountains, and are about to cross Green River.

whose vivid and poisonous-looking waters take their color from arsenical and copper deposits washed from the green shale abounding on its rocky banks. But we have no time for geological or scientific studies just now, and give but a distracted attention to the lecture of the *savant* at our elbow—whom the youth of the party irreverently denominate "The bureau of information"—while the rapidly moving train whirls us on through this region, where Nature seems to have indulged herself in mad, purposeless exercise of her vastest powers, with little heed for man's approval or convenience. In fact, so far from calling this country a new one, it impressed us as the playground of forgotten Titans : such lavish waste of color, of form, of power ; such gigantic forces brought to bear, and the result left idle, a mere waste of supernatural energy ; its only effect upon the world the blank astonishment and awe with which we—the nineteenth century flies upon the coach-wheel—stare, and gape, and shiver, and exclaim. To describe these wonders, to chronicle them even, is not our purpose ; are not the Guide Books intended for just that, and are they not excellent of their kind ? What matter, then, whether the grand mass of castellated, turretted rock one admires, with its low-browed gateway, its long, dark shot windows, whence Rebecca might even now be peeping to watch the siege of Torquilstone for Ivanhoe's benefit, be called Petrified Fish Cut, or the Giant's Teapot, or the Devil's Tavern, or the Tower of London ? For our part, we call them all the Castle of St. John, in memory of the enchanted tower described by the Wizard of the North, which

E

was now a castle full of wonders and delights, and ladie
fayre and belted knight, and now was but a mass of
cold, gray rock, according to the humor of the enchanter
and the character of the spectator.   The Church Buttes,
for instance, may suggest ecclesiastical architecture to
some minds, but to `ours the name seemed dwarfing
and unworthy ; since no cathedral built by human
hands, not St. Peter's itself, could for a moment bear
comparison with some of the Titanic piles here
upreared—could seem other than a paltry and puny
attempt of man to mimic Nature.

And now we reach Echo Cañon, and with bated
breath and a zest of terrible delight tingling in our
veins we sweep down with a grand rush and roar
between beetling crags, and toppling crests, and sheer
precipices, which now seem planted directly across our
path, as if in reaching them the solid wall must open to
admit us, or else we, striking full upon that impassive
barrier, must be hurled back to the opposite wall, like
the shuttlecock in a demoniac game of battledore.   But
the road winds, and doubles, and curves, and twists like
a snake—a miracle of engineering, as the Chief informs
us, but one has no thought for that just now ; indeed,
as the full breath of the mountain sweeps past and over
our car we seem lifted upon its wings, and fly exultingly
downward and onward, oblivious of engines and rails
and pounds of steam, which, nevertheless, like the
poet's roast beef, are the essential foundation of this
rare and æsthetic delight.   Speaking of wings, we well
remember a formation called the Winged Rock, where
a pair of eagle-like pinions seem struggling painfully

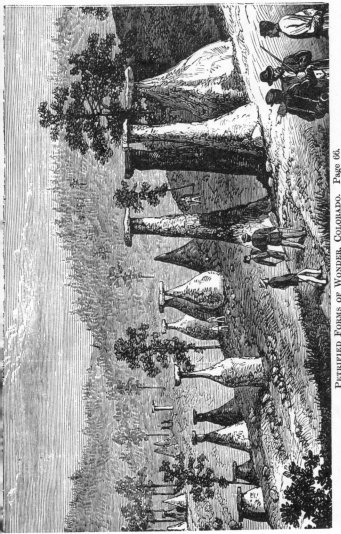

PETRIFIED FORMS OF WONDER, COLORADO.   Page 66.

out of the face of a precipice, and we can easily fancy how the poor bird of Jove was caught there just a moment too late, and petrified in his last wild struggle for freedom. Whether the shock deprived him of his head, or if he has since been decapitated by the elements, no man can say; but, certes, he is headless.

Many of these cliffs are curiously honeycombed by the action of weather and time, some of them appearing almost sponge-like in their reticulation; and we were grieved at being informed by our *savant* that, like most other peculiarities of this world, the buttes of this wonder region are doomed to be smoothed away by the hand of civilization; for the presence of such quantities of iron as go to the formation of the railway, and more especially the wires of the magnetic telegraph, have such attractions for the storm clouds that formerly swept harmlessly, or rather dryly, over this region, that the rainfall and the general humidity of the atmosphere have sensibly increased, and just in proportion the sharp outlines of cathedral spire, of witches' needles, of Titanic face, or soldierly sentinel have softened and crumbled, and " effaced " themselves, until some points of interest are already lost, others have altered to commonplace, and our *savant*, with a relish for which we could have set Follette at him, gave the region something over half a century to have lost every one of its special features. If ever poor Louis XV.'s *bon mot* is justifiable, is it not in the face of such a prophecy? "Après moi le déluge !"

On the overhanging edge of a cliff, high above our heads, appeared some mounds of apparently small

stones, collected by the Mormons in 1857 to serve as
missiles of war against the U. S. troops under General
Johnson, who was then marching against them. He
did not, however, pass through the Cañon that season,
and before another the domestic differences of Utah
and her mamma were so far adjusted that the piles of
stones remained. Beyond here we are called to observe
the resemblance of a huge mountain shoulder to the
prow of a steamship, and the resemblance is enhanced
by the waving top of a little cedar tree, obligingly growing in the place of a flag. They call it the Great
Eastern ; but considering the green banner, one must
conclude it an Irish emigrant ship, which, in some
forgotten age undertook to sail to America by way of
Japan and the Overland Route, and got caught in the
same fashion as the eagle. Why cannot some public-
spirited man quarry the mountain from above, in search
of the bodies of the hapless crew and passengers ?

And now a group of slender and fantastic rocks, sur-
named the Witches, appear, remarkable not only for
their weird shapes, but for the new combinations of
color exhibited in their snowwhite surface, banded
with red and yellow. Why some other rocks are
called the Witches' Bottles we know not, unless Mr.
Gough may have been this way and deduced from
petrified witches and petrified bottles a grand moral
tradition in the interests of total abstinence.

From Echo Cañon we sweep into Weber Cañon, and
are immediately struck both with the contrast of form
and color ; for here the detached and fantastic buttes
give place to grand sweeps of mountain sides, and bold

masses of rock, no longer of rich red sandstone, but of all shades of gray, from a tender, greenish tinge to a sombre hue just losing itself in black. The little Weber river, gray-green itself in color, winds timidly along at the feet of these overpowering crags, scarcely daring to murmur at the gloomy shadow which at some points forever excludes any ray of sunshine from its life, and yet she seems content.

Near the crest of one gray crag we were shown some little apertures, said to be the entrances to caves where, year after year, the eagles build and rear their young, defiant of their enemy, man, who has yet found no means to scale this aerie. Let us hope he never may, and that the bird of freedom may scream back for centuries an insulting echo to the train whirling like children's toys hundreds of feet below his home.

Presently we pass the Thousand-Mile tree, Nature's landmark for the round thousand miles west of Omaha; and here, a little farther on, upon a smooth mountain side, we see one of her very oddest freaks, in this, her old-time playground. Two parallel ledges of granite, in places fifty feet in height, crop out from the hillside, and, holding a uniform distance of about fourteen feet, extend eight hundred feet downward to its base, where they disappear in a little sheet of water. It is called the Devil's Slide, and it would be amusing, certainly, on a Winter's night, to see his Infernal Majesty disporting himself there in company with the harlequin Witches of Echo Cañon and their gray-clad sisters of Weber.

And now a grand, snow-clad mountain rears itself across our path, apparently forbidding all exit from the

vast prison house through which we have been borne ;
but a nearer approach shows a huge natural portal,
formed perhaps, for us, perhaps for the little river
which here suddenly throws off its late submissive
aspect, and after some wild plunges hither and thither,
sees its way of escape, and, rushing forth, becomes, in
later life, as commonplace and quiet a river as ever
turned a miller's wheel or floated logs to a lumber
yard.

Following the strange instinct which leads so many
of the godfathers of Nature's children to name them
after the Prince of Darkness, this mountain is called
Devil's Gate Mountain, and these portals the Devil's
Gate.   Gliding through, we cross the Weber River once
more upon a trestle bridge, with the waters roaring
fifty feet beneath, and get a last view of it twirling past
a huge gray wall of rock, in whose sunless shadows its
waters, but now so bright, show cold and green, and then
we look back at the crowding and apparently imperious
mountain range we have just passed, admire once more
their grand and snow-clad summits, piercing the cold
blue sky and frowning defiance on men whose puny
strength has conquered their inmost fastnesses, and
evaded their grimmest terrors ; and so we glide out
into the level plain, draw a calmer and freer breath,
and gaze around on scenes more familiar to our eyes
than the wonders so lately gazed upon ; for we are
in Utah, the land of thrift and industry, of agricul-
ture and irrigation.   We have been appalled by Nature
in her unconquered might, in her resistless grandeur ;
we are now to admire her placidly yielding to man's

dominion, and lending her creative forces to his guidance and direction.

The barren plains become verdant fields, the squalid cabin of the usual Western settler becomes a neat cottage, with flowers and garden-produce growing at its doors; the odious sage-brush disappears before the system of irrigation, which it dislikes as much as the more human indigenes of the prairies; men, women, and children are better fed, better dressed, and better mannered; in fact, as we stop in the first Mormon village, above whose single store are inscribed the mystic letters Z. C. M. I. (Zion's Co-operative Mercantile Institution), we feel a vague doubt and bewilderment stealing over our prejudices, not to say our principles, and are disposed to murmur, "Certainly, polygamy is very wrong, but roses are better than sage-brush, and potatoes and peas preferable as diet to buffalo grass. Also school-houses, with cleanly and comfortable troops of children about them, are a symptom of more advanced civilization than lonely shanties with only fever-and-ague and whisky therein. Why is nothing quite harmonious, quite consistent, quite perfect in this world?" and Echo Cañon echoes "Why?"

PRAIRIE DOG TOWN.

CHAPTER VII.

OGDEN, a city not otherwise remarkable, is the junction of the two great railways that unite sea to sea—the clasp upon the belt, so to speak, by which the continent is girdled. In point of fact, the junction was effected at a place called Promontory, some fifty miles west of Ogden, and readers of the illustrated papers eight years ago may recall the poetic and picturesque interest attaching to the scene that took place when an engine upon the Union Pacific road, and another upon the Central Pacific approached, the one from the East and the other from the West, until they actually touched, while a libation of wine was poured upon the last tie, the golden and silver spikes were driven by the hand of Governor Stamford, representing the C. P. R. R., and Dr. Durant of the U. P. R. R., and a prayer was offered by a Massachusetts clergyman—a combination of heathen, Christian and civil rites, characteristic enough of our great Republic, and also of a work carried on and completed by Europeans and Asiatics, with Americans directing both. Ogden is also the terminus, or rather starting point, of the Utah Central road, running south to Salt Lake City and beyond, and of the Utah Northern, running nowhere in particular as yet. These two great and two little roads have amic-

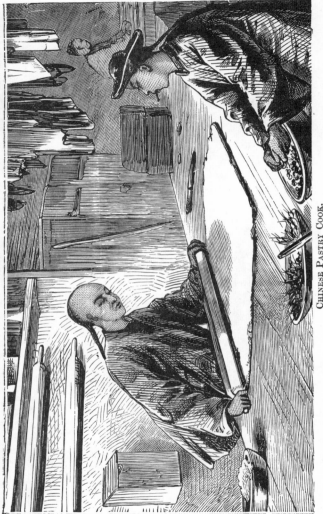

CHINESE PASTRY COOK.

ably agreed to build a large Union depot, to be occupied in common.

Our car being detached from the Union Pacific train, was connected with one waiting upon the Utah Central road, becoming, during that process, the nucleus of an inquiring group of Mormon and Gentile youth, and we were not sorry to find ourselves presently steaming southward at full speed, and enjoying a beautiful sunset scene, where the Wahsatch Mountains at the East and the Great Salt Lake at the West, with a smiling and fertile country between, make up a landscape one longs for time to dwell upon. The distance from Ogden to Salt Lake City is thirty-six miles, and we arrive at the terminus a little before nine o'clock, just in time to hear the last part of a service in one of the small churches scattered over the city, to serve when the weather is too cold to use the Tabernacle, which, from its vast size, cannot be artificially heated. The fragment of a sermon to which we listened seemed rather of a denunciatory than a benevolent nature, and turned upon the wrath of God toward apostates, and the propriety of rooting out those who had gone astray after Amalek. We wondered whether this meant Ann Eliza, but could not determine!

Those familiar with Mormon doctrines and preaching, although not of the faith, aver that the more usual Christian teaching of charity, humility, patience and forgiveness of enemies is rarely if ever made the leading topic of any sermon ; but that, as the Mormons are fond of likening themselves to the children of Israel and a People Peculiar to the Lord, their texts and lessons are generally drawn from the denunciations of the Prophets, whom they interpret with a literalness not found in other forms of faith.

The next morning we sallied forth to view the City of the Saints, with the same odd sort of excitement and vague expectation one must experience in Constantinople or Tangiers, or several other places which stand out in a traveler's memory as typical of a state of society utterly alien to his own. Nothing peculiar appeared at the outset, however, except that here for the first time did we perceive about the poorer houses that attempt at decoration, that consciousness that "a thing of beauty is a joy forever," which makes the difference between poverty and squalor; which shows that penury has neither broken the spirit nor crushed out the taste for refinement. Every house, however small or poor, had its little garden in front, filled with flowering shrubs or plants, many of them fruit trees, in this Spring time of the year rosy or white with bloom. Everywhere was thrift, care, the evidence of hard work, and a pride of ownership; and oddly enough, these homes of rigid, yet tasteful and dignified poverty, reminded me of nothing so much as a Shaker village, visited not long since—a place where nobody was rich, nobody poor, nobody idle, nobody overworked, and where a certain prim love of the beautiful everywhere gilded the necessity of the useful. Is it that a strong religious conviction pervading a community, a religion that permeates every phase of life, has this effect upon outward forms of living? We present the question to the psychologists. As for the better houses, they were many of them elegant, all of them comely and substantial; mostly built of yellow brick or stuccoed with yellow or white plaster, very few of wood; all had their own grounds, large or small, well cared for, and thoroughly irrigated by means of the streams of pure, bright water running along each street, and applied through branch ducts as required, to private grounds. These roadside streams also water the roots of the cottonwood and poplar trees which line the street on either side, and keep the grass vividly bright and green. There was no dust, no mud, no litter of any kind. Arrived at the main street, we noticed the Merchant's Co-operative Union Building, or "Co-op," as it is facetiously and popularly termed, with its inscription of "Holiness to the Lord," in black and gold above the door; a profusion of neat shops of all sorts, but more especially well-stocked and flourishing millinery establishments, and several fine book and stationery shops.

Reaching the principal photographer, who was an old acquaintance of our Chief's, we paid him a visit, and found a good assortment of views of the city and its surroundings, and a very civil and gentleman-like proprietor, who seemed quite amiably willing to impart the information we were thirsting to obtain. He freely admitted himself to be a Mormon, somewhat defiantly stating that he had nailed his colors to the mast. A picture of the Beehive, Brigham Young's principal residence, easily led to a discussion of Mormon houses and Mormon domesticity. But our new friend considered it very unlikely that we, even the women of the party, would be able to "interview" any of the upper class of Mormon wives. "The ladies here don't like being made subjects of curiosity," said he. "Their homes are just as sacred to them as yours in the East are to you, and they are very sensitive about being questioned." Then he cited, evidently as a timely warning, the case of a titled English lady recently passing through Utah, and remarkable, as our photographer seemed to think, in possessing more than the usual amount of cheek—"as much cheek as a government mule"—some artistic effect of which feature probably attracted his professional eye. This lady, as it seemed, possessed the troublesome characteristic of "wanting to know, you know," and attempted to gratify it in an artless manner by calling upon several of the Mormon ladies, and putting them to their catechism with the vigorous candor of a parish visitor. The consequence was that Miladi got terribly snubbed, and what was perhaps worse, learned nothing, and went away next day to make up her notes of travel as best she could. Having furnished this little narrative, our friend paused significantly, with a "*Hæc fabula docet*" air, and then indulgently added : "But I'll give you an introduction to the leading Mormon editor of the city, and you can see what he will do for you." Then he showed us some portraits of the various Mesdames Young, first of the recreant Ann Eliza, who "bolted," as he phrased it, upon the very day the President was about to present her with the title-deeds of the house she lived in. "And here's the house," continued he, producing a picture of a neat little villa ; "that's the hovel she talks about in the East." When President Young was informed that she was gone, or at least had removed with all her effects to the Walker House—the Gentile hotel, you know—he just opened his desk, took out the "title-deeds," and, tearing them across, said, quietly: "So much saved!"

The next picture represented a lady of about thirty, well dressed, a little stout, with a strong, sensible, pleasing face, and something of a stylish air. This was Mrs. Amelia, said to be Mr. Young's favorite wife, but this assumption our photographer scouted indignantly. "That was only Eastern talk; there was a lot of nonsense talked in the East about the Mormons, and Ann Eliza had set a whole raft of stories afloat, but all about it was that Mrs. Amelia was a born nurse, and had taken care of Mr. Young through some bad times, and so he always took her traveling with him and liked to have her near him at home." To a delicate suggestion about selling Amelia's picture, the artist shook his head; no, he couldn't sell that or the picture of any private lady. He had been offered a hundred dollars for it, but it was not for sale. We appreciated the fine feeling of this little speech, and mentally wondered how long our friend's position in Salt Lake City would be tenable if he offended Mrs. Amelia, and whether a hundred dollars would make up his loss in that case. On the whole, we concluded that he was a wise as well as an amusing and instructive photographer, and so took our leave.

The editor of the Mormon paper proved a very intelligent and cultured man, and after a little talk he

escorted us to see some of the lions of the place, first to
the " Woman's Union," a large establishment, where
the work of the women of Utah is collected and offered
for sale. It is under the charge of a lady called Miss
Snow—although she is one of Brigham Young's wives
—two of his daughters, and Mrs. Davis. The large
room on the ground floor was decorated with the
American flag and three large mottoes done in white
on a blue ground, to wit :

> " Knowledge is Power."
>
> " In Union is Strength."
>
> " Success to Industry."

The goods consisted of every sort of home manufacture :
clothes of all descriptions, shoes, bonnets, straw hats,
artificial flowers, laces, including some beautiful
wrought Honiton, and a piece of the first silk manufactured in Utah — a silver - gray fabric, resembling
Japanese silk. Miss Snow presently entered, and
greeted us pleasantly ; she is a lady considerably past
middle age, with a good and pleasing face, a quiet,
refined manner, although cold and reserved, and a very
precise and deliberate mode of speech. She seemed
perfectly willing to talk upon any subject which we
introduced, and quite able to give information in any
direction indicated. She had been abroad, and told me
she took cocoons of their own raising to Palestine, to
compare with those of that country, and that the Utah
article was pronounced fully equal to that of Oriental
growth. She quietly acknowledged herself the principal mover in the Woman's Union, the object of which

is to encourage self reliance, and perfect independence of the outside world, and added, with a smile of conscious strength and power: "We consider ourselves among the finest women in the world, and aim to compete with our sisters elsewhere in every pursuit and every branch of education." Women, she said, had as much interest as man in the prosperity of the territory, and their rights and privileges were equal. At the two colleges of Utah the course of study was the same for male and female students, and the progress of the latter was fully equal to the former. Education had necessarily been neglected among them in the first hard years of struggle, when every one had to labor for the means of bare existence; but now good schools were established everywhere, and the rising generation would be admirably trained.

In this connection she spoke of the hard journey across the plains thirty years ago, when, on the twelfth of June, leaving the place where Omaha now stands, they did not arrive at Salt Lake until the second day of October.

We touched slightly upon the peculiar institution of Utah, and I inquired if the various wives of one husband got along amicably among themselves, to which she decisively replied: "Perfectly so, their religion inculcates it; and besides, their work is so large, and their aims so high, that they have no time and no capacity for petty jealousies."

While talking we turned over some of the books by Mormon authors for sale here, and noticed a volume of Voyages by Miss Snow, and also a collection of poems, but she herself was more interesting than her books, and seemed so strong and earnest, and full of ideas and aspirations, and plans for the widest good of her chosen people, that we left her with real regret.

CO-OPERATIVE UNION BUILDING, SALT LAKE CITY.   Page 75.

CHAPTER VIII.

A FIRST-CLASS MORMON INTERIOR.

FROM the Woman's Union our cicerone led us to the Deseret National Bank, a substantial brick building, and presented us to Elder H——, president of that institution, and twice Representative from Utah to Washington, where he gave such satisfaction to his constituents as to win a most enthusiastic welcome on his return. We found him a fine-looking man, with marvelously expressive eyes, and as courtly and imposing in manner as appearance, and spent a pleasant hour as his guests in the bank parlor.

Mr. H—— spoke freely upon Utah matters, especially of its faith, professing himself a Mormon, but not a polygamist; having always, as he said, respected his wife's feelings too much to take another. In fact, he declared very few polygamic marriages now took place in the city, although still common enough through the rest of the Territory. He did not hear of more than half a dozen in the course of the year, and it was amusing to find this decadence from the primitive custom attributed to the same cause which excuses our city youth from taking matrimonial chains upon themselves, viz.: the increased cost of living, and growing demands of the fair sex. Formerly, as the Elder gravely asserted, polygamy had been a different matter, more patriarchal in its nature than was now possible;

the women had been content with the simple necessaries of life, and each had borne her share in the hardships and toil of the infant settlement, but now—

"But now," we interposed, "the railway has come and brought a whole train of French milliners and fashion plates."

"Yes," replied he, with a good-humored twinkle of the eye, "harbingers of a higher civilization I suppose you think."

"Yes," we responded, boldly, "for before them the evil of polygamy will melt away as it never would have done before either civil or moral legislation. Don't you think so?"

"Perhaps, perhaps," replied the Elder, stirring a little uneasily in his chair, and adding, cautiously, "that is, if it be an evil at all."

He then spoke of the position of women in Utah as being unusually elevated and respected; their actions were free, their opinions sought and regarded, and they had been offered the privilege of a vote on polygamy, which, however, they had declined to accept; they had the right of legislation in school matters, however, and could obtain almost any position they chose to claim and try for. Sounding him upon the subject of domestic peace in polygamic families, we received much the same answer as from Miss Snow; certainly the wives harmonized, why should they not? Each, if she chose, had her own house, where she lived in perfect privacy with her children; or, if they preferred, all combined in one united household. Pushing the matter home, we inquired if he would be willing to see his own daughters become wives of husbands already married, and he replied he should not seek to control their own choice in the matter. He might prefer to see them the sole wives of their husbands, but it would be as God willed and they chose.

At this moment a genial, hearty gentleman entered the room, and Mr. H—— at once presented him. He is, as we afterward learned, one of the principal merchants of Salt Lake City, and a man of large means; an Englishman, with the home accent still lingering in his merry voice, but quite free from English reserve and offishness; joining at once in the conversation, and speaking with enthusiasm of the beauty and charm of the women of Salt Lake City.

"Madame wishes to know if they are a jealous race?" said Mr. H——, with evident enjoyment of the idea of seeing some one else put through the same inquisitorial questionings, ordinary and extraordinary, to which he had just been subjected.

"Jealous!" exclaimed Mr. J——, "not they; they have no time for such nonsense. They have their houses, their children, their sewing, their affairs to attend to, and if idleness is the mother of mischief, occupation is the parent of contentment. Look at my wife, for instance: to be sure, she is an only wife, but if she were not, what time would she have for jealous fancies, with a large household, a family of fourteen children, their governess, and four servants to look after?"

"Fourteen children!" we echoed, involuntarily.

"Yes" replied Mr. J——, with pious fervor; "we

hold, with the psalmist, that 'children are an heritage of the Lord,' and man can have no surer sign of God's approval and kindness than a large family."

Mr. J—— mentioned that he had been seventeen years in this country, that he was the only Mormon in his family, and that he had never regretted the choice he had made in joining the sect. A short time since he took his two elder daughters and revisited the old country, spending some time upon the Continent, and bringing home a French governess for the younger children.

We spoke of Miss Snow, her remarkable intelligence and attainments, and, after heartily endorsing our encomiums, he remarked that she was one of Brigham Young's wives, but that she was merely "sealed to him for time," having been the widow of Joseph Smith, whose wife she would be in the next world. In fact, she had long since ceased to live among the President's wives, but maintained the most friendly relations with him and them. Inquiring into the nature of this temporary contract, we were informed that a woman once sealed or married to the man of her choice, was his to all eternity. So long as he lived she could think of no other partner, but after his death she might, if she chose, seal herself to another for the remainder of her mortal existence; a mere marriage of time, not at all to the prejudice of those eternal relations to be resumed at her own decease. One point striking us very forcibly in this exposition was the positive faith in another existence, implied by making such definite arrangements for its duties and pleasures.

Divorce is possible under the Mormon law, but is seldom applied for, and never granted except in case of ill-treatment, flagrant neglect, or the gravest offenses, and is not considered creditable to either party.

Mr. J—— closed by inviting us to call and see his wife in the afternoon, which we gladly promised to do; feeling that at last our fondest hopes were about to be realized, and we were actually to see the interior of a Mormon home and converse with a Mormon wife and lady.

While waiting for the hour appointed for this call we visited the theatre, where we found Neilson—the beautiful—rehearsing. It is about the size of the Fifth Avenue Theatre of New York, neatly, but not very expensively, decorated; the colors pink and gray. We did not see the rocking-chair in which Mr. Young is fond of sitting in one of the aisles to witness the performance, but two of the four proscenium boxes, we were informed, belonged to him, and some members of his family are generally to be seen there, as he is a zealous patron of the drama, and encourages a large attendance. We went behind the scenes, and found the green room spacious and comfortable, furnished with piano, sofa, chairs, and a long mirror; the dressing rooms commodious, and the "star" chamber luxuriously furnished.

From the theatre we drive to Mr. J——'s house, a really superb villa; the fine sweep of the carriage drive cuts a lawn of emerald-green velvet, and is bordered with symmetrical beds of tulips, geraniums, and other brilliant flowers, and although not so remarkable

here as in the humbler houses, we could but admire
the exquisite neatness and precision of everything we
saw.   Upon the doorstep we are met by our genial
host, who conducts us into a drawing-room noticeable
in any city for its elegant and tasteful furniture, ornaments and mirrors, and presents us to Mrs. J——, a
fine-looking, dignified English matron, surrounded by
several of her children—two young ladies elegantly
dressed and perfect in manner ; a young girl of twelve,
very pretty and stylish in her polonaise of brown
velvet ; a little boy of about three ; and a toddling
baby, sweet and dainty in its Valenciennes lace and
soft blue ribbons.   The other nine children did not
appear.

Mrs. J—— conversed much as any other cultivated
lady might do, upon all sorts of subjects, until the
gentlemen departed, *en masse*, for a visit to the stables
and conservatories, when, with much circumspection,
we introduced the subject of polygamy, and instead of
being snubbed, as our photographer warned us would
be the case, found our hostess as pleasantly willing to
converse upon that as all other subjects ; giving us such
information as we asked in a quiet and courteous manner, saying neither too much nor too little, but holding
herself so accurately within the golden mean as to give
all her words an additional force and weight ; convinc-
ing us that here, at least, we had the true woman view
of this great and vexed question.   And still the quiet
assertion was made that there was little or no dissen-
sion between the wives of the same household, but that
all united harmoniously in the effort to make the home

a happy one for the husband and a good one for his children.

Remarking, somewhat impetuously, that we could scarcely imagine such a state of things, and that we were sure no " Gentile " wives could live thus together, Mrs. J—— replied, with quiet significance :

" We control ourselves, and make it a duty to subdue all jealousies and tempers that would injure the harmony of our home."

" But are there no women among you of such disposition and temperament that they cannot endure a rival in the affections of their husband ?" we asked ; and Mrs. J—— replied, with an exceedingly subtle smile :

" If there are, and if they have accepted polygamy as part of their religion, that religion steadily trains them in the duties it involves, and enables them to carry out whatever it teaches."

" But does not the favorite wife assume authority and privileges which the others are slow to admit ?" we persistently interrogated.

" Oh, there are no favorites," replied the lady, confidently, and then added, a little dubiously : " or at least there should be none ; it is especially inculcated, that if the husband has any preference he should be very careful not to show it; and if a wife suspects herself to be the object of more than her due share of regard she should keep the suspicion strictly to herself."

" That is a very fine theory, Mrs. J——," we declared, laughingly, as we remembered Mr. J——'s declaration of monogamy. " But you have never tried it personally, and cannot be sure."

"Yes, but I have tried it, and am very sure," replied our hostess, as courteously as ever, and, turning with an affectionate smile to the eldest daughter, she added : "Jennie's mother and I lived in the same house for years, and were always the best of friends !"

The confusion at finding into what a horrible blunder we had been led, baffles all description. No doubt our hostess perceived it, but with perfect tact she went on speaking, without waiting for questioning, and we presently recovered ourself enough to listen. "The women of Utah," she said, " considered themselves quite on a par with the men in all respects, with equal interests and equal labor to perform for the welfare of the colony, education of the children, social growth and public refinement and elevation. These great aims naturally enlarged and strengthened their whole nature, and not only could they live happily and peaceably with each other, but they were faithful and devoted wives and intelligent and affectionate mothers. It is the duty or the privilege of the first wife to present the new-comer to her husband, and if she is an elderly and motherly person, she generally helps and guides the junior, instructs her in household matters, advises her in the conduct of her new life, and sustains and encourages her in every way. And I speak of these matters from experience," added Mrs. J——, quietly, as she finished this little dissertation ; and the writer, still a little nervous in pursuing this branch of the subject with her, turned to the young ladies, and inquired what were their views of Mormon life and Mormon marriages. They replied readily enough, and with the gay *insouci-ance* of youth, that they enjoyed themselves very much at Salt Lake, for the present at least; and as to the future, perhaps they should never marry at all, although it was evident they had no horror of polygamic union. Their mother, however, remarked, that although she should never interfere with the girls' own inclinations, she should prefer to see them each the only wife of a good husband. If otherwise, she had no doubt their religion would prove strong enough to enable them to bear cheerfully and patiently whatever might be in store for them.

The gentlemen here returned, and the conversation took a different turn, but in recalling it minutely after-ward, it seemed to me that in spite of all Mrs. J——'s insistance upon the enviable position of Mormon women, and the charms and advantages of their insti-tutions, the keynote of the whole system, so far as it related to women, was struck when she said:

"It is ordained by their religion, and their religion enables them to bear it!"

Cake and champagne were served, and the young gentleman of three proved himself a hero in the demo-lition of the former, somewhat to the distress of his sister. One of the young ladies cut us some beautiful flowers, and we took leave after a long and most delightful call, feeling that we had at last gained some reliable information and experience in the ways of Mormon homes and the feeling of intelligent Mormon women.

"And now," said the Chief, as we drove down the pretty sweep and out at the handsome entrance, "we have to do the Tabernacle, and pay our respects to his excellency the President, and we are done with Utah."

THE "TWINS," MARIPOSA GROVE.

CHAPTER IX.

FOLLOWING the suggestion of the Chief, we hastened from Mr. J——'s residence to Temple street, where, behind a plastered wall twenty feet in height, we found, not that gigantic monster of architecture, but the foundations of the new Temple which is to replace it as the scene of all the functional rites and ceremonies of the Mormon Church, such as ordination, baptism, "sealing" or marriage—both monogamic and polygamic—and burial; the Tabernacle to be reserved simply for preaching. This new building is planned in a very ornate and imposing style, and is built from white granite quarried in the northern part of the Territory; teams of oxen were dragging in great blocks of stone, and a score of workmen were busily hammering them into shape during our visit. But although five years and a good deal of money have already been expended upon this building, its walls are as yet only about ten feet above the ground, and the date of its completion is not named. One cause, if not *the* cause of its delay, may be found in the fact, that it is built entirely by voluntary contribution, and even Brigham's earnest desire to see the work completed has not brought in the funds with sufficient rapidity for any very rapid results.

The Tabernacle itself, as nearly all of us know from

pictures, if not personal survey, is a huge, bare, and very ugly building, with an oval, tiled roof, brick pillars, and no attempt at decoration outwardly. Inside it is quite as ugly, but a little less monotonous, for in the centre is a fountain with four *couchant* lions in plaster about it, and from the dreary expanse of white plastered ceiling, certainly concave, yet scarcely a dome, hangs a great star, with pendants of artificial flowers. Galleries supported by three rows of pillars, painted to imitate marble, extend along the sides, and the whole floor inclines like that of a theatre. The seating capacity of the building reaches twelve thousand, yet so fine are the acoustic properties that a speaker upon the rostrum is audible in any part of the house. In this respect the Mormons claim the Tabernacle to be unsurpassed by any building in the world.

At the end of this great hall, two hundred and fifty feet long, by one hundred and fifty wide, and eighty feet high, hung a monstrous blue banner, blazoned with a golden bee-hive and the inscription :

"Deseret Sunday-school Union."

At the other end was the great organ, of which the Mormons are justly proud, as it is said to be only second in size to the Boston organ—which is taller, but not quite so wide—and possesses a sweetness of tone really wonderful when the visitor is told that it is of absolute home manufacture, the wood and most of the other materials the growth of Utah, and the plan and construction are due to an English convert named Ridges, who prepared and built it in the Tabernacle

SOME OF THE LATE BRIGHAM YOUNG'S RESIDENCES IN SALT LAKE CITY. Page 83.

It contains twelve hundred pipes, and the case, although only of stained pine, is elegant in design. Between the organ and the auditorium, as it might be called, are the seats for the elders, and the leaders of the congregation : first and highest a little desk, with an ancient blue sofa behind it, used by Brigham Young and his two councillors ; below this a long straight bench and a small semicircular one, to accommodate the twelve apostles; and below this again a similar arrangement, where the elders sit and speak ; other seats around the organ may be used by the choir and dignitaries of the Church. Altogether, the Tabernacle impressed us as quite the sort of place where we would rather not spend the hours of a rainy Sunday in November; and having conscientiously looked it through we gladly turned our backs upon it, viewed the Endowment House in the same enclosure, where the ceremonies of the Church are celebrated, and where preaching went on until the Tabernacle was built, and then went to deliver a letter of introduction to Brigham Young himself, who had signified his readiness to receive us at his office at a fixed hour, now approaching.

We found the President's houses and other buildings enclosed by a high stone wall, well filled-in with adobe, with arched gateways and wooden gates before each building ; over that leading to the factories, stables, etc., is a double arch, surmounted by a beehive in the clasp of a monstrous eagle. The largest building, occupied by a dozen or so of the Mesdames Young, is also distinguished by a beehive over the door, and is called the "Beehive House." The other principal residence is called the Lion House, and Mr. Young generally breakfasts at the one and takes dinner or tea at the other, except when he visits either of his wives living in a house by herself; for each wife, we were informed, had the title-deeds of a house of her own, if she chose to accept the documents, and several of them having rural tastes live upon farms a short distance from Salt Lake City, and raise vegetables, etc., for the tables of the others.

The schoolhouse for the President's seventy children stands next the Beehive, and all these buildings, finished in smooth yellow plaster, with white trimmings and green blinds, are crowded close behind the high stone wall, shielding them from the street; in fact, we could think of nothing but the closely guarded seraglios of some Turkish Prince, and an odd desire to investigate the likeness and differences of Mohammedanism and Mormonism, the two polygamic religions of the earth, seized upon the writer, and may yet insist on gratification. Following this vagary of the mind came an overpowering sense of the rapidity with which this poor old world of ours is losing the romance of her youth, and how realistic is the spirit of her present epoch. In the days when the "Arabian Nights" were written, or rather orally handed down, what rapture it would have been to find one's self inside the precincts of the Harem of Haroun el Raschid, or even of the King of Oude ; what heart-throbbings of excitement, what thrills of mysterious delight one can imagine, or can remember one's self capable of imagining. But change the scene from Stamboul or Hindostan to these United

States of America, Territory of Utah; for Haroun the Magnificent or the Royalty of Oude substitute Mr. Brigham Young; for Zoraide, Zuleika and Dinorzade, read Ann and Harriet and Susan; and it will be more difficult to write a Thousand and One American Nights' Entertainments than a new bible called the Book of Mormon.

But apologizing for the digression, let us return to our tour, and look in at the Tithing House, whither in true biblical style, the people come, year by year, bringing literal tithes of all they possess, of whatever nature, and pay them into the common treasury. But the finest building within many hundred miles, perhaps, is the Amelia Palace, a really magnificent house, nearly finished, and designed for the wife whom our photographer sternly denies to be the favorite, and whose name it bears. It is really a splendid edifice.

Having looked at everything from the outside, we entered the Office, a large unattractive room, with a private sanctum railed off at the end, plainly furnished as a business room, and hung with portraits of the founders and leaders of Mormonism; among others that of Joseph Smith, who may be called the Father of that religion, although it is unfortunate that so blindly was it revealed to him, that one of the first laws laid down by him as an inspired direction to himself and his followers, was a stern prohibition of polygamy or concubinage, and his name is still on record as a President of the Church of Latter Day Saints in Nauvoo, Lapeer County, Michigan, excommunicating a certain Hiram Brown for preaching polygamy and "other

false and corrupt doctrine"; but in three years from
that time Smith and nearly all the Mormon leaders
were living in authorized and undenied polygamy.
But leaving the vexed question of Smith's first and
second revelations, and the glaring inconsistencies of
their record, which must be thorns in the side of those
whose duty it is to uphold and explain Mormonism, we
will speak of its present apostle, President (of the
Church) Young, whom we found standing in the middle
of his Office to receive us, with an expression of weary
fortitude upon his face, and a perfunctoriness of manner, suggesting that parties of Eastern visitors, curiosity seekers, and interviewers might possibly have
become a trifle tedious in Salt Lake City and the Office
of the President.

"How do you do! glad to see you! pass on, if you
please!" was the salutation, accompanied with a touch
of the hand as each guest was presented and named ·
and when nearly all had passed on and sat down, and
the host resumed his own seat, an awful pause fell upon
the assembled company, broken presently by a sonorous
assertion from the President that it was a pleasant
day. This was eagerly assented to by the Chief, who
added that the weather had been fine for some days,
and the conversation flowed on in this agreeable
strain for some moments, during which time we studied
the personal appearance of the lion we had come out
for to see. We found it both formidable and attractive:
a fine, tall, well developed figure; a fresh, ruddy
complexion almost befitting a young girl; keen blue
eyes, not telling too much of what goes on behind

them; a full mouth; a singularly magnetic manner; a voice hard and cold in its formal speech, but low and impressive when used confidentially; altogether a man of mark anywhere, and one whose wonderful influence over the minds and purses of men, and the hearts and principles of women, can be much more fully credited after an hour's conversation than before.

Perceiving that the interview was but a "function" for President Young, and one whose brevity would doubtless be the soul of its wit, we resolved to constitute ourselves the Curtius of our party, and, approaching the sacred sofa, remarked to the Chief, who was seated thereon, that we would change places with him as we had some information to ask of the President.

The Chief rose with suspicious alacrity, and for the first time a gleam of interest shone in Brigham's pale blue eyes as he turned them upon the bold intruder, whose first question was:

"Do you suppose, Mr. President, that I came all the way to Salt Lake City to hear that it was a fine day?"

"I am sure you need not, my dear,' was the ready response of this cavalier of seventy-six years, "for it must be fine weather wherever you are!"

The conversation established after this method went upon velvet, and, as the rest of the party began to talk among themselves, presently assumed a confidential and interesting turn, and we felt that what Mr. Young said upon matters of Mormon faith and Mormon practice he said with a sincerity and earnestness not always felt in a man's more public and general utterances.

Glancing at Joseph Smith's picture, we ventured the

criticism that it did not show any great amount of strength, intelligence, or culture. Mr. Young admitted the criticism, and said that Smith was not a man of great character naturally, but that he was inspired by God as a prophet, and spoke at times not from himself but by inspiration; he was not a man of education, but received such enlightenment from the Holy Spirit that he needed nothing more to fit him for his work as a leader. "And this is my own case also," pursued Mr. Young, quite simply. "My father was a frontierman, unlearned, and obliged to struggle for his children's food day by day, with no time to think of their education. All that I have acquired is by my own exertions and by the grace of God, who sometimes chooses the weak things of earth to manifest His glory." This want of education, he went on to say, was one of the greatest drawbacks and trials to the older generation of Mormons; they had been, almost without exception, poor and unlettered people, gathered from all parts of the world, and obliged, especially after their arrival in Utah, to use every energy and all their time to make productive and life-sustaining homes from the desert lands and savage wilderness into which they had penetrated; since, only thus shut off from other men could they hope to enjoy their religion and practices unmolested.

"But all this is over now, thank God!" ejaculated the President, with a gesture of relief. "Our homes are made, our country is prosperous, and our educational privileges are equal or superior to any State in the Union. Every child six years of age in the territory can read and write, and there is no limit to what they may learn as they grow older." I said that I had spoken of these matters with Miss Snow, " formerly one of your wives," as I somewhat diffidently phrased it, but the patriarch, with a calm smile, amended the sentence, " My wife still, if you please, my dear; once having entered into that relationship, we always remain in it, unless "— and his comely face clouded —" unless under very peculiar circumstances." We presumed him to be alluding to Ann Eliza, and longed to hear his views upon that recreant spouse; but not being gifted in the manner so liberally ascribed to the titled English lady by the photographer, we refrained, and only made a eulogy upon Miss Snow's attractions and merits, to which her husband listened graciously, and heartily indorsed, saying that she was doing a noble work among the women of Utah, and that he had placed two of his daughters under her training, and had the utmost confidence in her judgment.

We spoke of the magnificence of the Amelia Palace, and he characterized it as " absurdly fine "; but when we suggested that nothing could be too much for so good a wife and so lovely a woman as she was said to be, he assented, and added, emphatically, "She is all that, and more. Yes, Amelia is a good wife, an excellent wife and a lovely woman," with other phrases expressive of tenderness and esteem. "Besides," added the writer, " the Beehive, which is, I believe, your present residence, looks to me rather shabby for a man of your position;" but at this he shook his head, saying: " There it is, there it is; extravagance and ambition come creeping in, and destroy the simplicity of the first ideas. The Beehive was good enough for me, and has been so for many a year, but the world is changing—changing!"

"But nothing will change the Mormon ideas of polygamy, I suppose," suggested I, for having, by means of the parallel trenches of Miss Snow and Amelia, approached the subject, I could no longer refrain from a direct attack. Mr. Young glanced at me keenly, but replied, devoutly: "No, nothing can, since it is given to them by the grace of God. It is not obligatory, of course, but it is a blessing and a privilege vouchsafed by Him to his chosen Saints."

I broached yet once more the question of domestic harmony, and asked if the children of different mothers could live amicably in the same house.

"I'll tell you something about that," replied Brigham, emphatically. "My sister came to make me a visit some years ago, and staid here until her death. She was not a Mormon, and did not believe in polygamy, but she said she had never seen a family of four children as peaceable and orderly and happy as my family of twenty-four, as I had then. She talked of it all the time, and never ceased praising this domestic harmony of which you speak. You see, they are trained to it by their mothers from earliest infancy; it is made a part of their religious teaching."

"Yes, but who trains the mothers?" inquired I, audaciously; "what religion can make a woman happy in seeing the husband whom she loves devoted to another wife, and one with equal claims with herself.

Any woman, I should think, would spend all her strength, use every effort of mind, body and soul, to attract and retain his love, admiration and attention. Isn't it so, Mr. President?"

Mr. President shot a keen, inquisitorial glance at the face beside him, and answered, meditatively:

"You look like just the woman to do that sort of thing, but fortunately, perhaps, there are not many of that mind among us; as a rule, our women are content in trying to make their husbands happy and their homes pleasant ——"

"Just what I was suggesting," interrupted I. "That she should make it so pleasant that he would not seek another."

He laughed a little, but replied:

"That would be agreeable to the husband, no doubt, but it would be contrary to the teachings of the wife's religion. She would not be a good Mormon wife if she allowed herself to follow such a course, nor could it, in the end, make the husband happy to alienate him from those whom he was bound to love and care for equally. For my own part, I always endeavor to show perfect impartiality, and allow no one division of my family to claim time or thought too exclusively."

"Then do Mormon husbands feel no preferences?" asked I, ingenuously, and laughing outright he replied:

"Well, perhaps; human nature is frail, but our religion teaches us to control and conceal those preferences as much as possible, and we do—we do."

The conversation was here interrupted, but the

President himself resumed it by saying, in a confidential voice, that Utah was going, in two or three generations, to present the finest specimens of men and women to be found in this country, for they would spring from marriages of pure affinity, and a state of society impossible except under polygamy. "Why," said he, "I have walked the streets of your great city at night and my heart has bled to see the hollow eyes and painted cheeks of the women who walked them too, and who lead away the young men who are to be the husbands of this and the fathers of the next generation. Not one such woman is to be found in Utah, and our young men are pure, our women are virtuous, and our children born free from inherited disease." In fact, he said that the children of to-day were a finer race than were to be found elsewhere, and he was going to have all of his photographed as specimens of childish beauty.

"But are all the women of Utah sure to marry?" asked I. "Suppose nobody offers for them?"

"A woman feeling herself drawn in affinity to a man, and feeling inclined to seal herself to him, should make her ideas known to him without scruple. It is her duty, and there can be no indelicacy in obeying the voice of duty," was the reply; and with this cheerful and hopeful vision of Mormonism before our eyes, we at last obeyed the urgent gestures of those who had not been so well entertained as ourself, and rose to depart, Mr. Young taking leave much more impressively than he had greeted us, and retaining, it is hoped, as pleasant a reminiscence of the interview as the writer.

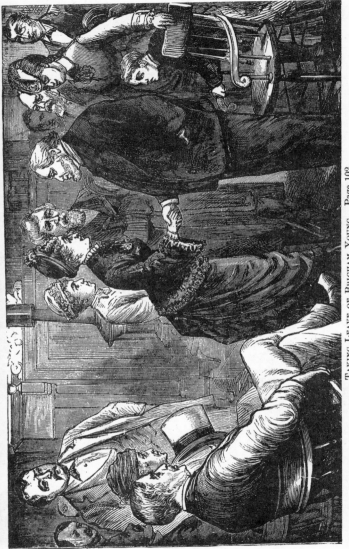

TAKING LEAVE OF BRIGHAM YOUNG.   Page 102.

A few hours later we had said good-by to Salt Lake City, with its many strange and peculiar objects of interest, and were steaming back to Ogden, there to reunite ourselves with the Great Pacific Road.

[Since writing the above, news comes to us of President Young's sudden death, and all that struck us as doubtful, or wrong, or ludicrous in the strange system of life he upheld, and of which he was the centre, disappears in the solemn respect and silence with which one remembers the dead whose lives have, even for an hour, intersected our own. He was an honest and sincere believer in his own theories, and lived up to his own convictions of duty; and how many of those who sneer at him dare say the same? A little selfish regret also mingles with the tribute we would fain pay to the memory of the kindly and courteous patriarch, who made us welcome, and exerted himself to entertain us even when ill and weary himself; for his parting words to us were: "And if you put me in a book, promise at least that you will print me as you have found me, and not as others have described me." We had tried to do so, and now he will never know it; never know how kindly and respectfully we remember him, or how honestly we regret his death. May the world deal as tenderly with his memory as we would do, and above his tomb let us inscribe: "**Judgment is Mine, saith the Lord.**"]

NEW MORMON TEMPLE AS IT WILL APPEAR WHEN COMPLETED.

CHAPTER X.

SOON after leaving Ogden we caught another fine view of Salt Lake, with its bold promontories, and blue waves dashing upon them quite in oceanic style, and listened to some valuable remarks from the *savant* and others as to what will happen when the waters of this inland sea, always gradually rising, shall overflow their bed, and demand the outlet they do not at present possess. I believe it was finally decided that they were either to adopt the Humboldt River as their channel, or to set up a certain valley, supposed to have been an arm of the Lake, and after cutting through a certain range of hills some fifty feet high, were to flow into Raft River, and so down to the Pacific.

"Après nous le déluge," remarked I to Follette, and we sympathetically fell asleep. Waking some hours later, we found ourselves in what is aptly called the Great American Desert, and surely Sahara deserves the name no better; and yet, as if to mark the different seal Nature has set upon the drowsy Orient and the laborious Occident, the Eastern desert is strewn with only yellow sand, of no possible earthly use except to inspire the venerable conundrum about the sand-which-is-there; while our American Desert is composed of alkali, suggesting at once manufactories, mills, factories, companies, washing soda and hot biscuit, with an infin-

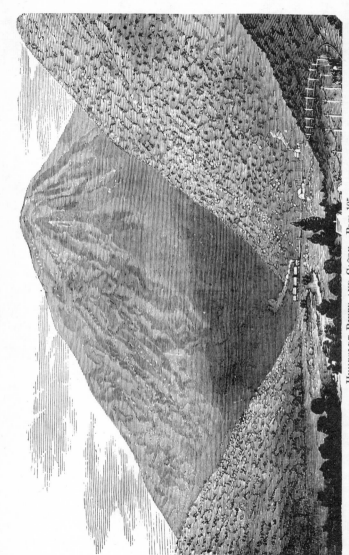

Humboldt River and Cañon.   Page 105.

ity of uses not yet discovered, and not more incredible
than the manufacture of Lubin's Extracts from coal tar.
Hundreds of miles of alkali going to waste, my countrymen, ye men of enterprise, of capital, of ingenuity!
Up, my friends, in the words of the immortal hero of
Waterloo, "Up, boys, and at them!" Before we have
quite done up the prospectus of the Great Anti-acid
and Baking Powder Company, we arrive at Humboldt
Cañon, and, albeit grown a little critical and fastidious
in such matters, wake up to a good deal of enthusiasm
and interest. Another valuable dissertation upon the
real destination of the waters of the Humboldt and
Truckee rivers now arose; the simple fact being, that
they pour their bright waters, year by year, into a lake
unsentimentally named the "Sink of the Humboldt,"
wherein they disappear, and are seen no more, except
in the shape of great white cumuli of clouds, which
drift away overhead to carry the evaporated moisture
back to the springs whence it came, for the "Sink of the
Humboldt" has no more outlet than has Salt Lake, or
many another Sink scattered through this Desert; and
after all, no theory seems more feasible than that this
entire region is the bed of an ocean whereon the unremembered people navigated their navies, lived upon the
islands which now are mountain peaks, and idly wondered what might be the secrets of the submarine
territory through which to-day we travel. When in
some great convulsion of Nature this ocean disappeared,
perhaps overflowing in the Noahcian Deluge a smiling
and prosperous land, now called the Pacific Ocean,
the Salt Lake, or crevice deeper than the general

ocean bed was left, and the Sinks were left, and the
vast barren plains covered with salt and other
alkalies were left, and the great process of evaporation
dried up such moisture as did not resolve itself into
rivers which seek these lower levels, and still evaporate
as much as they receive.

Quite fatigued by such a "breather" over the
hedges and ditches, swamps and brambles of science
and supposition, the feeble female mind turns with
interest to the contemplation of the noble savage, who
now begins to be frequent and importunate at every
station. There are women clothed upon with filth of
every shade and texture, woven or skinny; shawls and
handkerchiefs tied over their heads, and about half of
them carrying upon their backs a formless and silent
burden, which, for filthy lucre, they would unstrap and
bring forward, showing it to consist of a flat board, with
a headpiece projecting from the top of it, and two skin
flaps attached to either side of its length. Beneath
these flaps is strapped a pappoose, its patient face and
black bead eyes concealed by a piece of dirty cloth
thrown over the projecting board at the top. Of
course, the little wretch is very uncomfortable, and has
every reason to complain incessantly; but such is the
force of inherited nature, or of very early training, that
never a sound is heard from their grave little mouths,
and they probably have learned, thus early in life, that
very little sympathy, and perhaps considerable hard
usage, would result from any outcry. One young gentleman, aged about six, the son of a chief, was dressed in a
soldier's blue cap and a rabbit-skin cloak ; not made of

the skins sewed together, but cut in narrow strips, twisted into cords and then used as the warps of a fabric whose woof is sinews or stout twine.

The "braves," if they will excuse the sarcasm of so calling them, were somewhat more repulsive than the women and children, being equally dirty and more dangerous; as, for instance, a sewer rat is more disagreeable than a young pig. They were dressed in blue trowsers, the gift of their indulgent Uncle Samuel, striped blankets and low-crowned stiff hats, with feathers stuck in the bands, and a mane of coarse, dirty hair blowing about their shoulders. Many of the women had their faces painted in Turner-esque style of coloring, and begged vociferously for money, which they clutched with no pretense of gratitude or pleasure. The men stood magnificently aside while this was going on, and our young lady who had been vainly trying to recognize the Fennimore Cooper Indian among these squalid savages, was just exclaiming, "The men, at least, scorn to beg!" when one of the biggest, and probably the bravest of the braves, stepped up to the pappoose - laden squaw, and, with a persuasive twist of her wrist and wrenching open of her hand, relieved her of the burden of superfluous wealth just imposed upon her by our Chief.

"Lo, the poor Indian—squaw!" quietly remarked the cynic of our party, as the train rolled onward, and the young lady shut up "The Prairie," which she had been reading, and applied herself to Ouida.

At Elko we dropped the Shoshones and began with the Piutes, but did not perceive any great difference, except that the pappoose cradles were, in the latter tribe, made of basketwork, with a little perch woven out from the top to cover the baby's face, instead of the boards of the Shoshones. The fathers and mothers were as dirty and disagreeable in one tribe as the other, and the pappooses in both were so numerous, so flourishing, so fat and strong, as to quite calm the fears of those humanitarians who tremble lest these dear savages should become extinct in the next generation.

Now, too, we began to see the "Heathen Chinee" in numbers, and ill as their odor may be in Caucasian nostrils, we must say that their cleanly, smooth, and cared-for appearance was very agreeable in contrast with the wild, unkempt and filthy red man.

Toward night we began the passage of the Sierras with the help of an additional engine, for the grades are as steep as can be traversed, and occasionally the train seems to be plunging head first into some Avernus, from which return will be impossible, and anon scaling heights fitter for a chamois than a locomotive. If one only knew how to say them there are marvelous things to say about this Pacific R. R., and as the author of a nice book of California travel naïvely says, "If Americans were not the most modest people in the world," they would have, before this, convinced the public that no other piece of engineering, from Hannibal's eating down the Alps with vinegar, or the Great Emperor's road across the Simplon, to the present day, is to be compared with this passage of the Sierras from Ogden to Sacramento by Messrs. Stanford, Huntington, and the rest. We never scientifically examined either

Hannibal's or Napoleon's achievements, but we are very willing to accept the theory both that Americans err in lack of self-appreciation, and that the Pacific road is the road of the world ; and we advise those statistical souls which thirst for exact information about anything, to go and read all about this national triumph in any one of half a dozen most excellent books of travel, or even in the discursive and chatty Guide books which solaced many a weary hour for us in crossing the prairies and deserts which artistically throw out by contrast the wonders and beauties of the route. For ourselves, let us simply note the thrill of awe and wonder with which we gazed up the walls of the Blue Cañon, one thousand feet of sheer precipice, while far below winds a narrow ribbon of blue water curving to the curve of the foothills, and sweeping around their craggy feet, avoiding the jagged points, and lending grace and beauty to the stern and rugged scene in a manner altogether feminine. By the way, how true is that instinct which makes every one call a river she, and a mountain he!

But of all the scenery of the entire route, nothing can compare with the Great American Cañon, heralded by the rounding of Cape Horn, where the railway clings to the face of a precipice, with a thousand feet of crag above and two thousand feet below ; a river winding dimly through the ravine, and giant pine trees dwarfed to shrubs as we look down upon their crests. No blood so sluggish, no eyes so dull, no heart so numbed and encrusted by worldliness but that they must be stirred and thrilled, as few things in this world can stir its favorite children, by the sensation of thus flying like a bird across the face of this precipice, over the depths of this frightful abyss, suspended, as it were, between heaven and the inferno ; where the daring men who first stood here among the eagle's nests were lowered from the top of the cliffs by ropes, and where, to-day, one feels that at any moment the Titan slumbering within the mountain may by a single sleeping sigh fling off unconsciously the puny insect that dares thus to traverse his stupendous breast. The worst thing about language is, that it becomes so inadequate when anything of importance has to be portrayed. Talleyrand might well remark that words were given to conceal thought or feeling, if either is a little out of the common experience ; so, without attempting the impossible, we simply say to those of our friends to whom the Alps are a bore, Appenines and Pyrenees a weariness, and the Andes a tiresome impossibility, do go and see the American Cañon, Cape Horn, the Sierras, Donner Lake, Emigrant Gap, Yuba River with its dam, and all the rest of it. The journey is luxurious, the expense no greater than three months abroad, and the result something which will convince you that you did not know your world as well as you thought you did. Perhaps after all, however, the most original sensation is experienced as one from the level of the mountain tops looks across the sea of peaks to the horizon line on a level with himself, and feels that each of these crests represents a mountain which he would spend weary hours in climbing, if placed at its foot. It is a world above the level of the world we know and habitually live in, another strata of earth's surface, and gives far more idea of mountain scenery than anything we have ever beheld ; infinitely more than the passage of the Rocky Mountains.

At Dutch Flat, so called from being an unusually hilly and broken country, we came upon the first gold mining, the placer fashion being nearly out of style, except in some parts of California, where the root of all evil is still to be found on the surface, and small boys, when a circus comes into their town, borrow their mothers' tin pans and go into the field to wash out gold enough to pay for a ticket. Hydraulic mining is the same principle carried out, for instead of a dipper full of water poured into a pan of earth, whole tons of water are brought in iron pipes and hurled against the faces of hills and cliffs a hundred or more feet high, until the earth is all washed down into the flumes below, and agitated until the particles of gold settle at the bottom of the muddy mass. It is really wonderful to see what a force water thus applied can become ; some of these streams, starting from a head of five hundred feet in height, and directed through a nozzle six inches in diameter, assume a power nothing less than awful ; for great rocks, weighing hundreds of tons, are tossed out of their beds like the merest of pebbles, and the toughest clay and cement washed away like dust before their first approach. Such a stream is, as we were told, solid to the touch and cold as ice, and either man or beast, upon whom it was turned, would find as sudden death as in the track of a cannon-ball.

A verdant and picturesque hill subjected to a course

of this sort of hydropathy assumes, in a few days, the look of those landscapes Doré loves to depict in his Inferno : every particle of soil, trees, grasses, even the lighter rocks, are washed away, and lie in disordered masses at the foot, while the grim skeleton of the crag, if it was one, remains ghastly, naked, desolate, a monument of man's unmistakable greed of gain and reckless sacrifice of everything that stands between it and himself. It is to be devoutly hoped that the gold thus won is used somewhere and somehow to beautify the earth and the lives of its inhabitants, for surely the getting of it is a most defacing process to both the one and the other.

At Colfax the train stopped for breakfast, and the platform swarmed with boys selling strawberries, the first fruits of the new climate we were entering upon. At the right of the station stood a row of Chinese shops, each with its mysterious sign in red and gilded paper stuck up beside the door. At a stall stood · Chinese butcher, cutting up a sheep, and threading little morsels of the meat upon a long splint of bamboo, exactly as the Turks in Constantinople string "Kibaubs" for the watering mouths of the Faithful.

From this point the face of the country changed : vanished the mighty Sierras, the terrible abysses, the frowning black-green forests, the majesty and awe of the mountains ; vanished, too, the desolation and desecration of the placer mining district, and we were in a garden hundreds of miles in extent, and teeming with vegetation in every variety ; a lovely Summer land, fertile and blossoming spontaneously with a luxuriance the Mormons scarcely approach in Utah, even with the life-long and exhaustive labor they have bestowed upon their arid soil. Sacramento, the centre of this lovely region, is like a gigantic bouquet, every little villa rising from the midst of its *entourage* of clipped cedars, palm trees, cactus, prickly-pear, and belts of flowers, while the air, soft and caressing as that of the Spice Islands, was, like that, laden with perfume far fresher and less enervating than those.

"Sacramento!" murmured the young lady, as she buried her face in a mass of roses presented by our artist, who had secured them from one of the urchins clamoring upon the platform. "It is the oath of fealty by which man regains the Paradise he has lost."

"That sort of Paradise is regained by every woman somewhere between fifteen and fifty," murmured the Sultana, suffering her cashmere to drop altogether from her shoulders as the balmy air crept in at the opened window.

The only things that we never tire of are those that are snatched from us before we have fairly enjoyed them, and perhaps we should not remember this Paradise Regained so vividly but that we lost it directly in a region of the most commonplace and uninteresting prosperity, continuing until we reached Oakland, the end of the road, and standing in the same relation to San Francisco that Brooklyn does to New York.

Wearied, apathetic with over-exertion, and yet excited in feeling that at last we had reached the Eldorado, the City of the Golden Gate, the Mecca of our journey, we crossed the ferry, affronted the army of

H

hackmen raging upon the other side, and choosing the least vociferous of the crowd, were driven through dingy and unlovely business streets to the Palace Hotel, which we entered with something of the eagerness of "Noah's Weary Dove," when, after her long and fatiguing flight, she found the Ark of rest and comfort.

THE "NOBLE SAVAGE."   Page 107.

CHAPTER XI.

ONE of the most interesting sights in San Francisco
is the one that was first presented to our consideration, namely : the Palace Hotel. A certain Englishman described it as a huge building "broken out into
bird-cages," thus figuring the impression produced
upon his mind by the tier upon tier of bow-windows
which, whether they be considered as disfiguring or
ornamental to the general effect, are certainly very
comfortable to the inmates of the rooms thus beauti-
fied ; besides—and here we claim the congratulations of
those friends who have denied us a practical turn of
mind—besides securing to Senator Sharon a considerable area of territory not included in the ground-plan,
which, nevertheless, covers a whole square, measuring
about two acres and a half; and it will be a convenience
to conscientious pedestrians taking their matutinal
promenade to know that to go around the house upon
the street is to walk a quarter of a mile ; or if their
taste is feline, to go around the roof is to traverse
the third of a mile. Let us furthermore state, that the
corridors collectively measure two and one-half miles;
that twenty miles of gas-pipe are necessary to its illu-
mination ; that there are four hundred and thirty-seven
bath tubs, and accommodations for twelve hundred

guests. Having thus sacrificed on the altar of statistics, let us chronicle our own first impressions, which
are never by any chance statistical.

Driving in through iron gates and a stone archway,
we entered an almost regal inner court, reminding us of
the Grand Hotel at Paris on an enlarged scale ; seven
tiers of balconies surround the four sides, ornamented
with frequent tubs of flowering plants, cages of singing
birds, and sofas and chairs, where groups of guests sit
to chat, or promenade up and down. A glass dome
covers the whole, giving a soft and tempered light
during the day, while at night the place is brilliantly
illuminated by gas. On the ground floor the court is
faced with white marble, and a circular carriage-drive
sweeps around the centre, where stand groups of palm
and banana trees, and vases of beautiful flowers. Chairs
and settees are dotted around the pavement, where sit
the *flaneurs* who like to watch the constant arrivals of
guests, and the visitors' carriages standing in waiting
complete the lively and picturesque scene.

Mr. Warren Leland, that prince of landlords, welcomed us courteously and cordially, escorted us from
the largest and most elegant reception-room, upon
the easiest elevator in the world, to the suite of apartments on the second floor lately occupied by Dom
Pedro ; gave us the freedom of his kingdom, and at a
later hour caused the courtyard to be illuminated from
ground to dome, and a serenade to be given in honor
of our arrival. That evening we did little but make the
tour of the drawing-rooms and other principal apartments, which are as magnificent as befit a Palace Hotel,

listen to the statistics elaborately set down above, satisfy ourselves of the comfort of the bathing tubs, and go to bed tired, happy, and full of anticipating delight for the morrow.

Next morning, after breakfast, we received the visits of several photographers, who have probably learned by inspiration the Chief's amiable weakness for this school of art and artists, and who propose to immortalize us in a group. Not fancying that style of immortality, however, we compromise for large numbers of individual portraits. Our attentive friends claimed, and we believe the fact is confessed, that San Francisco is the place of all places for the perfection of their art, the peculiar atmosphere lending itself most happily to the combination of their chemicals.

Like Rome, San Francisco is built on seven hills —the foothills of the Sierras; and nearly every street sweeps up a steep incline to a bold, rocky bluff, crested with villas and other buildings, giving a wonderfully picturesque look to the whole. There are some stone buildings, but more of wood, and few exceed two stories in height, the frequent earthquakes, or "shakes," as they are familiarly called, making higher pretensions dangerous. The style of architecture has been justly denominated as "San Franciscan," and the bow window is its exponent: not a house, from the Palace Hotel and the sumptuous mansion of the millionaire to the cozy nest of "two young lovers lately wed," but is studded with bow-windows, very many of them filled with flowers and bird-cages. A lady to whom we noticed this peculiarity explained that the climate of

San Francisco is such as to seldom allow one to sit or lounge out of doors, the high, cold winds almost invariably coming in from seaward by noon, or earlier, and that after that time a sunny bow-window with a stand of plants was far more comfortable than a garden chair; and it is true that the sunshine is a luxury more highly appreciated in San Francisco than in most cities, for a room deprived of it is scarcely comfortable night and morning without fire during most of the year.

The most fashionable shops are on Kearney and Montgomery streets, the Broadway and favorite promenades of the city. The windows of these shops are large, and showily furnished, but the interiors are of limited extent, owing to the high price of land in these localities. Every imaginable object is to be bought in San Francisco, generally at very high prices; for, like most places of sudden growth, it is an extravagant place in dress, equipage, and general tone of living, the fortunes of the East becoming a modest competence here, and what would be comfort in Philadelphia or Baltimore dwindling to penury in San Francisco.

Many of the smaller shops are open to the street like booths, especially the cigar and liquor establishments, in one of which we saw a man throwing dice for a drink. Most of the sidewalks are of wood, and the street-car tracks are paved with that material, although we were told that none but the Nicholson pavement has proved a success here, as the long, dry heat of certain portions of the year, and the persistent dampness of others, shrink and swell, out of proportion, the blocks of all other kinds of wooden pavement.

The climate of San Francisco seems a point as difficult to settle as the standard of feminine beauty, or the intrinsic value of Wagner's music. Every one agrees that it is an exhilarating climate, that the air is more highly charged with ozone than in most localities, that the brain-worker can accomplish more here in a given time than anywhere else, and wear himself out faster; for dear Starr King died of exhaustion, of old age, in fact, after doing the work of a generation for his adopted State ; and such a career as that of W. A. Ralston would scarcely have been possible in any city other than high-pressure San Francisco. But this ozone, this fourth - proof oxygen, is borne upon the wings of high, cold winds, piercing the very marrow of a sensitive form, and alternating with fogs and dampness, fatal to any rheumatic or neuralgic tendencies, and unfavorable to pulmonary complaints. A few hours of nearly every morning are charming out of doors, and the rest of the day a fire or a bow-window full of sunshine is still more charming. One person says, "The climate of San Francisco is all that keeps me alive"; and the next one shudders, "The climate is killing me ; I must get out of town to warm my blood, or it will congeal altogether." All confess, however, that this is the chilliest and breeziest point upon the whole coast, for it stands in a gap of the hills, guarding the shore for miles above and below, and once in the sheltered valleys lying between this coast line and the Sierras, one comes into a tropical and paradisaical climate as enervating to the brain as the breezy air of San Francisco is exciting. Let us conclude that the climate, like the society, like the morals, and like the social habits of San Francisco, is a little mixed, and that a wise eclecticism is desirable in choosing a residence therein.

One feature of the street scenery in this city is the large proportion of foreign physiognomy and the accents of almost every language under the sun, which meet one's ear in all the crowded thoroughfares. The easy access of the Pacific coast from the other side of the globe has led thither a class of Oriental strangers who are seldom seen even in New York, and not only the Chinaman, but his neighbors of Asia and Africa— "Mede, Parthian and Scythian"— here find a home, a field of labor, and a share, however small, of the almighty dollar, which has proved more lovely in their eyes than the lands of the bul-bul and the rose.

To accommodate these various tastes, various amusements, shops, theatres, and especially restaurants, are established at every corner, and the Frenchman, scanning the *menu* of the Maison Dorée, may fancy himself at the Trois Frères, in Paris ; while the German finds his sauerkraut, the Italian his maccaroni, the Spaniard his picadillo, and the Welshman his leek, each at his own house of refreshment; and the Chinese eating-houses are a feature of their especial quarter, to be mentioned hereafter. To live in lodgings and to eat in a restaurant is San Franciscan as much as it is Parisian, and even families possessing houses and domestic conveniences are often to be found at one or the other of these establishments, dining or lunching, "just for variety"; and also, perhaps, to see and to be seen a little.

A fashionable restaurant for gentlemen is "The Poodle Dog"; "Campi's" is as Italian as Naples, and the "Maison Dorée" is Delmonican in every respect. The code of social law in San Francisco permits young ladies to freely visit these establishments, even at the risk of occasionally encountering a male acquaintance, and a cynical observer may find more refreshment in quiet observation of the scenes around him than in meat or drink. Perhaps, on the whole, we would not advise the widowed mother of a family of lads and lassies to carry them to San Francisco for social training; the Prunes, Prisms, and Propriety system is not universal, and although there is a large class of charming, unexceptional, and rigidly moral society, there are several other classes shading into it by almost imperceptible degrees; and the bygone days, when every man was a law unto himself in this city, have left their impress in a certain recklessness and willfulness of feeling pervading every circle.

The style of street dress is more gay and showy than is consistent with the severest taste, and an afternoon promenade upon Kearney or Montgomery streets reminds one of a fashionable "Opening," when the lay figures have suddenly received life and the power of locomotion. It has been said that in other cities the *demi-monde* imitates the fashions of the *beau-monde*, but that in San Francisco the case is reversed, and the caprices of the former class are meekly copied by the latter. It may be a libel; but we certainly saw very elegant toilets, and very fine jewels, both in carriages and upon pedestrians to whom we had no letters of introduction.

Noticing a goodly proportion of churches among the handsome buildings of San Francisco, we inquired if anybody ever visited them, and were indignantly informed that religion was one of the most flourishing imports of the City of the Golden Gate. Everybody knows, of course, that it was originally founded as a mission by the Franciscan Fathers, the first of whom, the Padre Junipero Serra, scandalized that no station had as yet been dedicated to his patron saint, prayed to him for a fortunate harbor in his next voyage of exploration; and being led or driven through the Golden Gate, considered that the Saint thus indicated the spot where he would have his altar erected, and so named the waters upon which the mission vessel floated, "The Bay of San Francisco." The Mission House and Church were more elaborately styled "Los Dolores de nuestro Padre, San Francisco de Assissi," and is still called the Mission Dolores; while the presidio and fort erected to protect the good monks in their holy work was called San Francisco, and the town that languidly grew around them took the name of Yerba Buena, from a medicinal plant growing abundantly in the vicinity. It was not until 1847 that the name of San Francisco was formally given to the little town, then just upon the eve of its marvelous upward bound to the rank of a great city. The Romish faith thus planted has kept its ascendancy in the city of San Francisco d'Assissi, and claims to-day about one-half of the population. St. Mary's Cathedral, St. Francis's St. Patrick's and St. Ignatius's, are all with large and wealthy congregations, and there are ten more Roman churches in the city. The Presbyterians are most numerous among the Protestant denominations, and Calvary Church is one of the handsomest in the city. Grace and Trinity are the most prominent of the Episcopal Churches, and both claim large and fashionable congregations ; and the Congregationalists, Methodists, Baptists, and other denominations are in a hopeful condition. Attendance at all of these churches for morning service is quite general, but the afternoon and evening of Sunday are devoted to amusement by the San Franciscan, and each in his degree seeks some place of public or private entertainment, or the day is spent in ruralizing, or in driving and visiting.

Returning from our first tour of the city we dined in the grand hall of the Palace Hotel, where stand four rows of tables, with space for three persons to walk abreast between them, the whole lighted by twelve great crystal chandeliers.

A note from Mr. Barton Hill, whose artistic ability, so well known at the East, is here united to a managerial position, invited us all to his theatre, where three boxes were set apart for our accommodation. The star was Alice Dunning, and our eyes were so abundantly feasted that the treat to the ears was a work of supererogation, the one sense absorbing all one's capacity for enjoyment. And so back to repose in Dom Pedro's sumptuous apartments and to dream of the morrow.

CHAPTER XII.

A PRINCE AND A PALACE.

A FEW days after our arrival in San Francisco we gladly accepted an invitation from Senator Sharon to pass some days at his country house of Belmont, a name so intimately associated with that of its late master, William A. Ralston, whose life and death form one of the most startling and extraordinary episodes of San Franciscan history, that we must pause here to speak one word of a man through whose means hundreds of persons fell from affluence to penury; and yet of whose death those very persons spoke with tears in their eyes, as a public loss and misfortune. Mr. Ralston was the Napoleon of speculators, and, like the great Emperor, his career of unparalleled success was closed by a Waterloo of utter defeat.

A self-made man, he rose from the smallest beginnings to the position of banker and broker before he was thirty years old, and in the time of the war managed the business of his firm so successfully that his correspondents in New York urged him to come hither and consolidate his business with theirs, promising that the firm thus formed should become the leading banking-house in the country. It was then that Mr. Ralston laid the corner stone of the monument to his own memory in San Francisco, which even the earthquake of his failure and death could not overthrow.

BELMONT, THE COUNTRY-SEAT OF THE LATE W. A RALSTON. Page 125.

and which long will stand an object of love and reverence to the generous hearts of the people, who forgave
their own loss in pity for his so much greater one.

"No," said he, in answer to Mr. Kelly's letter, "we
have made our money in California, and if it is the
nucleus of a business that shall bring credit and advantage to the city where it is established, that city shall
be San Francisco, and the men who profit by it shall
be San Franciscans."

That sentence was the key-note of his subsequent
career. Princely in his outlays, Oriental in his magnificence, audacious in his enterprises, the millions he
lavished upon business undertakings, or palatial residences, or hospitality such as seems only possible in an
Arabian Night's Entertainment, were all expended at
home; the money passing into his hands from hundreds of wealthy and confiding fellow citizens, passed
through them to the hands of thousands of other fellow
citizens, who lived by him and who adored him.

As President and Manager of the Bank of California, Mr. Ralston found ample opportunities for fostering
the prosperity and the interests of his adopted State,
and used them grandly and fearlessly. The mining
interests, manufacturing and commercial enterprises,
private schemes, if undertaken for the general good, all
derived sustenance from this rich fountain-head, and
the country grew and throve as thousands of little rills
trickled from it through arid and thirsting deserts.

It was in these days that Ralston built Belmont, a
palace costing a million and a half of dollars, standing
in the midst of two hundred acres of pleasure grounds.

Stables finer than many a good man's house are filled
with the best horses to be bought for money; green-
houses, graperies, ferneries, teem with all that is rare
and lovely in the world's flora; banana, orange, and lemon
trees grow in the open air; everything that the mind of
man can imagine in the way of luxurious living is here
collected; and in wandering through this palace and its
grounds, where everything seems to wear an invisible
badge of mourning for its ruined and dead lord, one
can only remember Fouquet, that other architect of a
colossal fortune and his own ruin; and Vaux, the
stately home built for his pleasure, whose magnificence
so filled the narrow heart of Louis le Grand with envy
and chagrin, that the favorite's death was decreed even
while the monarch accepted his hospitality.

It was no uncommon thing in the days of Belmont's
glory for its master to engage a special train of cars,
fill it with guests, a band of music, flowers, and all
that could add to the sumptuousness of a banquet,
and make a sort of royal progress to his palace, there
to spend a night and day of feasting and merriment.
Abstemious and frugal in his own habits, of the table,
of dress, or equipage, he never wearied of heaping
attentions and gifts upon his guests; and the story of
his sending a check of ten thousand dollars to the man
who in his early days had lent him five hundred
dollars, is but one of a score of similar anecdotes
lovingly told to-day by men not yet recovered from the
shock his failure gave to their own financial concerns.
It was in the very midst, at the very height, of his
splendor that the crash came. The Bank of California

suspended payment; the City, the State, the whole financial country stood aghast; the management summoned Ralston, in whom, up to that moment, they had reposed the blindest confidence, for an explanation. He had none to offer, but he offered instead every penny of his princely fortune to throw into the gulf. The sacrifice was accepted, and Mr. Ralston was removed from his managerial position in the bank. He acquiesced in this decision, spoke bravely and collectedly of the future and its possible successes, and then—went away from it all, drove to the North Beach, went into the water to bathe, and was brought to the shore a little later a corpse!

Some men gave a harsh and ugly name to this death; others, more charitable, named it accident. Who shall decide? who shall read the secrets of that proud, wounded, nay, broken heart? who shall venture to condemn this man, who dared and lost so much, and who, having reached the summit of earthly prosperity, found it easier, perchance, to fall from that into God's mercy than into man's contempt?

Senator Sharon was his friend and partner. Together they built the Palace Hotel, costing six millions of dollars. In addition to the four millions constituting his share of the property, Ralston was, at the time of his death, building a million-dollar private residence on Pine street, carrying a million or more in the Grand Hotel, supporting several manufacturing companies, and keeping the credit of the Bank of California to a ten million dollar standard, when it was really nothing but an insolvent shell. He died owing sixteen millions, and it is impossible to say what the real height of his fluctuating fortune ever was.

The public excitement at his death was intense: bankrupt men stood openly crying in the street—not that they were ruined, but that Ralston was dead; the garb or badge of mourning was everywhere displayed; the flags in the harbor drooped at half mast; bells tolled; business was suspended; great meetings of his friends collected to pass resolutions, to concert his obsequies, to pay him every honor that the dead can receive. The poorer people, who could do none of these great things, told of the benefits he had ever heaped upon their class, and on them; they gave him those words of praise and blessing which, from the lips of "God's own poor," are perhaps a more costly tribute than the flowers or the catafalque, or the music, or the stately monument that wealth can give. The funeral procession was four miles long, and when its head reached the grave the rear had not stirred from Calvary Church, where the obsequies took place.

SALMON FISHING, SACRAMENTO RIVER.

CHAPTER XIII.

A MEMORABLE VISIT.

BELMONT lies twenty-five miles south of San Francisco, and is reached by the S. P. R. R. after an hour's ride over a flat and uninteresting country, cut up into fields and market-gardens, irrigated by ditches, and cultivated by bare-legged Chinamen. Every house has its water tank, with a whirling mill to fill it; and the scene is quite Dutch, in spite of John in the foreground and the Sierras in the distance.

There is a pretty little station at Belmont, built by Mr. Ralston for his own accommodation, but we left the train at San Matteo, a few miles north, where Senator Sharon's four-in-hand and other carriages were waiting for our party, now pleasantly enlarged by the addition of Senator Conover of Florida, his beautiful young wife, her brother, and a distinguished Cuban friend.

The drive was through a region of delight for more senses than one, since not only were the eyes charmed with Nature's finest shows, but the scent and feeling of the soft air lazily drifting across our faces was delicious beyond account; surely the goddess of this land is sweeter breathed, as well as fairer, than our northern divinities, and the fruit she holds out with both hands to her guests more luscious.

We drove through the grounds of several private houses, as is the friendly custom here, and noticed that they are not as precisely laid out as is the fashion in the East; but Nature is allowed to display her own luxurious taste more freely, and with a wonderfully fine effect. The live oak is the principal tree, and many of the trunks are massed with ivy climbing riotously up the stem, and waving green tendrils from the upper branches. The wonderful Eucalyptus also abounds, and cypress, and palm, and olive ; while the roses blossom upon trees fifteen or twenty feet in height, each one a huge bouquet of bloom and fragrance. Every now and again we caught, through gaps in the foliage, glimpses of the distant hills and the crest line far away, and then drooping trees again closed around us.

At sunset we drove into the precincts of Belmont, passing a large pleasure-ground known as Belmont Park, the favorite picnic spot of the Italians in San Francisco. The carriages passed slowly on between rows of every beautiful, graceful, and rare tree that can be named; locusts laden with white blossoms, tulip trees, catalpas, magnolias ; and as we neared the house a lower growth of feathery pepper-trees, laden with dull red berries, hedges of geranium and roses, trellises of passion-flowers and stephanosies, until at last these artistically graduated into belts and plots of low-growing brilliant flowers, blooming up to the doors of the great house. This, made of wood and painted white, is not, perhaps, so imposing in its exterior as one is led to expect from so magnificent an approach, but like Oriental mansions it reserves its wonders and its luxury for those so happy as to enter.

The situation, upon a sloping hill, is quite artistic,

giving a very effective outlook from the house itself.
Driving under a *porte cochère* covered with climbing
yellow roses, we crossed the threshold, and entered into
what seemed more like the disordered vision of an architect than a sober American country house, for beyond
saying that there is everywhere a pervading effect of
lightness, and brightness, and airiness, and cool repose,
and luxury, and comfort, it is all but impossible to give
any idea of this delightful house. The first feature
distinctly appreciated is the absence of any doors
throughout the first story. A wide corridor, once a
piazza, runs around three sides, its floor of native
woods, polished like a mirror, in the style of old French
châteaux ; cane and bamboo chairs, Chinese settees,
inlaid tables, and tall vases of flowers furnish this gallery, and from it open, through great French windows,
the parlor, dining, billiard and drawing rooms, while at
the left hand lies a superb music and dancing room,
lighted through a glass dome by day, and at night by
graceful and elaborate chandeliers of silver and crystal.
The walls are paneled with mirrors and frescoed in
gold and neutral tints, and in a niche lined with mirrors
stands a grand piano, remarkable for its case of light,
satiny, native wood. Chinese furniture, light, elegant,
and curious, some statues, vases, and plenty of flowers,
furnished this room, one of the most charming possible
to imagine. The great dining and billiard rooms have
waxed floors, but the parlor, in which a bright, cheery
fire was burning, is a cozy little carpeted room,
eminently home - like in its aspect, with some fine
bronzes, a wonderful Chinese centre-table, and some

Indian arm-chairs of carved wood, big enough for three people. In the centre of the house, and upon which all these rooms open, is a square hall, from which winds up a great staircase. Here stands a tall, old-fashioned clock, such as was familiar to some of us in our childish visits to our grand-parents, with the sun and moon beaming jollily from its dial, and its *primo basso* tick of "For ever—never! Never—for ever!" Here, too, upon a pedestal, stands a brazen bowl of Chinese manufacture, which is used as a gong to summon the faithful to dinner. Some pretty tables, chairs, and a large mirror make up the furniture, unless one includes a gas bracket in the shape of a silver branch laden with leaves and silver flowers, the latter each blossoming into a tongue of flame. Up-stairs a balcony runs around the upper part of the wall, and is prettily furnished with couches, chairs, embroidered screens and footstools, and from it branch three corridors, contiguous to which are numerous bed-rooms, like those of an English country-house. Ours was spacious and luxurious, with dressing and bath rooms, every marble bowl in the latter fitted with a plated pipe, supplying a small shower-bath for washing the head—a great comfort, especially to gentlemen, in this dry and dusty country. A large picture gallery lies above the music-room, but is not yet finished.

Before dinner we took a little stroll in the grounds, looking at the stables niched into the side of a hill, with imposing stone front, and spending some time in the fernery, which is really exquisite, with a lovely stone fountain trickling into a mossy stone basin;

grottoes, rock work, and dewy coverts, where wave every graceful species of fern of which the world can boast. The barbaric tones of the gong summoned us away to a less ethereal feast before we had half done with this, and entering the dining-room we sat down fourteen at the table which, in Ralston's time, often accommodated a hundred guests. A great pyramid of flowers and a bouquet at each plate made the table as lovely and as fragrant as a garden, and the genial and interesting conversation was a dangerous rival to the sumptuous dinner set before us.

Mr. Sharon, as we have said, was the friend and partner of the unfortunate Ralston, assumed many of his debts, and accepted much unremunerative property in satisfaction of his own claims. He is a man of wonderful instinctive appreciation of character, a gift affecting his general manner; for, while remarkably frank and outspoken among those whom he finds congenial, he is chilling and reserved to those who impress him unfavorably. He is a man of great and comprehensive ability, and has need of it in attending, as closely as he does, not only to his duties as United States Senator from Nevada, but to the care of his own colossal fortune and domestic duties. But with all of these he has Byron, and Moore, and some of our more modern poets at his fingers' ends, and is a vivacious and most entertaining conversationalist. His immediate family is made up of two daughters: the younger a pleasant school-girl; the elder a fragile, graceful young woman, married to one of the most promising young lawyers of San Francisco, whose sister's marvelous musical talents added greatly to the charm of our stay at Belmont.

The most distinctive feature of the dining-room was a great sideboard of carved black wood, in which is set a broad mirror. Upon the face of this mirror, as on the dial of a clock, are engraved the numerals of the hours, and two slender gilded hands steal silently round, warning the reveler who chances to glance at them that no man's life is more than a question of Time, and not the wealthiest, not the most powerful of mortals, can hold one single moment in his grasp, be it never so delightful.

The works of this wonderful clock are entirely concealed, and the stately, noiseless motion of the hands across the mirror had a most weird and fascinating effect.

The dining-room opens into the billiard-room through a wide panel sliding up into the ceiling, and after passing through it we went to the music-room to spend the evening in conversation, in music—in which our host's son-in-law and his sister are proficient— and in dancing. We were also introduced to a novel and curious musical instrument, which, being set and wound up, goes on to perform the duty of a full band of instruments.

After breakfast on Sunday morning we again went for a drive. Taking the old San José post-road through the little town of Redwood, we wound among the picturesque foothills, saw lovely glimpses of sea and mountain scenery, and drove through beautiful private grounds, among others, those of the agent of the Rothschilds, a bachelor with an income of seventy thousand a year, who keeps up a perfect paradise of a place for himself, his dogs, and horses. Again we were struck with the superiority of Nature to man as a landscape gardener, and her general acceptance in that capacity in this region. Near the houses, to be sure, one sees carefully tended flower beds, and trim hedges but a stone's throw beyond; the Spanish moss droops from the live oak in all its unkempt luxuriance, and giant cacti, not unlike great green serpents, among the undergrowth. During the first part of this drive the air was mild, fragrant and warm as our New York July, but as we returned through Redwood the sea wind came in so chill and damp that we were glad to put on the sealskin sacques that it had seemed so absurd to place in the carriage, but whose warmth was now most welcome. Indeed, it is never safe in the neighborhood of San Francisco to leave home for an hour without some substantial wrap, and nothing is more common than for a lady to dress in white muslin or lace, find herself perfectly comfortable during two or three hours, and then be glad to wrap herself in furs or shawls above the gossamer draperies so pleasant a little while before.

We met with no reminder of the day during our drive; shops were open and business active in the little town, and people had neither the sedate and mortified air of a Northern Sunday, nor the festive and gorgeous aspect of that day among a purely Latin population.

At dinner we spoke much of Ralston, and Mr. Sharon, in eulogizing his singular unselfishness of life, pointed out that even this house, as well as others that he owned, was planned and adapted far more for the pleasure of his guests than for himself; the little parlor being the only purely domestic retreat in the whole house.

The next day we took leave of our courteous host and amiable family, and the palatial home, with its memorable history, satisfied that there is at least one palace near to the Golden Gate; and yet, as Aladdin's Princess-spouse missed the roc's egg in the palace the genii had built, we found one great and remarkable deficiency at Belmont: we did not, in all that mansion, see a book, or a bookcase, or any spot where one might fitly have been placed, or expected to be placed!

SWEETMEAT VENDER, CHINESE THEATRE, SAN FRANCISCO.   Page 159.

CHAPTER XIV.

ON Monday evenings the Palace Hotel is illuminated from top to toe, the band plays in the inner court, and the lady guests hold a reception, and dance. The upper floor, with its glass roof, and wide balcony overlooking the court and ornamented with vases and tubs of tropical plants in full bloom, is the pleasantest in the house, and is let in suits to families taking rooms for the season. As we have said, this mode of life is very popular in San Francisco, and all the hotels are built with reference to permanent lodgers as well as transient guests, and surely a lifetime might contentedly enough be spent in some of the apartments of which we had experience in the Palace Hotel. Among other guests with whom we made acquaintance were the Admiral and officers of the Russian fleet, then in harbor, and we especially noticed one handsome young Baron, for whom our sympathies were strongly enlisted a few days later, by the proclamation of the Russo-Turkish war, and the necessity for his sailing with his ship, leaving his heart in the custody of a fair American, to whom he could not even give an address, since the squadron sailed under sealed orders.

We also made the acquaintance of Mrs. and Mr. C., purchasers of Follette's portrait in Beard's admirable

painting of "The Streets of New York," now on exhibition in the Academy of Fine Arts. Mr. C.* was
presented as the Vice-President of the Union Pacific
Railroad, but, as I honestly told him, his appreciation
of my pet's beauty and grace, and his willingness to
pay three thousand dollars for the privilege of owning
her picture, was a higher title to my consideration
than even that which means for its fortunate possessor
a most honorable position and an income of millions.
Mr. C. is building one of the finest residences on the
hill, and the statuesque beauty of his wife would grace
a palace; her walk is the poetry of motion, and the
head so imperially set upon her shoulders loses none
of its beauty by being silver crowned.

The next day we visited the Board of Brokers, by
invitation of the President, and assisted at the throwing away, as he plaintively styled it, of some mining
stocks at a rate lower than they had ever been sold
at before. We had seats in a little private gallery
reserved for ladies, and from that coigne of vantage
looked safely down upon the ring of brokers in the
centre, with the circle of spectators outside. The
scene was one of the wildest excitement, reminding the
young lady of a gladiatorial arena, the Sultana of a
flock of hungry chickens, to whom some corn had been
thrown, and myself of the fact that I was only a woman,
and could never hope to join in such a soul-stirring
combat—for surely combat is but a mild term to apply
to the jostling, yelling, frenzied, purple-faced struggle,
roused into new vigor at each call of a new stock; the
bidders crowding to the centre, gesticulating, pushing,

ready to tear each other to pieces, or themselves fall down in a fit of apoplexy.

Not one word of all that was shrieked and shouted could we understand; but the excitement was contagious, and the writer would have given worlds to be six feet high, deepen her voice to a baritone, and be in the midst of it all!

The profound truth deduced from this visit is that a successful broker must be a tall, big man, with very long arms, and the theory was proven by a visit paid to our gallery by Mr. ——, the leader of the Bears, who is formed upon this principle, and who, although as meek mannered as possible with us ladies, and bland and courteous to a degree with everybody, had impressed me as quite the typical broker, be he Bear or Bull.

From the Brokers' Board we proceeded to the County Jail. Passing through China Town we entered a far more objectionable region, called the "Barbary Coast," inhabited by the vilest class of poor whites, as much worse than the "Heathen Chinee" as a vile woman is worse than a bad man, or any good thing gone to decay than one naturally vile. This region is said to represent, as clearly as the iron rule of the law will permit, the social status of San Francisco in the early days, when the report of gold attracted every desperado on the Continent to its search, and scarcely one respectable woman was to be found within the city's limits. Murder and debauchery of every sort ran riot, and it is surprising that out of such vile soil the fair flower and fruitage of the present city could ever have grown. In broad daylight, and protected as we were, we saw nothing objectionable except a large quantity of dirt, dust an inch thick upon the sidewalks, and numbers of hollow-eyed, sallow-cheeked, vicious - looking men and women lounging in the doorways and windows, or exchanging oaths and scurrility from house to house above our heads. By dint of much inquiry we presently found ourselves at the northerly border of this unhallowed region, in a street called Broadway, and opposite the County Jail, an unpretentious brick building, rather shabby and dirty. Mounting three narrow stone steps we were confronted by a placard upon the huge iron door stating that positively no visitors could be admitted. Ringing the bell we philosophically awaited the event, and presently perceived four human eyes inspecting us through a small grated aperture in the door. Making known our names and wishes, our escort so won upon the Cerberus within that the iron door swung suddenly open, admitting us, and swiftly clanging to, the moment we had entered.

The Jailor's rooms and kitchen lie in front, and leading back from these runs a stone corridor lighted from above, whitewashed severely, and with a row of black iron doors opening at intervals through its extent; in every door appeared a little window, scarcely large enough to frame a human face, but in every window appeared two human eyes, coldly and incuriously inspecting the visitors. No model prisoners these, cleanly, well fed, pious, industrious and sociable, such as were exhibited to us in England, but men of whose depravity no other warrant than those horrible eyes and so much of the face as could be seen was needed. So far from appearing ashamed or angry at our inspection, it was we who were compelled to lower our eyes and hasten our footsteps to escape from the bold and loathsome license of those looks. All were frowsy and unkempt, some were smoking, and the scent of the prison was so vile as to suggest that if the odor of sanctity pervades some holy places this must be the odor of depravity. Few of these men were imprisoned for less than four years, and one was to die on the morrow. He was a Chinaman, the second ever executed in San Francisco. He had committed a hideous murder, thoroughly proven, and well deserved his doom, but upon the yellow face and leering eyes showing at his window, one could read no remorse for the crime—no dread of the impending punishment.

Going up stairs into another corridor also lined with cells we looked down into the whitewashed stone yard of the prison. Among the men lounging about were a good many Chinamen, squalidly dressed in shirt and trowsers, barefooted and shorn of their pigtails — the greatest punishment, short of death, that the law can inflict upon one of their nationality ; one was brought in while we were there, and hurried across the yard to be clipped. They are said to cry and shriek like little children while undergoing this penalty ; and never recover the self-respect or confidence they previously had.

A straw mattrass, a tin-pan, plate and spoon constitute all the furniture of the cells, and no effort beyond occasional whitewashing is ever made for the physical, mental or spiritual improvement of the condition of these unfortunate beings.   Is there no Elizabeth Fry ready to take up this good work? no Bergh to do for men and women what he has so nobly done for brutes? Let the nineteenth century answer.

PROPITIATING FORTUNE BEFORE SPECULATING.   Page 148.

CHAPTER XV.

A DESCRIPTION of San Francisco which does not include Chinamen, China Town, and the Chinese question in some degree, at least, would indeed be Hamlet without the Prince of Denmark's character, and Heaven defend us from committing such a solecism! What could be seen in this direction we resolved to see, and one fine day made an experimental trip in company with a gentleman resident in San Francisco to some of the fashionable Chinese shops in the American quarter. We called first at Chin-Lee's, then at King-Lee's and Chi-Lung's, finding their establishments filled with much the same wares that flood New York since the Exposition; but the air of the shops is more foreign than is possible in an Eastern City, the atmosphere redolent of a pungent, delicious odor of sandalwood and Oriental perfumes, and the smooth, brown, quiet salesmen, in their loose, dark-blue sacks and trowsers, with shining pigtails depending from beneath their silken skull-caps, heads and faces smooth as a baby's, and their delicate slender hands, were altogether different from the Chinese laundry-men from whom we, of the Atlantic Coast, take our ideas of the citizen of the Flowery Kingdom. Among these merchants are the highest caste Chinese to be found in America, and their manners by no means lack the repose "that stamps the caste of Vere de Vere"; in fact, so reposeful are they that it is rather difficult to go shopping among them, for they only exhibit such wares as are called for, and that in a mechanical and abstracted manner, as if their minds were occupied rather with Confucius than glove-boxes, or some new astronomical discovery to the exclusion of *bric-à-brac*. The prices of their charming goods are fabulous, and one hesitates to cheapen anything under the melancholy and languid gaze of the almond eyes. We were willing to pay something, however, for the pleasure of fancying ourselves in Nankin or Pekin, and delighted to ask questions eliciting low replies in that peculiar lisping English, not broken, but only jarred just enough to let all the harsh consonants drop out, especially the rasping R, which becomes a liquid L in a Chinaman's mouth; and when I asked the price of the oddest possible little tea-pot at Chi - Lung's and was informed that the preposterous sum demanded was "Velly little for lich Mellican lady to pay," I bought it at once, not for the flattery but the l's of the statement! Well, the tea-pot was lovely, and it pleased the friend for whom it was bought, and so she and I and Chi-Lung were all pleased, and was not the money well expended?

From fashionable Kearney Street we turned into steep and dingy Munro Street, and were in China Town itself. No more *bric-à-brac*, no more silken caps or fine cloth clothes or languid grandeur of manner. Here all the houses are dingy, no two alike ; all the people are poor, and although universally clean in person,

CHINESE JOSS HOUSE, SAN FRANCISCO.   Page 145.

cultivate a squalid and odorous mode of existence, both in shops and dwellings, that makes extensive visiting among them rather distasteful to fastidious people.

Each little shop hangs out its sign of red and gilded paper inscribed with Chinese characters; and very little English is spoken or required, as these places are intended for native custom exclusively. We entered several, and found the stock in each to consist mainly of shoes, tea-pots and beryl bracelets — all cheap and all ugly; and there were three or four salesmen in each dark little shop to whom the same description might be applied. We passed along a row of butchers' stalls, and were glad to remember the impossibility of our own dinner ever coming from one of them, for the odors were horrible and the sights still more so—whole beeves and swine being hung up at the entrance and hacked to pieces almost any way, as customers applied. Smoked birds split and flattened out like a sheet of paper were also exhibited as imported from China, and fish so long divorced from its native element as to be fit for nothing but to return thither. We saw several Joss-houses, or temples of Chinese worship, decorated with lanterns, plenty of red and gilded paper, and scarfs and ribbons festooned across with peacock's feathers. The upper story of the house being thus sanctified, the ground-floor is devoted to trade, and under one of the Joss-houses Hoss, Wo & Co. conduct their Bureau of Emigration, and at the moment of our visit were welcoming a troop of newly arrived emigrants, who came pouring in, each bearing an immense parcel bound with straw ropes, and their wild and startled faces shaded by great umbrella hats of native manufacture.

But the mild and superficial view of China Town to be obtained at noonday by no means satisfied our determination to make its intimate acquaintance, and subsequently a formal expedition was organized under conduct of detective MacKenzie, the veteran of the San Francisco Police force, having served as detective and police-officer for twenty-two years in that and other cities. A little after eight p. m. our party started for the Bohemian Club Rooms, where we were joined by Mr. MacKenzie and five or six other persons, and at once sallied out. The detective gave me his arm, and as we walked down Kearney Street I tried to elicit some of the anecdotes and reminiscences with which such a man's mind must teem, but unfortunately he had so thoroughly learned that habit of discretion which must be part of a detective's training that he could not speak if he would, for I do not like to think that he would not if he could ; and the only memorable thing he said in all that walk was to point out a window on the corner of Portsmouth Square and remark : "Out of that window the Vigilance Committee of '51 hung their first man."

From Portsmouth Square we turned into Dupont Street and felt that we had passed from the familiar to the unknown. In Kearney Street, which we had just left, crowds of cheerful and busy persons with bright and expressive faces thronged the brightly lighted sidewalks and the elegant shops, or were merrily passing into theatres or concert rooms for an evening's entertainment; in Dupont Street the narrow walks were scarcely lighted except by the smoky glare from the shop windows, and the silent-footed, sad-eyed passengers crept along the wall, or stepped from off the walk at our approach, more like the shades encountered by Dante at the entrance of the Inferno than living and busy mortals. Nothing is more noticeable about the Chinese than this quietude of face, gait, voice and manner; their features never stir, their eyes never vary, their hands never gesticulate; they seem framed with fewer surface muscles than Caucasians, the whole system of training for body and mind seems one of repression, and it is nearly as impossible to judge by a Chinaman's face what he really feels, thinks, or wishes, as to guess the Sphinx's riddle by contemplation of her image. No happier hit was ever made than Bret Harte's poem of the "Heathen Chinee," but nobody can appreciate the phrase "child-like and bland" until he has looked into one of these smooth olive-colored, serene and utterly expressionless faces, and wondered, in vain bewilderment, what emotions, what passions, what opinions of one's self lay beneath it.

We stopped at the entrance to a black and narrow alley, its depths hidden in tenebrous shadow, and here our guide produced and lighted two candles, whose gleam faintly illumined the first few steps of a black and rickety staircase. Up this the guide led and we followed, walking purely by faith; since nothing was to be seen but the little patch of light, the dim roofs of houses beneath us, and, far above, the cold, pure gleam of the stars.   As the candlelight fell upon the wall at the left we perceived that it was closely covered with scraps of red and gold paper inscribed with Chinese characters.   These we were informed were prayers, and this was one of the principal Joss-houses, or temples, and the faithful visiting hither are in the habit of thus leaving a sort of a permanent petition behind them to supplement or perhaps to excuse the necessity for personal prayer.

Several Chinese men coming down from the temple passed us upon the narrow stairs, and very possibly felt disposed to fling us over the light hand-rail into the narrow court below.   At the top of the stairs we passed through a door and found ourselves in a dark room, quite bare except for a shrine at the farther end and a smaller one close to the door, containing the idol guardian of the temple, a very human (Chinesely speaking) wooden gentleman, who sits all day and all night in his grotesquely carved porter's chair of a shrine, contemplating a bronze bowl of ashes and some burnt out Joss-sticks standing as tribute before him.   The larger and richer shrine at the other end of the room contains the image of Troi-Pat-Shing-Kwun, the God of Fortune, who holds a nugget of gold in his hand, and is surrounded with all sorts of tawdry trappings of artificial flowers and tinsel.   His bronze bowl of ashes is larger and the tribute of Joss-sticks more plentiful; for, like some of his white brothers, John Chinaman's most fervent prayers are offered in the hope of temporal rewards and privileges.   Several devotees were lounging in the dark corners of the room regarding us with the

usual non-committal blandness, and the walls all pa-
pered over with the gay little prayers in scarlet and
gold, placed as perpetual reminders of the wishes of
his worshipers before the eyes of Fortune. In front
of this shrine stood a screen carved from a solid piece
of wood in all the minute elaboration we are familiar
with in Chinese work of this sort. It represented an
ancient battle, and was really a very wonderful produc-
tion. Its cost in China was about one hundred and
fifty dollars of our money. From this room we passed
through a maze of dark and dirty little rooms, each
presided over by a God or Goddess; all wonderfully
alike; all very ugly and grotesque; all surrounded by
a tawdrily decorated, carved shrine, gilded, arabesqued
and draped with more or less costliness and elegance,
according to the importance or power of the divinity.
Before each shrine hangs a glass lantern in which a
light is constantly kept, and in front of each is the
bronze bowl of ashes stuck full of Joss-sticks, most
of them extinct, but some slowly consuming and sending up clouds of stifling incense smoke. In some of
the rooms stood tables supporting handsome Chinese
vases filled with artificial flowers, and some pieces of
curious carved ivory, slips of paper, and split bamboo
sticks used in divination or interpretation of the will
of the deities were laid around. Also miniature copies
of the idols themselves, probably for sale, and various
toys representing beasts, birds, and fishes, objects of
worship or tradition in Chinese mythology. Before
each God of importance stands a table to receive the
offerings of food made by kind-hearted devotees, and

bowls of tea stand perpetually ready to allay the thirst of the immortals.

In several of the rooms we found worshipers before various shrines, but only in the case of a woman prostrate before a female deity, a sort of Chinese Lucerna, did we perceive any heartiness or absorption of manner. The men simply approached the shrines, without troubling themselves to cease their conversation, cease smoking, or uncover their heads, thrust a Joss - stick into the bed of ashes, bow three times, slightly and quickly—which ceremony is called Chinchinning Joss, and then retire, perhaps posting up a scarlet prayer as they go. In every room stands a tall wooden structure, like a very high four-legged stool, with a bell hanging inside of it, while above it is suspended a gong or drum, and both these are used by the priests upon occasions to arouse the attention of the meditative gods, or to awaken them from their slumber. On hearing this explanation we could but recall the magnificent irony of Elijah as the priests of Baal raged and howled around his altar, hacking themselves with knives, and shrieking to him in vain for a manifestation of his power, and the grim prophet taunted them with : "Cry, aloud, for he is a God ; either he is talking, or he is pursuing, or he is on a journey, or he is asleep!"

In the corner of one dismal little room, enshrined in a rickety wooden box, stood Shon - Ton, or the Devil, represented with a very European cast of countenance and dressed in dirty white ; he is especially entreated in time of sickness, the friends of the suf-

ferer bringing all sorts of delicate food, the essence
or substance of which he is supposed to imbibe as they
stand before him for two or three days, when the
remains are removed to be distributed among the poor
at the sick man's door. The other divinities are Kovan-
Tai, a most bellicose and violently whiskered personage; Wah-Taw, the God of Medicine or Chinese Escu-
lapius, who performed his cures in the remote antiquity
by laying-on of hands; Yun-Ten-Tin, the God of the
Sombre Heavens, who presides over the elements,
and is represented as sitting in a tree, and preventing
or dispersing fire and drought — two of the principal
errors of the Chinese; the Goddess of the Lake, rising
out of a lotus flower, is said to have emigrated from
Egypt to China and established a code of laws there.
Side by side in one shrine sat the Goddess of the Sea,
and the Goddess of Love, the Chinese Venus—to whom
our guide applied a more emphatic name. These, with
the God of East Mountain, one of the three sacred
mountains of China, were the most prominent of those
we saw; but there were quite as many others, petty
divinities, each devoting his attention to some venial
sire, for whose forgiveness and correction he is implor-
ed, and not one of them, from the great Joss to the
Devil, or any ornaments of the temple, but may be
bought, even by the "white-faced devil" in whose land
John has made his home!

In one room was an adobe oven, where, at certain
times, Satan is burned symbolically by means of red
paper. Across one of the little rooms extends a
counter, and behind it stood two or three priests, who

sell Joss-sticks, Joss-paper, incense candles, and little images, for the support of themselves and the temple. They beamed upon us a little more blandly or a little more innocently then their subtle lay-brothers, and one of them offered a little idol with the soft inquiry "Mellican lady want?"

Making our way down the dark stairs we strolled along Dupont Street for a short distance; wherever we paused, a crowd of blue-bloused, olive-skinned pig-tailed figures gathered silently and closely about us, contemplating us with melancholy, moony faces, and rayless eyes. At a broker's or money-lender's we stopped to look in through the window at a bright little Chinaman counting silver money in a most marvelously rapid manner. He looked up and smiled, and we all walked in without further invitation, followed by as many of the street crowd as could enter, all beaming with delight at having us so much more under observation than in the street. The young man informed us that he was seventeen years old, high-caste, as denoted by his long finger-nails. A sketch was made of him by the young lady while the rest were talking, and about a dozen Chinamen gathered about her to watch its progress, and seemed highly delighted. She gave them her sketch-book to look at, and they laughed over it, talking glibly among themselves, and expressing admiration in broken English. Bidding the pretty lad, whose name was Lee-Yip, good-by, we made our way into the street, not without difficulty, owing to the crowd, which evidently discussed us freely, and, as we could not but suspect, in a jeering and uncomplimentary manner, although on every face beamed the child-like and bland smile, and whatever was spoken in English was of the most flattering nature.

The barbers' shops are numerous and well patronized, since it is impossible for any man to himself perform the complicated and tedious process, of which we caught glimpses now and again in the bare little basement rooms, whose only furniture consists of a bench, a chair for the patient and a washstand and bowl. Once in that chair the applicant for "a shave" had need assume his whole stock of patience, for out of it he does not rise until every inch of skin above his shoulders, except the small portion of scalp whence the queue depends, is shaved, scraped, washed, polished, and minutely inspected. The pigtail is unbraided, cleansed, re-oiled and re-braided; the eyes, ears and nose are manipulated; and certainly whatever may be said of his style of beauty, a Chinaman just out of his barber's hands is about as exquisitely clean, from his shoulders upward, as it is possible to imagine.

The small dimensions of the shops and their crowded condition both as to animate and inanimate stock impressed us strongly, and Mr. MacKenzie inormed us that this is due solely to the home-training of the Chinese, who, having been educated to economize every square inch of space, every handful of earth, and, as it were, the oxygen of an atmosphere inadequate to support all who are born to breathe it, find themselves more at ease in these narrow quarters than in wider ones; and the first operation of a business firm in renting a shop or warehouse, or of a family in hiring a house, is to cut it all up into little tiny boxes of rooms, put in any number of shelves and cupboards, stretch lines over head to hang things upon, and reduce themselves generally to a condition of crowd, discomfort and clutter most repugnant to the American's habit of mind, but apparently the height of convenience to that of the Oriental.

CHINESE BARBER, SAN FRANCISCO.   Page 153.

CHAPTER XVI.

OUR next visit was to the Royal Chinese Theatre on Jackson Street. The drama is one of the greatest luxuries of the Chinaman, who frequents it constantly when in funds; nor does this imply great wealth, since the admission fee is two bits—twenty-five cents—at the beginning, fifteen cents toward the middle, and only ten cents near the end, of the performance. This frequently lasts six or seven hours, closing at two or three o'clock in the morning, and a single play requires three months or longer for one exhibition— an act or two being rendered each evening. These plays are nearly all based upon ancient historical events, the conservatism of the Chinese objecting to any modern innovations, and disdaining all sensational effects. There are no great playwrights in Chinese literature, and the profession of actor is not considered creditable, so that no great exertions toward superiority are made by those filling it. Actresses are unknown, the female parts being filled by men coarsely painted and tawdrily dressed. Nearly all the performance is in pantomime, and when speech is considered advisable it is uttered in a high, harsh falsetto, entirely unlike the human voice.

Entering from the street we passed through a long passage where a Chinaman behind a counter was selling native delicacies, such as figs, dark-looking sweetmeats, sugar-cane, betel-nuts wrapped up in green leaves and decorated with red paint and slices of citron. Inside we found a perfectly bare and undecorated auditorium, the parquette filled with rude wooden benches, a gallery above and another smaller one for women, who are not allowed in the body of the house. The stage was a mere raised platform like that in a lecture-room with a flight of steps at each end descending to the parquette. There was no scenery of any kind, but at either wing a red-curtained doorway, through which exits and entrances are made quite without disguise or ceremony; even when a death is represented, the actor, after going through the contortions and struggles of the last agony, gets up and quietly walks off through one of these doorways, nodding and smiling to his fellow actors or the musicians. The latter sit in a row at the back of the stage, between the two doors, pounding away industriously at the gong or cymbals, or scraping the little Chinese fiddles. They seem to have no method in their madness, but just bang away independently—each man making as much noise as possible.

When we entered, three actors were upon the stage, going through a stormy pantomime to the accompaniment of the orchestra. The man seemed to be having a stirring scene with his wife, who was aided and abetted by her maid in a most un-Celestial domestic rebellion; finally he gave her a push, closed an imaginary door between them and stood triumphant, while she—or the man representing a she—ran up and down, pushed against nothing, beat the air supposed to be the door, until finally both walked calmly off and the scene ended. The curtain at the other end of the stage was then withdrawn, and a warrior stalked forth who might as well have represented a Pawnee Brave as a Celestial hero, for his form was swathed in a mass of indescribable and very gaudy raiment, and his face painted in stripes of brilliant color. He wore clusters of flaps at each shoulder like wings, his head was decorated with pheasant's feathers, and his beard and moustache were fearful to behold. This champion strode across the stage, whirled round and round, stood on one leg, shook his fists, and generally expressed defiance and combativeness until some more warriors rushed in through the other doorway, apparently accepting the challenge, and these were followed by an army of women under the leadership of an Amazon, who was rather the most manly man present. Then these grotesque and phantom-like figures began a series of the strangest evolutions, marching in and out, around each other, backward and forward, all making the same ferocious and monotonous gestures, to the accompaniment of that frightful discord of barbaric sound, until it all seemed more like a feverish dream, the fancy of a lunatic, or the vision of an opium eater than an actual stage peopled with human beings. Each warrior as he entered threw one leg in the air and spun round upon the other; this represented the act of dismounting from his horse; and regardless of the fate of the imaginary charger he plunged at once into the battle, which finally culminated in the most grotesque scene possible to imagine, when ten or a dozen men, stripped to the waist and ranged in a line, turned somersaults across the stage, a row of whirling figures hurled through the air like so many balls, each one flinging himself fully six feet in air and spinning round like a wheel so fast that the eye could scarcely follow him. Presently the battle seemed to be forgotten, or to have resolved itself into a friendly acrobatic struggle, for the warriors began to vie with each other not only in the length and rapidity of their somersaults, but they jumped over large tables, alighting on the flat of their backs with such a jar that one would expect every bone in their bodies to be broken; but every man leaped up so nimbly as to prove that no harm was done, and directly did the same thing or something as remarkable, with unabated force. Finally the scene culminated in the performances of a half-naked man, with his nose painted of a glaring white, who did every thing but turn himself inside out: he tied his legs around his neck, jumped on his elbows, stood on the crown of his head with his arms folded, and propelled himself around the stage on acute angles of his frame without the aid of either legs or arms, until there was absolutely no contortion of the muscles left for him to achieve, and then he left off! Our party, the only Americans in the house, gave him a round of applause, at which the silent Celestials turned and grinned at us in wonder and derision, and we got up and went out. They never applaud or disapprove anything, but sit stolidly and smoke throughout the performance, the women in the gallery also indulging in this luxury, and patronizing the vender of sugar-cane and sweet-meats, who walks about with a basket of these dainties on his head, but does not break the sombre silence by crying his wares.

From the theatre we were taken to visit an Opium Den, as we of the East are prone to call the *tabazies,* where the Celestial seeks respite from toil and privation and home-sickness in the indulgence of a habit not so horrible after all as drunkenness of another nature; since the opium smoker injures only himself, and the man crazed by liquor is dangerous to his family and the community at large!

Passing through an alley-way, we entered a perfectly dark court where nothing was to be seen but so much to be smelled that the imagination became more painful than the reality could have been. A light twinkled from some windows on a level with the side-walk, and our guide unceremoniously pushing open the door led us into a small, close, but apparently clean room, filled with the fumes of burning opium—resembling those of roasting ground-nuts, and not disagreeable. A table stood in the centre, and around three sides ran a double tier of shelves and bunks, covered with matting and with round logs of wood with a space hollowed out, cushioned or bare, for pillows. Nearly all of these were filled with China-men, many of them containing two, with a little tray between them, holding a lamp and a horn box filled with the black, semi-liquid opium paste. But although every one was smoking, it was so early in the evening that the drug had not as yet wrought its full effect, and all were wide awake, talking, laughing, and apparently enjoying themselves hugely. The largest of the Chinamen was lying upon the shelf nearest the door, preparing his first pipe. He looked up and nodded as we crowded around him, and then calmly continued his occupation, we watching the *modus operandi* with considerable interest. The pipe was a little stone bowl, no larger than a baby's thimble, with an orifice in the bottom the size of a pin's head. This bowl is screwed on to the side of a long bamboo stem, and the smoker, taking up a mass of the opium paste upon the end of a wire, holds it to the flame of the lamp until it is slightly hardened, and then works it into the pipe, inhaling strongly as he does so, and drawing the smoke deep into his lungs, where it remains for a moment and then is ejected through the nostrils, leaving its fatal residuum behind; for opium is an accumulative poison, and when once the system becomes saturated with it, there is no release from the misery it entails but death. The tiny "charge" constituting one pipe-full is soon exhausted, and holding the last whiff as long as possible, the smoker prepares another, and another and yet another, as long as he can control his muscles, until, at last, the nerveless hand falls beside him, the pipe drops from his fingers, and his head falls back in heavy stupor, the face ghastly white, the eyes glazed and lifeless, the breathing stertorous, the mind wandering away in visions like those De Quincey has given to the world in the "Confessions of an Opium Eater." Looking at the stalwart Chinaman, with his intelligent face and fresh, clean costume, we tried to fancy this loathsome change passing upon him and felt quite guilty, as he looked up with a twinkling smile and offering us the lighted pipe said : "Havee Smokee?" and when we declined, held out the wire with the little ball on the end for us to smell. As we talked to this man, we were startled by perceiving two persons curled up in the bunk below his shelf, both smoking and watching us with their narrow slits of eyes like crouching wild beasts. They did not speak, but our friend above answered all our questions in a cool, matter-of-course sort of a way, and with an amiable superciliousness of manner. We bade him good-by and went out, his eyes following us with a look and a laugh strangely resembling a sneer. Perhaps, carrying out the proverb *in vino veritas*, there is something about the first stages of opium intoxication dispelling to customary caution and disguise, for in that sneering look and laugh we seemed at last to get the true expression of feeling which forever haunts the writer as the real meaning underlying the bland, smiling or inane exterior, presented to us by these Celestials.

We looked into another room in the same court much smaller but better furnished, the bunks neatly fitted up with mattrasses and each containing its little tray with the lamp, pipe, and opium all ready for the smokers not yet arrived. Our guide informed us in a mysterious tone that there are yet other opium dens to which access is impossible except to the initiated, where may be found at a later hour of the night young men and women as "white as you are" as he said, and with no drop of Mongolian blood to excuse their participation in this imported vice.

"Not respectable Americans?" asked some one incredulously, and the detective, with a glance inscrutable as the Sphinx, replied:

"That's according to what you call respectable. The women I don't suppose are generally received in your society, but as for the men—well, a lady would be surprised, sometimes, if she knew just how the gentleman she has danced with all the evening spends the rest of the night!"

"If Asmodeus could visit San Francisco and take us on one of his flying trips over the tops of these houses with the power of unroofing them as we passed, we should see some strange scenes," thoughtfully murmured the poet of the party, and officer MacKenzie, with one of his keen glances, replied:

"I don't know much about flying through the air, but I reckon I can show you as strange and tough a sight as you want to see, if you like to risk it, for the ladies."

.OUR "HIGH CASTE" CHINESE ACCOUNTANT. Page 152.

CHAPTER XVII.

WORSE THAN DEATH.

"THIS is pretty rough," said the guide, stopping at the entrance of a dark and dismal court, whose odors seemed even more sickening and deadly than those we had breathed before; "but say the word and I will take you in."

The word was said, and stumbling up some crazy stairs we found ourselves at last in a narrow balcony overhanging the reeking court. Some Chinese women clustered at the end of this balcony staring at us, behind them was a shrine containing the Goddess of Love, with gilt paper and Joss-sticks burning in the tray before her. From this gallery we passed into the house and became involved in a perfect honeycomb of little rooms, dimly lighted, or not lighted at all; no doors were visible, the doorways being shaded by long, pink calico curtains, and as they blew or were drawn aside we saw every room crowded with men and a few women, smoking, drinking tea, or playing at dominoes or cards. Every room we entered was exceedingly clean, and the inmates looked remarkably neat and tidy. Some effort at decoration was visible in the way of gilt and red paper, bright-colored scarves and peacocks' feathers upon the walls, and pretty little Chinese tea-pots and other pottery upon the tables and shelves. Everyone was smiling and

bland as possible, and seemed overjoyed to recei
a call; in one room especially, where a man a
woman and some boys were all squeezed up togeth
in a space of six feet square or so, they all chatt
and laughed and stared as if we were long lost brot
ers at least, asking " What you wantee? Where y
comee from?" and saying " Glad to see you, co
again velly soon!" at parting, in the most sociab
manner possible.

In another room was a fat, good-looking wom
of thirty or so, with her hair elaborately coiled, puff
and ornamented with bright gold pins, making t
at a little table set out with queer cups and sauce
which excited our ceramic covetousness; the ro
was very small and very neat, with a bed in one corn
enclosed with white curtains tied with scarves
the corners, and upon the bed a little tray holding t
vases of lilacs and other common flowers, besides
lamp, pipe, and opium box; curled up beside this f
tive preparation lay a man who arose and welcomed
with great enthusiasm and seemed so much at ho
that we concluded he must be the host, and aft
complimenting him upon the flowers decking l
opium tray, the neatness of the room and the pre
tea-service, we inquired if the woman were his wi
but at this he seemed very much amused, laugh
a great deal and said: " No, no, me no mally, no wi
no mally at all!" and the woman seemed as mu
delighted as himself at the absurd mistake.

In another room we found a dozen men or m
and one woman crowded around a table playing card

e woman was by no means unattractive and wore
autiful earrings and had a large diamond ring, and
her fat and pretty arms bracelets which our guide
id were twenty-carat-fine gold. She showed us these
naments with much pride, and on our admiring them
id us the Spanish compliment of saying they would
tter become us than herself. When asked if they
ere gifts from some of these gentlemen she answered
th a sudden assumption of dignity : "Me got velly
od husband, me mallied woman !" We assured her
at we were delighted to hear such favorable accounts
her condition, and so passed on, peeping into a
zen or more little rooms, all crowded with men and
few women, but no babies, no little children, nothing
relieve the brazen face of the whole establishment.
e women were mostly without beauty or grace,
d usually dressed in dingy blue sacks with huge
eves, their hair drawn back and curiously puffed,
led or plaited behind. They all wore the mechan-
l smile which seems part of the national character;
t their faces were thin and haggard, and the paint
l not disguise the wan weariness which was eating
ay their lives. These poor creatures are most
them bred to evil from infancy by parents who
ke merchandise of them in early girlhood. Some-
es the wretched creature sacrifices herself, signing
ontract and receiving a certain sum in advance for
rvices during a term of years or for life; the larger
rt of which sum goes to the broker or intermediary.
ese slaves — for they are so considered, and, as a
neral thing, are very harshly and penuriously

treated—receive only a maintenance and coarse clothin
during their brief period of health, and when overtake
by sickness are turned out to die in any hole they ca
creep into.

Great discontent exists among the better clas
of San Franciscans at the constant importation c
these slaves from China, the open and revolting traffi
forming a terrible satire upon the hecatomb of th
best lives of our own country sacrificed in the lat
war to abolish Negro Slavery!

Coming out of this house, we passed a row of tin
windows, breast-high to a man, looking out upon th
narrow sidewalk of the court, at each of which appeare
the face of a woman, the little room behind her a
bright and attractive as she knew how to make it
one in especial was quite illuminated and decked with
flowers and draperies, and the inmate, a rather prett
young girl, was singing in a sort of cooing little voice.

These unfortunates are seldom reclaimed; the
feel no sense of sin or shame in their lives, and if wel
treated are quite content. Occasionally the Christia
Missionaries who wage an unequal and all bu
hopeless warfare against heathendom in San Francisc
succeed in persuading one of them to escape an
accept such refuge as charity provides for them; bu
as a general thing their masters succeed in tracing
them and show willingness to expend more money an
time in repossessing themselves of them than th
victim can possibly be worth, and the last state of thes
reclaimed slaves is worse than the first.

There are said to be about fifteen hundred Chines

women of this class in San Francisco; seven-tenths
of all who come to this country belonging to its dismal
ranks, and it is surmised that not more than a hundred
reputable Chinese married women are to be found
in the city, the inducements to the better class
of men to bring their families to these shores being
small indeed, for the free and noble principles of our
government suffer insult and wrong, not only at the
hands of slave-dealers but at those of our own people,
who permit the ruffians infesting San Francisco to rob,
insult and maltreat the Chinaman at every turn, reveng-
ing upon him, as is the habit of degraded natures, the
galling sense of their own baseness and inferiority.

Let us close this painful subject, with a confession
of its most repulsive phase. We were informed that
the most beautiful and accomplished imported Travia-
tas in China Town were intended for and maintained
by white gentlemen exclusively. Let us subscribe
liberally to the mission to Borrioboola Gha, and send
flannel waistcoats to Afghanistan, and then let us
devote what is left of our money and energy and
Christian zeal to the conversion of these "gentlemen,"
and the Hoodlum who maims and insults and robs
the honest Chinese laborer!

POISON OAK, CAL.

CHAPTER XVIII.

SUPPER AT A CELESTIAL RESTAURANT.

"THERE were about one hundred and fifty gam-
bling-houses in China Town a year ago, and
I suppose there are fully half as many now, and I wish
I knew the precise address of one of them," remarked
officer MacKenzie pensively, as we stood once more in
the open street. "When the outcry against Chinese
cheap labor started up, the authorities made a raid
upon all sorts of little games down here, and managed,
not to cure John of gambling, for that can't be done,
but to teach him to hide himself so cunningly that
no one but the Father of Lies himself can find him
out. If we hear of a house and make a descent upon
it, we never find anything but the sleepiest, honestest,
smilingest old Chinaman, just getting out of bed and
maybe offering us a cup of tea because it is such
a cold night. Every gambling-house has three street
doors to pass through, and at each one sits a man with
the string of a bell close at hand, and the minute there
is trouble, the bells ring, the porters disappear, and
the company inside scamper away like rats into their
holes. It don't pay to look 'em up, and in a few
months things will get back about as bad as ever!"

"What is their favorite game?" asked "our"
artist with interest.

"They tell me it is a game called Tan, very much
like the game of 'Faro,' if you ever happened to hear

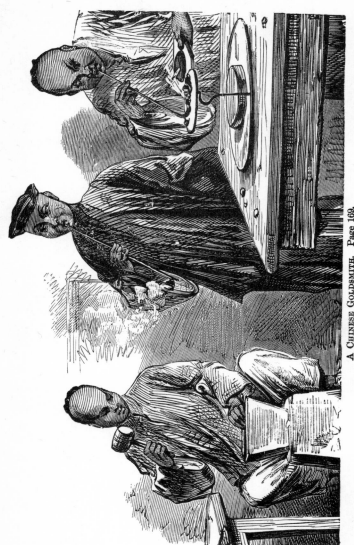

A Chinese Goldsmith. Page 169.

of that, young man," replied the detective, coolly ; " but they can take a hand at euchre."

" Yes, Ah-Sin played at that, played it on William and me in the game he did not understand," put in somebody else ; but our guide, more realistic than poetical in his temperament, suddenly paused, and, pointing to two alleys branching off at right angles from the court where we stood, informed us that one was Bull Run, and the other Murderers' Alley, so named by the Spaniards, who had given this locality a bad reputation before the Celestials dawned upon it. Our friend had been a policeman here in those days, and said it was unsafe for any man to walk through these alleys after dark. "And just about this spot," said he, " we used to find a man almost every morning before break-fast, served up all stark." It made one's blood run cold to hear such things so spoken of, and then to look up between the dark rows of frowsy houses to the stars whose cold, clear, eyes had looked down upon all these scenes.

We wandered on through little alleys lighted only from the provision shops which abound, and crowded by Chinamen talking, laughing, singing, shrieking the wares they carried for sale, hung in baskets from the end of long bamboo poles, or else gathering in knots to gaze at and discuss the strangers. Nobody seemed to think of going to bed or to sleep, although it was now very near midnight.

We went into one more shop, a gold and silver-smith's, where five or six men were as busy as if at mid-day, drawing the gold out in wire, beating it into thin plates or engraving and chasing. The lamps illuminating this midnight toil, and indeed almost all the lamps we saw in China Town, were common glass tumblers, filled with oil, in which floated a substance like vermicelli, and said to be a weed, imported from China for this purpose.

Weary in body and mind, we accepted the suggestion of our guide, and were conducted to the best purely Chinese Restaurant in this quarter of the city, although finer ones are to be found a little out of China Town, to which the wealthy merchants are in the habit of inviting their customers and friends. Our desire, however, was more to see the true national *cuisine* than to indulge in a feast, and we presently stopped before a house with a provision shop occupying the ground-floor and the two stories above used as saloons and refreshment rooms. The furniture was all of carved ebony or some other black, polished wood, very rich and tasteful, and the rooms were divided by archways. On one floor was the great saloon used for banquets, with an alcove for musicians who were not there, although the musical instruments hung ready upon the walls; queer little round guitars covered with serpent-skin and a little drum mounted on a tripod to beat time. Outside the window hung a little balcony filled with flowers in pots and tubs, and from it we enjoyed a wide and wonderful view of China Town, with the brighter gas-lighted streets of the city beyond.

We seated ourselves at several small tables, and were first served with tea prepared in little Chinese

cups with covers to them, and drank without sugar
or cream, and not acceptable to a palate educated
to their use; although we meekly bow to the decision
of those tea-epicures of our acquaintance who insist
that tea is not tea unless taken *au naturel*, and that
Chinese tea prepared by Chinese hands, and drank
from a cup with a cover to it is the only true realization of this æsthetic beverage. The tea removed,
an army of little blue Canton china plates was presented, containing squares of white cake, with a white
glazing covered with red characters, olives, salted
almonds, candied water-melon, little white cheeses,
several sorts of dark and dubious-looking sweetmeats,
and a good many unnamed and uninviting compounds
of a gelatinous and saccharine nature. We tasted the
cake, the sweetmeats and some of the anonymous
dishes, and found everything strange and disagreeable,
having a prevailing taste of lard, and that not of the
freshest. The banquet finished by a dessert of fruit,
and an orange was as refreshing as if it had not been
called *channg*, and the grapes bore up well under
the ignominy of being styled *po-tie-chee*, and the bananas were none the worse for the name *heong gav
chew*.

We finished with a course of Chinese liquor corre-
sponding with our whisky, and which we tasted in tiny
glasses and found fiery to the taste, and now as it was
well on toward morning and about half the party declared themselves thoroughly worn out, the dauntless
spirits who still clamored for more sight-seeing were
compelled to give in, and we presently stepped from

Jackson Street into Kearney, from the Celestial and flowery kingdom back to our American Republic, from an Oriental dream into a very wide-awake reality.

We did not organize another as formal visit as this to China Town, but made various little raids and exploring trips to the less objectionable portions, and heard a great deal of most conflicting testimony about the Chinese question from our acquaintances in San Francisco. Nearly all housewives agree that Chinese servants are the best in the country—neat, quiet, apt at learning and reliable in emergencies; *per contra*, they are, above all flesh, deceitful, devoid of personal attachment, and suspected of cultivating the most odious vices beneath a demure and discreet exterior. Of course, there are good and bad among Chinese servants as among all other classes of men, and the virtues of the good are patent upon the surface ; unfortunately no man has penetrated sufficiently beneath his smiling and subtle exterior to tell with certainty what underlies it, and I think that, after all, my own greatest personal objection to the Chinaman is the *arrière pensée* of which we were always uneasily conscious when in his society ; so that on the whole one would not wish to set up a house in a lonely neighborhood with a numerous retinue of Johns. One might take to reading the old letters from India which told at first of the skill and faithfulness of Ali, and Nana, and then of the horrors of the Sepoy rebellion, and then came no more ! In all branches of industry the Chinese workman ranks above the average. Having once been thoroughly shown the details of any handicraft, he carries them out with a patient fidelity and exactness seldom possible to the more nervous and speculative temperament of the European or American; and although he copies the errors as faithfully as the perfections, he may be trusted to "do as he is bid," unwatched and unwearying as long as he holds to that form of employment. The cry of "cheap labor," so furiously raised against the Chinese, principally by the classes to whom any labor is abhorrent, is as unfounded as it is malicious. A good man-cook in a family gets $35.00 per month, and a waiter $25.00; nor are the wages of inferior servants, mechanics, laundry-men, or laborers below the average of white labor in the Eastern part of the country. What makes Chinese labor cheap is its excellence and reliability, the absence of a disposition "to strike," and a quiet and gentle acceptance of the disagreeabilities of labor and poverty which many of our native workmen seem disposed to treat as unmerited hardship and injustice on the part of their employers. Meek, gentle and unobtrusive, John is, withal, persistent; whatever business he edges and glides into, he generally ends by mastering and excelling in, and so simple are his wants, and so close his economy, that a little capital is soon amassed from the wages an Irishman would eat and drink in the jolliest possible manner, and at the end of his career we find John modestly drawing his little account from the savings' bank and setting up for himselt or buying a small store in some establisned business.

Whether we like him or not, the Chinaman in California has become a fixed fact, and one not to be done away with except by giving the lie to our own Institutions, especially to that clause of the Constitution which declares all men to have a right to life and liberty "and the pursuit of happiness," and to those laws which welcome the emigrants of the world to our shores and offer them a share of that freedom and manly self-government we are so justly proud of. Accepting the fixed fact, therefore, and giving up any great hope of modifying it, since very few Chinamen have ever been Christianized, and only the weaker brethren have consented to exchange the social customs of their forefathers for ours, all that remains is, for us to make the best of it as it is, and treating John liberally as a man and a brother, cultivate such of his qualities as we esteem, deal with what we do not like, justly, impartially, and honorably, and wait for Time, the great assimilator, to soften the differences, subdue the Heathen's vices, and elevate the Christian's charity until it becomes the law of the individual and of the State.

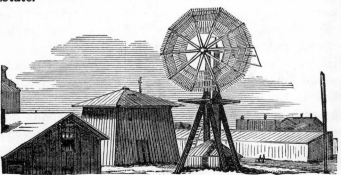

THE INEVITABLE WINDMILL.   Page 129.

CHAPTER XIX.

WOODWARD'S GARDENS AND SEAL ROCKS.

WE passed a delightful morning at Woodward's Gardens, a spot so well known to every one who has visited San Francisco, talked with any one who has been, or read the book anyone having been is sure to write, that we will not minutely describe it here; merely saying that Mr. Woodward is one of those happy individuals who have had the opportunity given them of leaving the world undeniably more beautiful than they found it. The place was originally his own private grounds; the building now serving as the museum, his own private house; and having transformed the grounds into a terrestrial Paradise, and the house into a rare collection of every sort of curiosity, he throws the whole open to the public, who, for twenty-five cents each soul, may spend the day in rambling among shady groves, verdant lawns, flowery bosquets, lakes, streams and waterfalls, conservatories, ferneries, using the swings, the trapezes, the merry-go-rounds at will, or listening to the fine music and witnessing the theatrical displays often given in the great arena surrounded with seats, which is also used for dancing, parlor-skating and acrobatic performances. Connected with this is an excellent refreshment-room, whose dainties are more to be recommended than those described in the last chapter.

Such a garden as this is only possible where frost is unknown, and the Summer's growth is never nipped by Winter's snows. Why does not human nature carry out the rule of inanimate nature, and why are the persons who have never known a sorrow, or a want, or a cloud upon their day, by no means the sweetest, the fairest or most perfect?

An underground passage leads from the gardens proper to the Zoological Gardens, so called, and here is a fine collection of wild animals; the ferocious ones as languid and disgusted of mien as wild beasts in iron cages always are; the beautiful ones more beautiful than we often see them, because they are at liberty, within their fenced paddocks; and one gets a better idea of an ostrich in seeing him upon a sunny hillside, even with a fence in the perspective, than in a cage six feet square with his beautiful plumes as broken and worn as an old feather duster; and the deer in their park are as free and graceful as in their native wilds. The most amusing feature of all was the bear-pit; tall poles were erected in the middle with little platforms on top that Bruin might pretend to himself that he was climbing a tree and resting in the branches. We were presented to an infant black bear aged three months, a perfect darling, with innocent blue eyes, and the sweetest little fat palms to his feet, and as full of fun and harmless antics as a kitten. In a cool grotto was an admirable salt-water aquarium supplied constantly from the Pacific Ocean, and fitted up with stalactites depending from the roof, and barnacled rocks, masses of coral, and sand at the bottom, imitating the bed of the sea. A similar fresh-water aquarium adjoins this, and also a machine for hatching fish-spawn of every variety. The tanks for seals and kindred monsters were large and well kept, and seem a very popular feature of the collection, especially at feeding time, when the barking and roaring are really terrific.

Quite tired out with walking, standing, looking, laughing and admiring, we returned to the hotel and found a vase of roses awaiting us with the card of a lady resident in the house ; the roses were the largest I had ever seen, even in Lima, Peru—too large, indeed, for beauty, and only curious as mammoths. In the evening we returned the call, and found Mrs. S—— a most charming and individual person. She rarely leaves her apartments, being extremely stout, yet with the smallest feet and hands imaginable, but she has brought the world to herself; her wonderful conversational ability, sunshiny nature, and rare literary attainments making her drawing - room the centre of one of the brightest circles, intellectually, in San Francisco, and reminding one of the traditions of Madame Récamier and the galaxy of wits and savants that gathered around her.

Beside these living ornaments, Mrs. S—— has been able to make a collection of pictures, books, carvings *objets d'art* and *bric-à-brac* fit to drive a rival collecto- mad. Among other items in the latter direction, one may mention three hundred tea-pots, each named after a friend, and the tiny ones after baby friends. A Japanese puppy, precisely like the little monsters one is familiar with in pottery, should, as he was alive, occupy a third place between the coterie of friends and the coterie of tea-pots and *bric-à-brac*, although he was so excessively ugly as to be perhaps more charming than either. Mrs. S——, besides being *au fait* with every book of the day, is an admirable artist; and her young and pretty daughter is a musician of no mean merit, and studies the art diligently in her private school and music rooms attached to the suite. Mrs. S—— has resided in California for twenty years or more, her childhood having been passed in China; so that she is one of the best possible exponents of both the Chinese and San Francisco questions, which, in these latter days, have become so curiously mixed.

The next morning we drove out to the Cliff House, the most popular resort of the pleasure-seeker in this city. We started in the fog nearly inevitable, at this season, every morning, but warranted to clear by nine o'clock. This especial morning the warrant failed, but unlike gloves and boots, the day could not be returned to its manufacturer, or exchanged for a better one, so we made the best of it and took it out in grumbling and seal-skin sacks. The drive through the suburbs is not especially attractive until one enters Golden Gate Park, the principal driving-ground of San Francisco, and destined, like many other things in this wonderful city, to become by-and-by one of the finest, not only of America but the world. Just at present, however, things are in a rather rudimentary state, the four years of its

The Cliff House.   Page 179.

existence having done a large work upon the thousand acres of shifting sand-hills and wild ravines, thinly clothed with cacti and evergreen—its original status—but leaving much still to be accomplished. The first object to achieve was to form a soil, or rather to hold the restless sands in one spot until a soil could be laid upon them, and this has been done by the extensive planting of lupins, whose spreading roots interlacing between the surface make it permanent, while the coarse leaves and flaunting flowers, not very lovely in themselves, form a shelter and foundation for finer growth. Trees are profusely planted already, and the hard red roads are perfect of their kind; the commissioners are active, the citizens liberal, the climate propitious; so that the baby of to-day, on her bridal tour to San Francisco, may find the melancholy waste of sand-dunes, which Padre Junipero reported as cutting off the site of the Mission Dolores from the ocean, transformed into a park which shall be the delight of the Continent. Presently, after a three miles' drive, we emerge from the great gray drifts which end the grounds upon the western side, and see the long level line of the Pacific stretching to the horizon, its breakers rolling heavily in upon the flat beach and their low roar filling the air.

The Cliff House perches on a steep, rocky eminence, sweeping up abruptly from the beach, so that its piazza literally overhangs the surf. A few hundred yards from the shore rise the picturesque mass of broken crag known as the Seal Rocks, and the long swell of the Pacific meeting this obstacle, breaks from its majestic placidity into an angry rush and roar of surf, sweeping over and among the rocks and churning itself into a foamy fury that fills all the space between them and the shore.

The ocean was of a dull green that day, the sky gray, the wind blowing a gale and wildly scattering the feathers of the sea fowl who fled before it; far to the left stretched the sandy beach with the soft fog drifting down upon it, while to the right the steep and jagged cliffs cut sharply against the sky; from their summit we could have looked across the Golden Gate and the lovely bay to Part Point, with its lighthouse, but we did not do it, sitting instead upon the piazza to watch the sea-lions or seals which swarm upon the rocks bearing their name, playing, eating, fighting, barking, and filling the air with shrill cries and deep roars which mingle in discordant music with the dash and tumult of the surf. Every age, size and description of seal is here represented, from the soft baby of a few weeks old, to the barnacled and clumsy patriarch, turning the scale at three thousand pounds, and rolling hither and thither in majestic disregard of the small fry, who scuttle out of his path to avoid annihilation.

The biggest, ugliest and most belligerent of the seals is called General Butler, and he evidently is not considered an agreeable or safe neighbor, for every one else gave place to him with a haste more of fear than of reverence.

After breakfast—a most elaborate, prolonged, and admirably cooked and served meal — several of us

SEAL ROCKS, HARBOR OF SAN FRANCISCO. Page 180.

descended the cliffs by a winding wooden staircase of
one hundred and forty steps to a little sheltered bay
and lovely sandy beach, with a huge rock towering up
just on the edge of the surf and dividing it into two
shining channels. We stood upon the sands and gazed
far out upon the lovely opal-green expanse of water
which in its great heaving swells seemed lifted above
our heads and gathering all its forces to roll over and
submerge us while the foam and din of the surf close
at hand was the onset of the battle. On each side
of the little bay the gray rocks towered up, all water-
wasted and honeycombed, their surfaces fretted like
lace-work and crusted over with a kind of coral deposit
and clusters of muscle and snail shells. One of the
Seal Rocks has an arch cut completely through it,
presenting a charming effect.

On the drive home we passed Lone Mountain, a
solitary peak upon whose summit stands a gigantic
cross — mute memorial of the Spanish Fathers who
worshiped and buried their dead in its shadow. The
hills around its base are covered with gleaming stones,
and the Romanists, the Protestants and the Chinese
have their cemeteries here.

The sun came out during the return drive, and
by the time we reached home, about two o'clock, it was
overpoweringly hot and we were glad to shelter in the
house.

CHAPTER XX.

THE TIES OF CALIFORNIAN BUSINESS PARTNERSHIPS.

WE received a pleasant call from Mr. Bryant, the Mayor of San Francisco, a most genial gentleman, with the frankest and most honest of blue eyes and a mouth and teeth just formed for gracious and contagious mirth. His manner especially pleased us as lacking that reserve and *arrière pensée* one learns to expect in all men connected with political life. He is hospitable as a prince, and deservedly popular with all classes of his constituents, while his amiable wife is an able and active coadjutor in the social duties of his position.

Mr. Bryant is a New Hampshire man by birth, and came here twenty-seven years ago with a schoolmate, his partner. There is something very touching in this peculiar relationship which formed so marked a feature of early Californian life, and lasts down to to-day. A man's " partner " here is not simply his business ally and perhaps personal enemy, but, following out the picturesque and chivalrous scheme of life that was the first outgrowth of Californian society, these partnerships were a reproduction of the sworn brotherhoods among the Knights of the heroic age, or of the similar tie so common with German students of to-day ; the partner is more than friend, more than a brother, he is an *alter ego*, whose interests, wishes, pleasures and profit are as valuable to his other half as his own; his loves, his quarrels, his ill or good luck are shared with eager partisanship, and whatever comes between, the tie of loyal good faith is very seldom broken. Read Bret Harte's "Tennessee's Pardner" and you will see what it all means better than I can tell. Mr. Bryant and his friend live side by side to-day; they toiled and fought side by side in the wild old days, and the tie remains strong and bright as ever.

The mayor had brought his horses, and presently took us out to see something more of the city than we had yet beheld. We went first to the new City Hall, which will not be finished for about three years more. It is of brick, and cement, plastered outside—San Francisco architecture eschews stone, finding brick and cement with iron beams and cross-ties and iron pillars running from floor to roof more nearly fire and earthquake proof. They claim that this City Hall will outlast any public building in the country, and will be the strongest and most perfect of any structure of the kind ever erected. The Hall of Records is quite separate from the main building, circular in shape and finished with a beautiful dome; two galleries run around the interior, and the floor is of Georgia pine and black walnut, with a very handsome marble centre-piece.

We went on the workmen's elevator to the roof of the main building and saw tantalizing glimpses of a magnificent view partially hidden by the Summer fog, which, as usual, rested soft and gray and fleecy upon the Bay and crept up over the foothills—Goat Island heaved its round back up through it in one spot, and in another we caught a lovely vista of bright blue water, and the city with its rush and roar lay spread out at our feet.   The wind blew a gale, but it was so soft and fresh and warm a wind that one forgave its rude toying for the sake of the relief it brought from the sultry heat of the day.

From the City Hall we drove up the steep hill-streets to look at some of the handsome residences on the cliffs.   Many of them are perfect palaces, generally built of wood, and ornate to excess.   Ralston's city house is a huge caravanseri absolutely without beauty or ornament, the grounds a mere waste of weeds and rubbish.   Most of these places, indeed, fall short in the matter of grounds, everything looking crude and unfinished to Eastern eyes.

Two fine houses are in process of building by Mr. Hopkins and Mr. Crocker.   On the estate of the latter gentleman stood a small cottage which he wished to purchase and take down, but the owner refused to sell under some fabulous price, and Mr. Crocker, declining to be imposed upon to this extent, has instead built a high frame wall around three sides of the cottage, completely shutting it out from his view and also from viewing.   The proprietor threatens to erect a Chinese laundry on the roof of his house, by way of revenge !

We called upon Mrs. Bryant, and after lunch took a Market Street car for the Mission Dolores—the nest-egg, so to speak, of San Francisco.   It was built in 1776 by the Jesuits, but the original adobe building has

been restored almost to annihilation; however, the
church front and most of the interior remain as they
were. Over the low-arched doorway with its four columns are three little arches and two large bells; on
the right are the priests' apartments and rooms for the
Mission schools; on the left, one passes through a little
wooden gateway into the graveyard, a wild and tangled
place overgrown with ivy and myrtle, the blue flowers of
the latter as large as morning glories; the graves, like
those at Lone Mountain, each sheltered in its own little
picket fence with a high board at the end like the head-
board of a bedstead. We left the sunshine outside and
entered the church, where a century's gloom and damp
seemed centralized. One aisle divided the rows of
uncushioned benches, and the floor was bare and worn
by the feet of those who now filled the neglected graveyard outside. A single arch spanned the church, and
upon it was inscribed: "How dreadful is this place;
it is none other than the House of the Lord and the
Gate of Heaven." The main altar was rather bare and
rather tawdry, and at each side of the chancel was a
shrine containing statues of saints not badly executed.
The altars are old and decaying, the gilding tarnished
and the paint dingy; there were many little bouquets upon them all, and the smell of the roses was
heavy and sweet as incense.

In the evening, by way of severe contrast, we went
to Baldwin's Theatre, attached to the hotel of the same
name and just finished. It is really the prettiest to be
seen in any part of the world—a perfect little gem,
fitted up like a *bonbonnière* in crimson satin and gold.

The six proscenium boxes on either side, and the row of French boxes at the back are marvelously pretty. Nothing could be more rich and exquisite in refinement of taste. The symmetry of the house is unmarred by rows of pillars, the galleries being suspended from the roof.

Next morning we went up Clay Hill, on the Elevated Railway, the cars being dragged up the steep ascent by wire cables beneath the wooden track. There is a little engine in the middle and seats around the four sides where you sit and dangle your feet into space; the grade is 376 feet, and one wonders how the inhabitants ever went up and down before the railway was laid. We came home through China Town, never missing an opportunity of visiting it, and saw a woman sitting in a doorway dressed in white trowsers and a pea-green sacque, and a man leading along a little mite of a girl gotten up in a pink silk sacque and trowsers, silver bracelets on her wrists and ankles, and her hair dressed in two flat round whirls at the back, stuck full of artificial flowers. We ventured into a tenement-house, its corridors and stairs filthy and odorous, but its many rooms and more inmates neat and well kept, and the former almost invariably decorated with flowers and globes of gold-fish. These people enjoy inconvenience and prefer to exist five or six together in one little room, men, women and children, cooking, eating, sleeping, and living generally in a space rather scanty for one Englishman or American. Yet all seem happy and content, and all smile upon us persistently and blandly.

CHAPTER XXI.

ONE lovely Sunday morning, following the fashion of the Romans among whom we found ourselves, we started at eight o'clock to pass the day at San Rafael with Mr. Coleman. Going on one of the comfortable boats of the Oaklands and Alameda Ferry Company we found ourselves in the midst of a festive throng of pleasure-seekers who, accompanied by a brass band, were bound for the picnic grounds of San Rafael, one of the most popular resorts for that class of San Franciscans who look upon Sunday as a day of wholesome recreation and rest.

The sail, northerly up the Bay, is one of the most charming imaginable, crossing the channel of the Golden Gate and passing close by Alcatraz with its green breast-works and red roofed forts, then winding between the coast range on the east, and on the West the Mission Hills, Saucelito and Raccoon Straits, while northward lies the great dark peak of Tamalpais, seamed from top to base by a white sand slide where a "cloud-burst struck" some years ago. The soft, bright haze only made the landscape lovelier in a rosy-purple light, and the water was green as emerald and dappled with flashing white caps; presently the sun came out, the sky grew blue and deep, and every-

thing was delicious except the long, slow, swell of the
sea, which rocked the little boat like a cradle.

We disembarked at Point San Quentin and found
the narrow gauge train of cars for San Rafael awaiting
us. Besides the usual carriages we noticed a series of
picnic cars consisting merely of platforms quite close
to the ground and furnished with bare benches. A
passage of twenty minutes or so along the shores of the
Bay brought us to to the pretty village of San Rafael,
nestling at the foot of a great conical hill, half covered
with wood. Mr. Coleman's carriage awaited us, and
the four admirable horses whirled us away, Elijah-like,
in a cloud of dust to the hills above the town. Nothing can be lovelier than the position of San Rafael, the
beautiful Bay at its feet and great Tamalpais shelter-
ing it from the cold winds that sweep in through the
Golden Gate. The valley runs back from the coast
between swelling ranks of hills covered with verdure,
for in the warm, still air and sweet sunshine, every form
of vegetation revels and luxuriates. We drove along
the old post - road running twenty miles inland to
Petaluma, passed the old Mission House now convert-
ed into the Court House of Marion County, and the
Mission gardens and orchards still luxuriant with
flowers and fruits planted by the dead and gone old
monks, and so, through hilly by-roads and glimpses of
lovely scenery to Mr. Coleman's great nursery gardens,
where we left the carriage and walked about to pick
flowers, taste of fruits and enjoy ourselves *à la* Adam
and Eve in Paradise *sans* the serpent. In the garden,
roses were running wild in all directions, the blossoms

as large as great peonies—deep yellow, pale buff, the darkest crimson, pure white and lovely pink; honey-suckles, geraniums, verbenas, pansies, California ever-lastings, every blossom fit for a flower-show, and crowd-ing each other in a mad luxuriance of bloom which made it a charity to pluck as many as possible ; be-sides these, were wildernesses of trees all in flower or fruit, acacias, varieties of eucalyptus, guavas, blue and red gum trees, rhododendrons, and tulip trees, locusts and magnolias. A little wearied at last, we, accompanied by Mr. Coleman, returned to the carriage, and continued our drive through roads scarcely more than projected as yet, some of them no more than mere trails among the grass and wild flowers. Mr. Coleman owns the whole of the San Rafael valley, about forty-five thousand acres of wild land, and he is diligently employed in planting it with trees from his nurseries and laying out roads commanding the loveliest views. He expects by-and-by to sell portions of the grounds as building lots, and the whole region will become one continuous garden. Always, as we wound in and out among the hills and paused for a fresh aspect of the charming view we found Tamalpais in the middle dis-tance, as distinctive a feature as Vesuvius of all Neapol-itan scenery, and Mr. Coleman averred that, owing to its protecting influence, the climate of San Rafael is quite different from that of the coast towns—softer, more equable, and having a larger rain and dew-fall. Nature is so spontaneous and lavish here that she leaves but little for man to do ; on all his vast estate Mr. Coleman employs but eleven men as nurserymen

or gardeners, and the trees once planted are self-sus
taining, never dreaming of withering or dying. Afte
several hours' drive we stopped at a lovely spot an
partook of a picnic lunch under a great laurel tree, an
then, laden with flowers and memories, said good-by an
took the homeward route, pausing to visit the littl
village of San Rafael, a sleepy, peaceful spot, with n
merous pretty white cottages buried in flowers an
shaded by palm trees, and in one garden a centur
plant, its blossom spike twenty feet high and ju
ready to burst into bloom, after which the plant die
Near San Quentin we passed a settlement of shrim
fishermen, a knot of little low huts, the red pape
above their doors betraying the presence of the heatl
en Chinee. The black nets were drying upon the gras
and the fishermen, blue bloused, pig-tailed and bar
legged lounged about staring at us and commentin
in the usually outwardly bland and covertly snee
ing manner. The shrimps, when caught, are passe
through a machine which takes off their shells, whic
are ground up for compost, while the meat is salte
and packed for transportation to China.

The sail down the Bay was as lovely as that of th
morning until, in the purple light of early evening, w
passed the Golden Gate and saw San Francisco, sleepin
upon her seven hills; Lone Mountain, with its grea
cross towering to the sky; Telegraph Hill, overhangin
the bay, and the sunset glow making one great op
of the quiet sea. A little later we reached the Palac
Hotel, made our rooms beautiful with the wealth
flowers Mr. Coleman had lavished upon us, dressed f

dinner and in the evening received all the world just as one might do in Paris or New York, or anywhere else; for the world of people does not present half the charming varieties in different latitudes that the world of roses and eucalypti does.

The next day we dined at Ex-Governor Stanford's, who has the most magnificent house on this Continent; it covers an entire block and its appointments are simply palatial. One drawing-room is furnished in Pompeian style from designs which were the joint work of its tasteful mistress and her friend Miss Hosmer, the sculptress of whom America is so proud. The dining-room is as superb as it is spacious, and nothing that taste could suggest or wealth provide is there wanting, while the sleeping and dressing rooms are as luxurious as they are dainty and magnificent, and the picture gallery is a worthy home for its choice paintings and statuary, where all of our native as well as foreign artists of distinction are worthily and characteristically represented.

The dinner was superb, the thirty guests well-selected and harmonized, the hostess a tall, stately woman, with regal manners fitly borne out by her costume of crimson velvet softened with rare old lace and embellished by a magnificent *parure* of diamonds and glowing opals. Her unmarried sister, who aided her in doing the honors, is a charming lady, both genial and courtly of manner; but the pet of the house is a splendid boy some ten years of age, the only child of the parents, who waited nineteen years for his arrival. The little fellow was presented after dinner and charmed us by his pretty and very graceful manners.   He has great artistic as well as other talents, and all are carefully fostered under the charge of his adoring mother, who, on a subsequent occasion, took us to see his apartments. They consist of study, music and play rooms, bath-room, dressing-room, and bed-room, all fit for a prince, or better, for the splendid American boy, whose manhood should be the perfection of our race, so nurtured and protected.

Next morning, after breakfast, we were invited by Mr. Baldwin, whose unique theatre we had visited to go over the hotel connected with it and likewise bearing his name.   It is not quite complete as yet as to furniture, but has been opened for visitors for a couple of months and is a most admirable house.   We viewed the offices and were shown the improvements such as the revolving post office with boxes arranged in a cylinder; the chronometer which regulates the sixty clocks of the hotel, timing them all to a second; an apparatus for gauging the heat of each apartment or suite ; another for reporting the movements of the bell boys ; passenger elevators, and one for sending up parcels to each floor; each department provided with an office and set of boys independent of the rest.   Each department has also its individual fire apparatus, and a well runs the height of the building, having a small window at each floor, and behind it a coil of hose connecting with the tank, so that at the most sudden alarm of fire any one can rush and turn on a stream of water. On the lower floor is a waiting-room, a reading-room, a barber's shop and a fine billiard-room for gentlemen and at the opposite extreme of the house, in the roof, a reading and billiard room for ladies. The parlors were unfurnished, but we could admire their graceful proportions and elaborate frescoing. The suites of private apartments were charming, finished in black walnut and furnished, many of them, in crimson velvet and gray satin, with fine large, light bath-rooms, rich in hooks and shelves, unlimited closet room and all the accessories of each suite daintily matched and harmonized. The rooms of the suites connect but have double doors to insure perfect privacy. The upper floor, or sixth story, furnished in light California wood, is devoted to bachelor apartments, where smoking is not forbidden!

The theatre connects with the hotel, and two minutes before each act the prompter touches a bell ringing in the bar, so that thirsty souls may appease the pangs of drought with no danger of losing any part of the play. Altogether, we must confess that Mr. Baldwin's hotel, like his theatre, is quite the model building of its class in this our model country.

SETTLERS IN ECHO CAÑON. Page 71.

CHAPTER XXII.

THE ROSES OF SANTA ROSA.

RISING at six one fine morning we ate such breakfast as was possible at that crude hour, and embarked for the first stage of our journey to the Geysers. The sail up the bay was a repetition of Sunday's experience, and at Donohue Landing we took the train for Cloverdale, and were soon flying through the loveliest country imaginable —a perfect Arcadia. The land was level and an almost unbroken mass of verdure and bloom, field after field of wild grain, which in California holds the place of grass with us, with great wide-armed trees brooding over it, live and white oaks, garlanded with gray moss, laurels and chestnut trees; here and there were tracts of wild poppies, great solid sheets of golden bloom without a blade of green, flaming in the sunshine until the eye was dazzled with their glory, broad patches of blue and purple and orange flowers of names unknown, and, darting over and among them, whole flocks of birds with colors as vivid as the flowers—blue-jays, blackbirds with scarlet epaulets, burnished blue-black magpies, and quails with oddly plumed heads, sitting fearlessly upon the fences. Here and there were great herds of cattle and flocks of sheep, but happily very few signs beside of the occupancy or dominion of man.

At Santa Rosa we left the train for a little exploration, and found the Mayor and some of the dignitaries of the place awaiting us with hospitable and courteous intent, and three vehicles in readiness to carry us around the town, which certainly is well worth the seeing. Santa Rosa is named in honor of the first and we believe only American saint in the Romish calendar. She was an inhabitant of Lima, in Peru, a charming girl, endowed with numberless graces of body and soul, and enthusiastically given to practices of religion, sighing in her fervent devotion for the palm of martyrdom, even of the most terrible nature. After her death, the Pope then occupying St. Peter's chair was requested to canonize her, but refused to do so, expressing the greatest incredulity at the notion of a holy virgin having lived and died in Lima, of all places. Urged yet farther, he exclaimed, " Yes, when roses fall from out the skies upon my head, I will believe that this Rosa was all that you claim, and will surely canonize her!"

No sooner had the words passed the lips of the holy father—you will not doubt the legend surely—than a heavenly perfume filled the apartment and a shower of the fairest and sweetest roses fell upon his head and hands, and slid meekly to his feet. Astonished and humiliated, the Pope hastened to fulfil his pledge, canonized the fair Limeña without delay, and named her Patron Saint of her native America. Churches and convents have been called in her honor, and in one of the finest of these latter at Lima her remains are religiously preserved. No doubt it is in consequence of her fostering care, but surely roses never bloomed more beautifully or perfectly than in this little Californian town whose name is hers.

In one garden was a giant rose-bush twenty-five feet high, with a sturdy trunk like a tree, and the top one snowy globe of blossoms. In another garden we saw an evergreen, up which a climbing white rose had made its way and thrust forth sprays of creamy roses from among the dark foliage with a wonderfully pretty effect.

The Mayor was a jolly sort of personage, with an uproarious laugh and a thoroughly hearty manner, who addressed the Chief simply as " Colonel," and invited us all into the bar-room for a treat of beer. The editor of the *Sonoma Democrat,* Mr. Thompson, accompanied the Mayor and made a very agreeable addition to the party. He has lived in Santa Rosa for twenty years, and is enthusiastic both as to its present and future. Still one could but wonder that a man of Mr. Thompson's rare erudition, intellect, and refinement could be happy so far away from a great literary centre. The Mayor also was enthusiastic about his pretty little town, averring that it possessed the best climate, less high wind and more rainfall, and the healthiest influences of any in California. Fruit and flowers, he said, could be had for the picking eleven months in the year, and grew with scarcely any cultivation. There is a church in this town eighty feet deep, forty wide, and thirty in height, every plank and shingle of which were cut from a single red-wood tree. This wood is beautiful for building purposes, requiring only a coat of varnish upon the surface to bring out the richest warm color imaginable.

The Sonoma red-wood grove is near Santa Rosa, and the Mayor and his party proposed escorting us thither. Upon the way back to the station we craved and obtained from Mr. Thompson a few statistical items, such as that the population of Santa Rosa has within five years advanced from one thousand to six thousand, and that she possesses five churches, and two colleges, one under the Methodist, the other under Campbell-Baptist patronage.

From Santa Rosa we passed through the rich and lovely scenery of the Sonoma Valley into a region where the track began to wind and curve between steep hillsides black with huge pines and cedars, crossing and recrossing the little deep-green stream of the Russian River. We were in the red-wood country, and the trees began to shoot higher towards heaven tall, dark trunks, straight as masts, and beginning to throw out branches at about the height common trees leave off altogether; here and there were patches of blackened giant stumps, and here and there lumber yards, until of a sudden the trees seemed to crowd down and close across our path, the train stopped, and we dismounted in the heart of the Sonoma red-wood forest. Those who knew told us to restrain our superlatives of wonder and admiration until we saw the really "big trees" of Calaveras and Mariposa, the world-famous Sequois; but after all, size is not the only measure of beauty, or astonishment the highest proof of delight, and many of us enjoyed more in wandering through the cool dark depths of this grove, looking up to the rustling roof of foliage so far above our heads that we could scarce distinguish the leaves, and listening to the roar of the wind in their unseen crests like the roll of surf upon a distant shore, than we did subsequently at Mariposa.

The rest of the journey was pleasant, but uneventful, and we reached Cloverdale in time for dinner in the big, bare dining-room of the pleasant inn. These country inns of California were quite charming—more like those one finds in the heart of rural England than those to be seen elsewhere in America—long, low, two-storied houses, with plenty of cosy little rooms, clean and homely, but, unlike England, with no arrangements for fire, and with a long, wide piazza across the front. We saw nothing of quiet little Cloverdale except the inn, and after dinner found the stage awaiting us—a great open vehicle with five seats, capable of accommodating three persons on each—and a big black-bearded driver. We started at once; and much as we had previously enjoyed California scenery, this afternoon's experience was the climax. The air was warm and peculiarly sweet, the slanting lights exquisite, the shadows artistic, and the rapid Russian River, which we waded twice, with the water up to our horses' girths, full of life and *verve*.

Presently we struck into Sulphur Creek Cañon, a wild and wonderful mountain gorge, where the road is hewn out of the face of a precipice, with a sheer descent of three or four hundred feet between it and the river-bed below, and a wall of rock above, crowned with a fringe of dark-green trees. The road is safe, no doubt, but there is not a foot of ground to spare between the wheel-tracks and the unguarded edge, and as it winds and doubles around a series of capes and promontories, succeeding each other like the links of a chain, the leaders of our spirited "four-in-hand" were often invisible to the occupants of the back seat of the coach. Our driver at least knew no fear, and dashed along in grand style, grinding the edge of the precipice with his outer wheels as he swung round the sharpest curves at a dead run, often lashing his horses into a gallop, and laconically answering the timid and respectful inquiry whether such a course was quite safe, with the phrase "You bet!"

This gentleman was not a conversational person, and, it is to be feared, was something of a misogynist. At any rate, he expressed great contempt for the terror of the ladies, and sneered cruelly at our desire to see a grizzly bear, which amiable creature is still occasionally to be met with in this vicinity.

"I'd like to see you hold them horses if a grizzly showed his snout. I couldn't do it," remarked he, and then in a burst of confidence went on to say that this road had been opened only a few years, and that he drove "the first wheel" that ever passed over it. We longed to inquire if this wheel was attached to a wheel-barrow, but refrained, and found ourselves rewarded by the farther information that our friend had been "staging it" for twenty-five years without a single accident; that he was both owner and driver of this entire line, consisting of five coaches and twenty horses, and that his net profits at the end of the year were just about enough to keep him in clothes.

"I go stagin' for glory, I do," remarked he, and then evidently feeling that he had sufficiently sacrificed to the

curiosity of the female sex and the duties of hospitality,
he closed his mouth like a steel trap, and opened it no
more, except for the surliest monosyllables, only unbending
so far as to point out the Madrona trees (big mothers), so
called by the Spaniards, from their size.   They are wonderfully beautiful, their great, glossy trunks and branches
glowing with a color like burnished copper, shading into
cinnamon flecked with gold, and having a curious grape-
like bloom upon them.   The glossy, green leaves, too, are
touched with gold, so that even in shadow the trees look
as if the sun were shining upon them, and in sunshine
they blaze with splendor against the deep-blue background
of the mountain sky.

The white oaks, too, were very attractive with their
broad, low crests, the gray Spanish moss flaunting like
banners from their sturdy arms, mixed with great knots
of mistletoe, enough to furnish forth a whole college
of Druids, or all England's Christmas festivities.   The
birds flitted in and out of this dark foliage, bright as
winged flowers, and about sunset gave us a grand vesper
chorus, at sound of which the gay little lizards, gray, and
brown, and bright blue, slid out of sight beneath the
stones ; the shadows stole from the depths of the pine
trees, and crowded down to fill the depths of the cañon,
and Nature was so obviously preparing for her night's rest
that we were quite relieved when, at a sudden turn of the
road, we came in sight of the Geysers. whose steamy vapor
gleamed purple in the sunset light.

We passed an abandoned quicksilver mine, gaping and
desolate, with its ruined roofless buildings, and just as the

sunset chill began to creep up from the cañon, arrived at the little mountain inn where we were to pass the night. It was a little straggling low-roofed building, from whose windows gleamed the welcome of a blazing wood-fire. Cold, weary, and hungry, we stiffly descended from our perches, and were shown into the cosy little parlor, where, beside the fire, we found welcome from some travellers already enjoying it, and were glad to recognize the bride whose nuptials made so great an excitement in the fashionable world of New York last winter.

Herself and husband had been at the Geysers earlier in the season, and were pleased with the quaint little mountain inn, and they had returned to pass another week there. The bride seemed happy and cheerful, and had lost nothing, in her newly-acquired matronly dignity, of the genial grace of manner which had made her, as Miss R——, so many friends in her widely-extended circle. The handsome young husband, with his thoroughbred, rather English air, seemed born to the millions which had come to him by kind fortune and with his amiable and accomplished wife, and we passed a pleasant hour chatting of mutual friends and acquaintances, of our own city, and of others that both parties had recently visited, of the bridal party's abandoned trip to China and approaching European tour, until we parted for the night with a cordial grasp of the hand, mutual good wishes, and, on our side at least, with a fervent and heartfelt prayer for future happiness and prosperity among the chances and changes of this most uncertain life.

A little later we all enjoyed an entertainment certainly
9*

not set down in the programme. The Geyser Hotel is constructed upon a novel and decidedly breezy plan, the corridors being all open to the outer air, and the bedrooms each having a door upon the piazza running around the house; besides these conveniences for communication, the partitions are nothing but thin boarding, considerably shrunken, and conversation can be carried on with perfect ease from one end of the establishment to the other, even after every door is shut that CAN be shut. The consequence of this arrangement, on this particular evening, was that we all heard ourselves discussed with a frankness and candor not usually granted to one's own ears.

The little inn was full of guests, and probably no two of them failed of some remark upon the new arrivals. The rival claims to beauty of the various ladies of the party—for our ranks had been recruited by a lovely widowed friend from California—their toilets, manners, and identity were all freely discussed, and the two married gentlemen of our company had the satisfaction of hearing their wives freely bestowed upon each other or upon the bachelors, while the charming widow was made a wife once more, and one of the wives set down as a widow, the maiden married, and a general new distribution of the party effected with the most charming celerity and certainty.

We must confess, however, that nothing malicious or slanderous was heard, and when the subject in the adjoining rooms turned from ourselves to the personal affairs of the gossipers, the rap of a brush-handle upon the door secured silence and the possibility of slumber.

CHAPTER XXIII.

THE GEYSERS AND FOSSE OF FOSSEVILLE.

IT is proper to begin a day at the Geysers by visiting the baths, of which there is quite a variety. Passing down the canon opposite the house, and keeping along the bed of a stream, one arrives at a little rustic bridge, and crossing it to the bath-houses, takes one's choice between hot sulphurous water, dense steam—also sulphurous—and a cold plunge in the river.

The odors of the sulphur baths were odious, but the waters felt pleasant, and left a delightful sensation upon the skin.

Coming out of the houses we wandered a little farther up the cañon and seated ourselves upon the dry, crumbling soil, through which jets of vapor were spouting here and there, some close beside the river, as if its clear, cold waters had been subterraneously boiled and were throwing off steam.

The Geysers are seen to greater advantage at early morning than later in the day, as the vapor condenses more in the chill hour before sunrise than afterward, and we sat for awhile content to watch the Afrit-like shapes of the columns of steam rising and forming, and then dissolving in endless succession, while the level rays of the rising sun touched first the crest of the rocky walls of the cañon, then crept slowly down, lighting the cold, gray rock and black-green evergreens to warmth and life, and making prisms and irises of the cloudy stream-wreaths.

But even the sunlight and the morning could not alter the general mournful, uncanny, blasted look of nature in all this region, the soil, apparently of crumbled pumice stone, is ghastly in its pale-gray color, unenlivened by verdure or the tender brown of arable earth; the river moaned and murmured as if those subterranean fires were scorching its life-springs, and clouds of vapor assumed more and more fantastic shapes.

After breakfast we set forth for the regular tour of the Geysers, crossing the stream at the foot of the cañon, and winding a little trail into another gorge, wild and steep, and gradually bringing us into the region of purely mineral and chemical life, with little trace of vegetable or animal existence.

The soil, after passing a landmark called the Devil's Arm-Chair, and the Magnesia Spring, is a mere crust of crystallizations of sulphur and lime, beds of cinnabar, like wet red paint, green incrustations of copper, and brilliant yellow patches of brimstone, everything wet with the oosing mineral waters, and scalding hot to the touch, the air dense with horrible fumes and clouds of hot steam puffing up into one's face, jets of boiling water spirting under one's feet, and black, bubbling pools lying ready to entrap the unwary; the loose and friable soil crumbles beneath the tread, and seems to breathe heat, so that one feels as if walking over an endless series of registers, with a seven-times heated furnace underneath.

THE WITCHES' CAULDRON, CAL.   Page 205.

Few mortal experiences can give so vivid an idea of the infernal regions, and were I a great reformer of the Calvinistic school, I would simply engage Mr. Cook to take all my converts to this valley, upon a gigantic excursion, sure that it would do more to frighten them from evil courses than any amount of preaching.

The Witches Cauldron, black as ink, leaping, bubbling, and hissing, is all but hidden in the dense clouds of vapor, so that one only sees it through the rifts, and may fancy it limitless in extent, and peopled with the spirits of the damned; there is a continual rumbling and roaring in the bowels of the earth, which suggests the pleasing idea of an earthquake possible at any moment. The utter absence of vegetation and of animal life adds a certain horror to the scene, suggesting a world in process of extinction, where man, the latest and highest form of creation, is also to be the last to perish.

This gorge is appropriately called the Devil's Cañon, and the heat, and the steam, and the sounds, and the smells, and the vague horror of the whole intensified, until we reached the Devil's Pulpit, a huge crag, closing the valley and commanding its whole sweep, the pools in the bottom round which our path had skirted, and the steep bare sides, patched all yellow and scarlet, and ashy white, with hundreds of jets of steam and smoke bursting out in every direction. Such a picture must have been in John Bunyan's mind when he described Christian's journey through the Valley of the Shadow of Death, and we were fain to fancy the dark evergreen forests of Sulphur Cañon, which closed the distant view, as representing the

Delectable Mountains, and the little white hotel nestling in its fertile clearing, as the House Beautiful with its fair inmates.

Perhaps the gray-headed and learned looking man, in a linen duster, whom we found wandering in the Valley, was the Interpreter. At any rate, he joined himself to our party in a friendly manner, and informed us with the voice of authority, that the phenomena of this spot was occasioned by the action of various chemical agencies meeting and conflicting just beneath the surface of the ground. Our guide, however, not a bit like Great-Heart, by the way, pooh-poohed this theory with great scorn, insisting that the region was volcanic, and the commotion we witnessed was but a feeble exponent of much more terrible disturbances deep down below our feet. In fact, the *savant* would have the trouble a mere cutaneous disorder, of little real importance, while the guide considered it symptomatic of deep organic disease. I myself inclined to the latter theory as being more terrific and exciting, and walked gingerly about on the crisp lava-like surface of the subterraneous volcano, expecting each moment when it should explode and blow our theories and ourselves sky-high, whence we might take a wider view of the matter!

In support of his side of the question, the guide presently led us past the Devil's Pulpit, through a pretty little path suddenly blossoming out of the waste, to the crater of what he declared to be an extinct volcano. It was a great circular depression in the earth, its surface dry and baked with patches of mineral deposit, variegating its dull ashen color, and sounding hollow beneath our feet as we stamped upon it.

Especially, we noticed some lovely needle-like crystals of sulphur, so delicate that they crumbled at a touch, and altogether could well believe that in some unremembered age, this mournful basin was filled with boiling lava, and sent forth its desolating streams to fill the valley beyond. The little track wound on in a gentle curve, passing a great white oak bent nearly to the ground, with a hole in the side where visitors are in the habit of thrusting their cards for the benefit of acquaintances who may chance to come after. Some grass and bushes timidly appear here and there, but the path presently curves away from them, and sweeps into the region of Geysers again.

The Indians' vapor bath is a deep cave in the side of a hill, filled with scalding hot steam, which rises and hangs around the entrance in a dense cloud; the Indians used to resort here yearly for this bath until within a brief period, but now come no more. Near by is a safety valve through which the hot air puffs in regular blasts with a hoarse roaring sound, and such force as to eject pebbles thrown into the opening some three or four feet into the air.

As we passed we saw a picturesque group of hunters on horseback and on foot, slowly climbing the steep foot-hill beyond, with dogs and a pack-mule following, and were told that game is various and abundant in this region, ranging from grizzly bears to woodcock.

The trail wound around the steep sweep of the hills a little farther, and then down to the little stream at the bottom of the cañon, and so by the bath-houses to the hotel where we rested an hour, lunched, and were ready at one o'clock to mount the open stage-wagon with its four fine horses driven by a son of Fosse, the celebrated horse-breaker and stage driver of this region, although, indeed, his reputation extends all over California.

The stage was to convey us to Fosseville and Calistoga, where we were to take the cars again for the home trip, travellers generally preferring to go by the Cloverdale and return by the Calistoga road, instead of retracing their steps. We had been assured that this part of the route would prove far more terrific than that we had passed on the previous day, and had braced ourselves to a pitch of unshrinking and unshrieking courage quite beautiful to contemplate, but altogether wasted as the event proved, for the road was, if anything, a little less dangerous, and the scenery even more beautiful than that previously passed.

Both road and scenery presented the same general features, a deep cañon with the road cut in the side of one of the ranges enclosing it ; the same curving and doubling and serpentine festooning around head-lands, and capes of rock rising hundreds of feet above our heads, and falling hundreds of feet below to the sombre depths of the gorge, and the all-but inaudible river far beneath. To-day, however, the cañon was wider and the scene more extended ; at almost the highest point we passed a little cabin perched like an eyrie above the world, and commanding a view of the whole Sonoma Valley, a great green trench, with no track through it except this one clinging to the side of the cañon, and the bright watercourses sparkling through it.

Beginning to descend, we passed over the Dog's Back, which some one has described as a most awful and perilous pass, but to us it seemed no worse and no different from several similar points of the route; the precipices above and below were steep and the road not the one we should select to train a frisky four-in-hand team upon, but it was wide enough for our safe passage, and the curve not nearly so sharp as some around which we had jauntily swung.

The view from this point was sublime, but although a succession of slightly varying views bring with themselves a sufficient difference of charm to sustain the interest for days and days, the English language contains but twenty-six letters, and no very varied vocabulary of adjectives, so that we spare all farther description of the fringy mountain lilacs beside the road, and the great splendid Madrona trees ablaze in the sunshine, and simply say that descending precipitously from the heights whereon we had dwelt for two days, we came into a green and level region, and by and by stopped at a little wayside station consisting of half a dozen houses hidden in a grove of pine trees.

This was Pine Flat, of poetic celebrity, but now falling to decay, the population having within two years dwindled from six thousand to fifteen souls, its present census. The abandonment of the quicksilver mines in the vicinity is the cause of this exodus, and the only present industry of Pine Flat is the collection of minerals and crystals which are offered for sale to travellers, just as similar products are at Vesuvius and Pestum.

From Pine Flat we drove through a pleasant uninteresting country of several miles, and finally arrived at Fosseville and drew up before the castle of Fosse himself; it was a charming white house with a huge white-oak before the door, and quantities of flowers both inside and outside of a huge garden. The great Fosse came forward to meet us, or rather to upbraid and reprove us, for it seems we had been expected to dine and perhaps pass the night, and a banquet had been prepared and spoiled by waiting; furthermore, Fosse himself had driven out six-in-hand to meet us, and coming home disappointed had solaced himself with whiskey to an- extent not increasing his natural amiability. He is a great, burly fellow, a native of New Hampshire, and so long accustomed to autocracy in this region, as to bitterly resent such disregard of his plans and efforts, as we unwittingly had shown. He accordingly received us very gruffly, and evidently had resolved to make us feel the penalty of his displeasure.

We were shown to the charmingly neat rooms prepared for us by his amiable, pretty, young wife, and spent half an hour in removing so much as was possible of the coating of red dust, in which we were encased like mummies in asphaltum. Descending, we found Fosse himself seated upon the driver's seat of the wagon prepared to take us to Calistoga, but no sooner had we started, than it became apparent that his ill-humor had only increased by expression, and had reached a pitch beyond the power of the softest words to turn away—even the Sultana's eloquence being tried upon him without the slightest effect. What was worse, this mood found expression in his mode of managing the six horses who tore along at a rate threatening to project us all into the road at the slightest notice, and the result of the whole was, that it was considered wisest to bend to the offended power and return to pass the night and eat the funeral baked meats as best we might.

The word was said, the six horses wheeled as if on a pivot, and we tore back again, having been absent from the house about ten minutes, and traversed about three miles. A supper was served which did ample justice to the landlord's grumbling complaints as to the trouble and expense of the wasted dinner, and while it was preparing we walked in the pretty garden, and down a planked path to a little cottage buried in roses and white blossomed vines; it is let to lodgers and is quite the ideal nest in which a pair of newly-wedded doves might pass their honey-moon.

Our lovely young widow decked herself in roses and made her travelling dress fit for a ball-room, but she herself was still the freshest and sweetest rose of all, as both eyes and whispers told her. After supper a roaring wood-fire, and a new upright piano and the widow's sympathetic voice made the little parlor charming, and we passed a happy although short evening, for every one was weary, and at an early hour sought the sweet, fresh bedrooms where rest and sleep awaited them.

Breakfast was as good as the supper had been, and at last with lightened consciences and somewhat lightened

purses, we again mounted the big stage, and were driven
by the comforted but not quite genial Fosse, to Calistoga,
making the six miles in twenty-one minutes!

The four-hours journey by rail from this place is
through the Napa Valley, a lovely cultivated country, with
miles of vineyards, where the vines look like a bouquet of
leaves tied to a sturdy stalk, hardly a foot high. We
passed Mr. Woodward's charming country seat, saw the
State Lunatic Asylum, and, as we took the steamboat, had
a glimpse of the Navy Yard.

Then another delightful sail with old Tamalpais welcoming us back to the region where he presides, until at
length tired, dusty, disordered, but rich in new experiences
and pictured memories, we arrived at the Palace Hotel
and revelled once more in all the appliances of the highest
civilization.

A DRIVE WITH FOSSE OF FOSSEVILLE.

CHAPTER XXIV.

IT had been decided that after the visit to the Yosemite Valley, which is, of course, inevitable in every
Californian tour, we should explore the Southern part of
the State to some extent, and return to the direct homeward route without revisiting the Golden Gate, and as
the day of our departure drew near, every member of the
party began, each in his or her own fashion, to make
those frantic and futile snatches at the special delight
they were about to lose, which are a feature of almost
every departure whether from a scene of enjoyment or
life itself.

For our own part we haunted the Chinese quarter,
greedily gathering up every item of novelty, every inti-
mation of the hidden life of this strange people, and so
many tangible memorials of our visit as the limits of our
purse and trunks would allow.

We visited Lee Yip and his silver " eelings " as usual,
and found the shop crowded with customers; in especial
we noticed the prettiest little China woman imaginable,
dressed in dark blue silk trousers and a purple silk sack,
her long hair braided with scarlet ribbons, and wearing
rich bracelets, and ear-rings of green stones heavily set in
gold. Her expression was marvellously sweet, and her

complexion a wonderfully clear golden white with a faint pretty color in the cheeks. She spoke no English, but our little high caste Lee Yip informed us that she was "mallied," and indicated a fat aquiline-nosed disagreeable old fellow as the husband, although both his own expression and the giggling of the spectators gave us a most uncomfortable sensation of being hoaxed. We invited her to sit for a picture, and for reply she tried to run out of the shop, but being caught and brought back, she finally submitted with a good grace, and sat still while a pretty little picture was made of her, the "husband" and a crowd of friends looking on, laughing and criticising, in Chinese.

Lee Yip gave us his autograph, and he and the rest amused themselves by examining our jewels and the young lady's purse, which they opened, discussed and handed it round, finally returning it with the contents intact. From this favorite haunt we wandered away through several little dark alleys, seeing the dirt we had only smelt during our evening expedition. The sidewalks are only wide enough for one person to pass at a time, and the doors of the houses open directly upon them, and as each door is provided with a sliding panel at the height of a man's head, one cannot fail to get a pretty clear idea of the internal economy of the houses; in many, however, the view was obstructed by a female face highly decorated, perfumed, and painted, looking out as earnestly as we were looking in; over many of these panel-windows a bunch of joss-sticks, or some red and gold paper were slowly burning away, probably on the horse-shoe principle, although I fear quite as much evil dwelt within as could approach from without.

In one of these alleys we passed a doctor's office, with two great paper signs on rollers outside the door, covered with illustrations of the most hideous forms of disease depicted in the reddest possible paint, and a great deal of it. Also we saw a poulterer's shop, with hundreds of bamboo cages of live hens and pigeons. Near the Bureau of Emigration we again met a throng of newly-landed emigrants with umbrella-shaped hats and great bundles and bales done up with straw-ropes. They were all chattering like magpies, and stared and laughed at us even more boldly than we did at them.

Just back of China Town is the French quarter, and we coyly promenaded through two or three streets of little one and two-storied houses, consisting, as the open window assured us, of little more than a front-parlor, and a bed-room behind, some of them elegantly furnished. The half-doors are finished with a little cushioned ledge at the top, where the occupant may stand and lean with folded arms to enjoy the outer scenery when so disposed, while a little silver plate below is engraved with her Christian name only; a glass door within is decorated with lace-curtains and the air of the whole is prettier and more graceful than the Chinese houses. There are, however, no joss-sticks or gilt paper above the doors, no amulets or charms, alas! to avert the evil that stalks boldly through all these quarters of the town.

In one of these last days, Mayor Bryant invited us for a parting drive behind his elegant four-in-hand team.

We went to Oaklands, which rather disappointed us, being more city-like and less rurally beautiful than we had anticipated, but passing through the city we wound up into the hills, between high wooden slopes and constantly catching glimpses of the bay and the Golden Gate. We passed several ranches, and some green meadows completely perforated with the burrows of the gray and brown ground-squirrels, who scampered about quite tame and undismayed.

Live-oak and chaparral were abundant, but everything looked brown and dusty until we reached the Mayor's own grounds, where care and irrigation will soon make a paradise around the pretty cottage which he has recently purchased as a summer home. Everything looked green and smiling, plenty of roses and other flowers, a rustic bridge, and a little summer-house, all home-like and rural.

We lunched in a pleasant company, and then walked up the hill behind the house to see the trout artificially hatched in a pool and brook, manufactured for them, as nearly as possible, on the model of their native New Hampshire streams; after this we visited the stables and horses, of which the Mayor is justly proud, sat in the cosy little house with Mrs. Bryant and her other guests, and then enjoyed one of the fastest of fast drives home in the purple twilight, and devoted the evening to the painful task of packing.

The next day we made a sorrowful promenade through some of our favorite haunts; we liked the steep hills which slope up and down from Kearney Street, with its

macadamized side-walks and cobble-stone pavements, the
background of the brown foot-hills circling the town, and
the heights crowned with the ambitious homes of rival
capitalists, which a vivid imagination can readily convert
into castles; one of the characteristic sights, and a very
pretty one, are the flowerstands enclosed in glass and
mounted on wheels filled with bouquets for sale.

Then the fascination of climbing Sacramento or Washington Streets and finding one's self in that swarm of
Chinese is one that never wears out for us, and were it not
for wearying the reader, we could go through unnum-
bered pages describing the quaint, queer, outlandish
sights and people, whom nobody comprehends, and who,
while we arrogantly try to civilize and Christianize them
by our own standard, complacently seat themselves upon
the heights of their own civilization, their own religion,
and consider us as outside barbarians whom it is not worth
their while to convince of error and ignorance.

ON THE ROAD TO THE "BIG TREES." Page 243.

CHAPTER XXV.

A LODGE IN A VAST WILDERNESS.

AT three in the afternoon we said good-by to the
Palace Hotel, and laden with flowers and pleasant
adieux, and friendly wishes from a host of new-made, but
not soon-to-be-forgotten friends, we embarked upon the
Oaklands ferry-boat, and when well off discovered that a
large portion of our luggage was left behind, and still ru-
minating on this disaster, took train for Merced, at which
place we arrived at ten at night and were welcomed by
Senator Conover and his party, whom we had arranged to
meet at this point.

In spite of a driving shower we sallied forth to visit
the lions of the place, the principal of which seemed to be
the Cosmopolitan Saloon, large billiard and refreshment
rooms handsomely furnished in native woods, gorgeously
fitted up and said to be the finest establishment of the kind
in California; its attractions for us, however, were soon
exhausted, and we were all glad to return to our hotel for
rest and sleep.

Seen by the gray light of early dawn next morning
Merced showed itself a flat, straggling, dismal town
enough, planted in the midst of a bare and level plain,
destitute of trees, or verdure, or anything to be called
scenery, unless the white sails of numberless windmills

may be so called. The hotel is large and commodious and quite an important point of junction for various lines of roads and coaches.

The great entrance hall was piled with luggage and crowded with travellers each intent upon his own especial box, his own especial route, and his own especial comfort. One of our party was quite amused by a conversation rehearsed in this hall where an angry gentleman, disappointed in obtaining places in a coach secured entirely for ourselves, exclaimed: "Now that is what I call too bad, too —— mean, if we have got to travel to the Yosemite in the wake of that Leslie party! We were behind them all the way to the Geysers and back, and it was like travelling in the wake of a swarm of seven-year locusts. Not a carriage, not a house, not a bed, not a guide, not a decent dinner to be had anywhere, 'they had all been engaged or gone with or devoured by Mr. Leslie's party,' was the universal cry, until I was sick of the name and now we are going to have it all over again, it seems."

In spite of the lamentations of this modern Jeremiah, however, the best coach was soon laden with as many of us as it would hold, and the second best nearly filled with the remainder of the party, and we all drove cheerfully out of Merced, perfectly content with the dispensations of Providence, and wishing that everybody else was so also. In the suburbs of Merced we saw in some of the barnyards a kind of plough peculiar to this region, having ten or a dozen blades or plough-shares, and intended to be drawn by as many horses. Except for this contrivance it would be impossible to cultivate these immense fields, hundreds of acres in extent.   The road was fine, hard as a floor, and perfectly level, but scarcely distinguishable in color from the barren plains stretching away from it on either hand, brown, bare, and dry.   Far more desolate, to our mind, than the Great Plains.   There had been so little rain here during the past winter that vegetation had nearly died out, and the only green things to be seen were some stunted willows growing beside a dried up river-bed.

On these plains we saw the first jack-rabbits, as large as a great cat or small dog, who sat upon their haunches to contemplate the coach as it went by, and hardly seemed at all alarmed ; we also saw gophirs and ground-squirrels playing around their burrows, and an occasional reed-heron whirring up from among the willows.   We drove for miles over this weary and desolate plain with no sign of human life except a packtrain, two wagons hitched together and a string of mules.   As our course began to tend toward the hills we passed ranges of buttes looking like breastworks, with arches hollowed in them as if made by man ; sharp, splintery slabs of stone cropped out here and there, looking like tombstones, crested over with bright orange and crimson lichens, and the whole surface of the country became more broken and rugged.

As we entered the more hilly region the thunder clouds gathered, a flash of vivid lightning nearly blinded us, and, contrary to all California precedent, the rain descended in a sudden flood just as we drew up at the first station where we were to change horses.   It was a very Bret Harte-ish little place, consisting of a narrow street of wooden shanties, a bar-room, a few shade trees, and a corral with some frisky horses plunging about inside; these, with a few wild-looking men and a swarm of children, seemed to make up the population of Indian Gulch, where we stayed but a few moments, and dashed on with the fresh team, into a more wooded and mountainous country than we had yet seen to Bootjack Hollow, eighteen miles distant, and finally reached Mariposa about noon.

It is a pretty place in itself, with a wild rolling country and wooded hills as a back ground, but like so many places in the West, its days of life and prosperity are over, the mining interest being in the hands of a few Chinamen, who " pan out" about a dollar a day.

We dined excellently well at Callison's, a tidy house, kept by a Pennsylvania woman who has lived in Mariposa for eighteen years; she amused us very much by her candid style of conversation, and in especial by her persistent inquiries as to which lady was the wife of the chief of our party, hazarding various ludicrous guesses, and coming to the right one last of all. Having established the identity, she warmly grasped both hands and shook them heartily, exclaiming:

" Well, now, is this really Mrs. L.! I've read lots of your writings, and there's nobody I wanted to see so much as you and Theodore Tilton!" But why this remarkable collocation she did not explain nor we inquire.

The rain was over, but the sky was dark and lowering as we set forth for the long stretch of our last stage, including the ascent of the Sierras, and descent to Big

Tree Station, where we were to pass the night. The road lay along the bed of the old Fremont lead, filled with broken rocks, washed bare by placer mining, and the soil seamed with little trenches for leading the water in every direction.

A ruined bridge once spanning the gulley, and an abandoned flume running along one of the steep banks, gave the place a wild and picturesque interest, culminating at Mormon Bar, where we turned off from the old " lead," and passing the row of tottering cabins, crowding and elbowing each other along the gulley, took the winding up-hill track, which brought us presently into a pine forest, through which we wound, catching occasional glimpses of the Merced Valley behind us, vast, desolate, and wild, while before us lay the level crest-line of the Sierras, dark, gloomy, and snow-clad.

About three o'clock the rain came down again in a cold drizzle, then in a steady pour, beneath which the picturesque was forgotten, the front seat abandoned, umbrellas went up and w aps went on, and every one devoted him or herself to the futile effort of keeping either dry or warm.

The road grew slippery and painful for the animals, and finally, when at five o'clock we stopped to change horses at Cold-Spring Station, a settlement of two houses and a watering-trough, Hiram, our driver, suggested the expediency of spending the night there, representing that we were just at the foot of the ridge between us and Big Tree Station, and confessing himself very reluctant to undertake it after dark in this condition of the roads and the weather.

It was already dusk, the forward route looked dismal and forbidding, and a ruddy gleam of fire-light shot through the window of the little cabin, half posting-house, half grocery-shop, before whose open door we sat. The prospect of light, warmth, and rest, was too inviting to be resisted, and with one accord we dismounted from our dripping chariot, and entered the cabin *en masse*.

It consisted of only three rooms, the first and largest fitted up with a counter, and the flickering light from the fire glimmered upon raftered ceiling, unplastered walls, bare floor, two or three rickety chairs, and a table upon which stood a single dip candle. An open door revealed a little kitchen in which another fire was blazing. Over this door a shelf crammed with old newspapers testified to the literary tastes of the family, consisting of two women, two tiny boys, and a baby, now in arms, but whose permanent resting-place was a queer high-posted crib covered with mosquito-netting, and occupying a prominent place in the shop. On one side of the room some trunks were arranged for a settee, and on shelves behind the counter were piled the heterogeneous contents of a country grocer's shop. On the floor at one end lay a heap of bags of flour and salt, and on these poor little Follette took refuge from the damp and dirt of the floor, her depressed tail, an unerring thermometer of her spirits, and general meekness of appearance, eloquently testifying to her appreciation of the situation.

We clustered around the fire, drying ourselves and our

garments as best we might, the ladies alternately occupying the three chairs, while the gentlemen assisted at the
driver's survey of the weather, the road, and the possibili-
ties of the future.   The report was unfavorable, Hiram
averring that the storm was increasing, the darkness
deepening, and the narrow road-bed would be washed
into impassable gullies before midnight.   Under these circumstances there seemed to be no choice, and the mistress
of the house being called to council, concluded, with the
aid of Minerva, her "help," that she could both lodge
and feed us, "after a fashion."   The fashion proved a
new one, if not likely to become a favorite one.

The house boasted three beds. One of these the
hostess, with Minerva and her baby, reserved for herself.
The second, a trundle bed, was devoted to her own children and Senator Conover's little son, and the third she
placed at the disposal of her sixteen guests !

The women were hospitable and well-meaning, but
one found enough to do in supplying the fires with fuel,
and the baby was like the cherubims and seraphims who
"continually do cry," and required all the attention of
the mother, so that no preparations of any consequence
seemed likely or possible for the appeasing of the clamor-
ous hunger which asserted itself in every breast.

The forlornness of everything was beyond words, and
reminded me of a lifelike picture which in sympathetic
childhood excited my most poignant grief by its representa-
tion of poor Marie Antoinette, her children, and her lump
of a husband in the grocer's shop at Varennes, surrounded
by articles of commerce much like those we contemplated,

and by the rude and exultant family of the grocer and the municipal soldiery. True, that this being a republic, there were half-a-dozen queens instead of one, and true, that nobody was exultant or insolent ; but still—at this point of comparison my reverie was broken by the hostess, who, probably fancying from my dejected attitude and utter silence that I was the meekest of the party, thrust the baby into my arms, exclaiming : "Here, you hold bub, and I'll get a meal of victuals !"

The shock roused me, and I mentally rose to the occasion. What a pity that there was nobody to thrust a baby into Napoleon's arms at Waterloo ! He would have *invented* a victory.

Retreating a pace from the offered burden, I hastily replied : "No ; you hold the baby, and I will get the supper !" A derisive shout from those best acquainted with my abilities bespoke their appreciation, and even Follette whined feebly, as if resigning her hopes of sustenance ; but, nothing daunted, I sternly ordered her to remain quiet upon her briny couch, then dragging forth a table, spread some sort of cloth upon it, confiscated a quantity of delf displayed upon the shelves for sale, struck a hasty bargain for some canned oysters, sardines, and peaches, set the gentlemen to work in opening them, found a saucepan, and filling it with oysters, put it in charge of the Chief, of whom yachting experiences had made a tolerable cook, and made requisitions upon Minerva for butter, milk, and bread.

The staff of life proved but a broken reed in this instance, being small in quantity and largely compounded

10*

of pearl-ash, but the hostess produced a "kag" of crackers from under the counter, and some enterprising explorer wildly announced a "treasure trove"—not of our favorite Pomery Sec, it is true—but bottled ale and a jug of whiskey. With these materials and plenty of zealous, if not very experienced help, the commissary, as she was dubbed, soon produced a composite and harmless meal, which was presently eaten, amid much noise and mirth, after the fashion of the Israelitish Passover, all standing and ready for a journey, a mode selected not for traditional, but very practical reasons, it being impossible for sixteen persons, however affectionate, to sit, all at once, upon three chairs!

Empty bottles did service for candle-sticks, and the winter's supply of dips were merrily consumed by lighting every nook and corner of the dingy little place.

Supper over, some daring souls raised the question of sleeping accommodations, but, catching the blank and bewildered expression upon the faces of their less practical and more imaginative friends, dropped it for awhile, and while one little knot fell into vehement discussion of Tannhauser and Wagner generally, some of the rest strayed out into the kitchen to watch Minerva wash the dishes, an operation in which she was helped or hindered by a Mexican Indian called George. He knew very little English, and quite brightened up when our Cuban friend and myself spoke to him in Spanish, which was his vernacular; he had just come from Kansas, and was "staying along" with our hostess, an Englishwoman, who came here five years before, and engaged in mining interests and trade.

MAKING A NIGHT OF IT.   Page 227.

But at ten o'clock the question of repose could no longer be deferred, and the whole female intellect of the place being brought to bear, it was decided that three ladies should take the one bed recommended by the hostess, with the naïve remark that: "As only me and baby had slept there, it wouldn't be worth while to change the sheets!"

Hearing this, the three looked at each other, and then assuming a mien mingled of Joan of Arc, Iphigenia, and Charlotte Corday, they wrapped themselves in shawls and lay across the couch without disturbing its coverings. The pretty widow posed in a rocker tilted back, with her feet in another chair, and a blue and scarlet silken kerchief wound, gypsy fashion, around her waving golden locks, making a picture which I contemplated with great satisfaction by the flickering fire-light during a large portion of the night, for I had become so in love with the table I had laid for supper as to select it for my resting place, pillowing my head upon a bag of salt, which towards morning fell upon the bare floor with such a thud that I was sure it must be myself.

Two of the gentlemen stretched themselves upon the counter, one perched upon the trunks, several lay in a layer in a lair of straw upon the floor, and some youthful and enthusiastic spirits thought it fine to sit all night by the kitchen fire telling stories and asking melancholy conundrums.

The hostess and Minerva retired to their own little den, and as it was only divided from the shop by a shrunken board partition, we were edified by a loud al-

tercation as to the propriety of the latter's drinking any
more beer.

The rain fell in torrents, cold gusts of air blew shrilly
through the ill-jointed walls, the lock of the outer door
was broken, and we had heard horrible tales of a gang of
thieves and murderers pervading this vicinity.   These
items, combined with the peculiarity of *breathing*, not to
use a stronger term, of several members of the party,
thoroughly banished sleep from most of our eyes, that is,
of the weaker sex, for I believe it is conceded that a
tired man can sleep anywhere and anyhow.

The beau of the party occupied himself during a large
part of the night in keeping the fire alive, or we should
certainly all have frozen, and when in the early morning
the comfortless couches were abandoned, and the pallid,
sleepy, unkempt occupants looked the situation, themselves, and each other in the face, a more dejected party
of pleasure-seekers cannot be imagined; to divert our
misery we saw that the rain still fell in torrents, we felt
that the cold was biting, and we presumed that breakfast
was to consist of only the remains of last night's supper.

A small diversion to the gloom was caused by the
young lady of the party, who had hung some of her garments to dry beside the kitchen fire, and now found a
difficulty in collecting them, all finally were recovered,
however, except a basque, of which no account could be
obtained until a susceptible and romantic widower of the
party emerged from the straw with it gracefully draped
about his head to protect it from the draught inhabiting
his corner.   He acknowledged that the sleeves, with their

pendant cuffs, buttons, and pins, had rather disturbed his slumbers, and plaintively remarked that he didn't know how a crown would feel as a night-cap, but he could now testify from experience that "weary rests the head that wears "—a woman's basque waist.

I found myself far too dejected to offer any help in getting breakfast, and was in fact so crushed that I think if the hostess had insisted upon my holding the baby she would now have found a submissive and passive victim. With matters in this condition we were startled by the abrupt entrance of several men of rough exterior, but whom we presumed to be " to the manner born," by the directness with which they made for the whiskey jug hidden beneath the counter. They were in fact members of the family detained from home by the storm and now returning with materials for a savory breakfast, upon which we at once pounced, they sitting by while we consumed it, and entertaining us with a little history of their estate or rancho.

It was formerly owned, it seems, by a party called A., who gave a piece of his land to his friend C., who built a cabin upon it, but subsequently went farther up the hills, seized upon another piece of A.'s land and built another cabin. A. considering this an abuse of good-nature, tried to turn him out, but unsuccessfully, and the quarrel became so bitter that A. swore to have C.'s life. One night both men were drinking in the bar-room of A.'s rancho— the very room where we then sat at breakfast—and the quarrel running very high, when A. got up and went behind the counter for something; C., supposing that it was a pistol, and following in blind fury, stabbed him to the heart. C. was arrested and sent to the Penitentiary for two years, and when liberated did not return to this neighborhood; his widow still lives in the other house of the settlement.

This cheerful tale did not lessen our willingness to leave the locality, and about eight o'clock, as the rain had ceased for awhile, the stage-wagons were got out, and after paying for our accommodations a price sufficient to hire an Italian palace for a year, we embarked and began our five-mile ascent of the Sierras. It was slow and dismal work, and the poor horses evidently did not see the sense of it, but we got on, and by and by met two return stages, whose drivers reported three feet of snow higher up. We soon came upon wreaths and little drifts of it beside the road, and a fine drizzling rain again beset us.

In spite of all, however, we could not but enjoy the scenery, the great sugar-pines with their monstrous cones, occasional red-woods, and gaunt shapes of great trees, with their hearts burned out by the Indians, or herdsmen, or bush-burners. Over everything, dead and decayed, the yellow Yosemite moss began to appear, creeping in parallel lines up the trunks of the trees, and clothing the dry branches with a sunset glow. We passed the cabins of the Chinese road-menders, and some ruined huts forlornly picturesque, and once we saw an Indian, wrapped in his blanket, gliding between the ranks of black-green pines and never deigning to turn his head towards us.

The snow grew deeper, the cold was intense, the rain heavier, and the romance of travel less and less perceptible in spite of occasional glimpses of valley scenery behind, and the summits of frowning Sierras piercing the clouds in front.　About noon we crossed the summit, and began to make better time upon the downward course, striking the Merced River, a clear, foaming stream rushing through a channel reminding one of the granite beds of the New Hampshire streams.　A mile from Big Tree Station we crossed a covered bridge, whose rattling echoes, as a team crosses, can be plainly heard in the settlement, and finally about two o'clock drove up to the Big Tree Hotel and joyfully dismounted.

EN ROUTE FOR THE YOSEMITE.　Page 219.

CHAPTER XXVI.

THE YOSEMITE VALLEY.

THE hotel at Big Tree Station is a building of the composite, or rather, detached style of architecture, the parlors and dining-room occupying one building and the bed-rooms others at some little distance—a matter of importance in such a rain as welcomed us to our resting-place. There were some straggling barns, corrals, etc., with a background of tall slender pines merging into the dense mountain forest behind.

It rained incessantly all the afternoon, so that we deferred our visit to the Big Trees until our return, and contented ourselves with sitting on the piazza and watching the Mexican herdsmen, in their big blue army cloaks and picturesque sombreros, and the Indians in ragged shirts and pantaloons, with their shaggy hair falling over their faces and shoulders.

A flock of four thousand sheep were driven into a corral near the stables that afternoon to be separated according to their brands, and sent out in several directions. Among the lookers-on was a fine, handsome old Mexican, who officiates as bootblack at the hotel, reminding one of King Alfred and the oat-cakes, although Esteban does not forget his work in dreams of former grandeur, but blacks shoes as if Montezuma had never been his ancestor. We

A Peripatetic Cobbler.

talked Spanish to him while he was being sketched, and were amused at his persisting in addressing me as Señorita, even while removing Mr. L.'s boots from my chamber door.

At half-past six next morning we started for the valley, driving along the south fork of the Merced up a steep and narrow road, winding almost as much as that at the Geysers, with a magnificent sweep of mountain-side opposite, at least two thousand feet in height, and clothed thick with pines crowding down to the brink of the little green brawling river below. At Lookout Point the road makes a sharp narrow curve, and there is a magnificent view down the cañon and the valley beyond to where the crowding peaks of the Sierras fade away into the pale blue horizon.

Flocks of sheep dot the landscape here and there, and the woods are full of deer, wild-cats, California lions, and grizzly bears, one of which appeared in the road a few days before our visit, and frightened the horses half to death. It grew cloudy and cold just before we reached the valley, and we were afraid the views would be obscured. We were still discussing our fears and hopes, and had no idea that their end was at hand, when a flash of snowy white struck through the trees, and then a sudden curve of the road showed us a great white gleaming wall reaching to the clouds—a mountain of ivory, as it looked, with a streak of bright water flashing down at the side.

It was El Capitan, the King of the Valley, the monarch for whose sake it would be worth while to make the long journey, if there were nothing else to see. El Capitan is not a peak or a summit, hardly to be called a mountain, but rather, as we have called it, a wall, two miles in length, 3,300 feet in height, white as ivory and of a grandeur, majesty, and power of expression inconceivable to one who has not seen and felt its influence.

As we first saw it with the clouds resting upon its summit, and a great patch of sunlight lying across its seamless front, it impressed us even more than Mont Blanc or many another more elevated and famous mountain. Winding round Inspiration Point we came in view of the whole valley, the pale silvery gray mountains ranging away at either hand from the great white king. We looked, drew breath, and gave vent with such powers as God had given us to the wonder, delight, admiration, and awe which all persons, I believe, experience in first beholding this marvel of nature. But who ever could put such emotions into words that conveyed them to any other mind?

To know the Yosemite, to see El Capitan, to get a picture into your mind which will be a lifelong delight to yourself, but utterly "not transferable," you must do just what we did, go yourself and bring it away. Leaving Inspiration Point, both literally and metaphorically there, we wound round the sharpest of curves, down the cañon into the valley. In reaching the bottom it seemed as if we had left the surface of the earth, and entered a mere crevice of its granitic foundations, a fissure in the great chaos of everlasting rocks; and the towering peaks and overhanging crags seem marching down upon one, and pressing and crowding one in, until it seems almost a struggle to breathe.

Literally the valley is so deep that in winter the sun rises after ten in the morning and sets about three, and yet several families live here the year round. The forms of the various summits are varied and majestic, their height varying from one to six thousand feet, but after all it seemed to us that the variety and wondrous beauty of coloring is even more marvellous than the form, height, or grandeur of the scene. From El Capitan's creamy, ivory whiteness the rocks deepen through every shade of pearl, smoke, and gray tints to great black patches here and there frescoed upon the silvery gray granite, and the masses of dusky oaks and dense green pines that cling to the face of the range.

Next to El Capitan, we were most impressed, as we drove on through the valley, with the South Dome, or, as the Indians called it, Tis-oa-ack, the Goddess of the Valley, a great shining silvery dome, as perfect as if one cut a globe through with a knife. A little patch of snow rested upon its summit and glittered in the sunshine, and at its edge one tiny shrub, as it looked, which our guide told us was a pine tree of goodly size, as seen through a telescope, for no one has as yet been able to reach the summit of this mountain, the dome itself being tiled as it were with great, smooth, overlapping slabs of granite, curving at an angle of about sixty degrees, and impossible of passage to any natural appliances except wings. No doubt the craving curiosity and love of dominion inherent in man will impel somebody before long to drag all sorts of tools and laborers up the miles of precipice to the foot of this dome and construct some means of ascent, but for the present it lies beyond his grasp, and, if we had our way, should never be invaded.

We drove five miles down the valley beside the clear waters of the Merced, rippling over their bed of silvery pebbles, past Black's Hotel and the Cosmopolitan bath-houses, to the Yosemite House, constructed like the Big Tree Station Hotel, in detached buildings—dining-room and kitchen offices in one, bed-rooms in several others, and the parlor over the way from all. Opening from the parlor is a room built round the trunk of a huge oak tree, and embellished with a great open fire-place built of stones rudely fitted together and whitewashed. A big fire was blazing here, but the room was a most distracting place to me, as it was impossible either to feel one's self either in the house or out of doors in it, and one could never tell whether to sit down in slippers with a book beside the fire, or don one's hat and take a walk beneath the tree.

After dinner, and about sunset, we started to walk to the foot of the Yosemite Falls, just behind the hotel. It is a pleasant stroll over a green field or two, and crossing upon a little bridge over the Merced River, whose bright waters enter the valley by a plunge over its rocky wall in the Vernal and Nevada Falls. The foot of the fall is en- cumbered with great boulders and masses of rock and fallen trees ; but scrambling among them as best we might, we approached the great wonder through clouds of driving mist and spray that would soon wet one to the skin.

The highest of the falls is 2,600 feet, and Niagara is 163, and yet the two are kin in the sensations of slowly gathering delight and awe that they evoke. It was but a glimpse that we could take, for dusk was already upon us, and after a few moments of silent admiration we turned our backs, resolving to perfect our acquaintance on the morrow.

Descending from our seventh heaven of romance and delight, we sought our sleeping-rooms, and found the accommodations of the most primitive description—the chambers small, sparsely furnished, and with but a single window, and door opening upon the piazza, the former provided with no shade but a wooden one, quite effectual in shielding one from the world's rude gaze, but also effectual in excluding all light. The struggle to dress under these adverse circumstances was rather a severe one, but at a very respectable hour in the morning the party assembled in the parlor-house, adjourned to the dining-room house, and after breakfast separated, some to pay a second visit to the Yosemite Falls, some to sit placidly upon the piazza and contemplate them from that point, from whence, indeed, one gains an admirable view.

Some of the party, however, found energy to set off on horseback, under the charge of two guides, to ascend Glacier Point and obtain one of the wildest and most impressive views of the whole valley. One of the guides was the owner of the trail, and the other, in consequence of being snowed up over night in the Sierras, had totally and permanently lost his voice, and conversed altogether in a hoarse whisper. The Merced was crossed over a tall bridge, and after this the steep, zigzag trail was soon struck out along the face of the precipice, and just wide enough for a horse to pass. At some points the curves are really frightful, and the horse in rounding them seems to hang on by his feet, his body overhanging the precipice. The beasts utterly ignore any attempt at guidance, and pursue their course with a calm confidence and phlegm which is, after all, their riders' best guarantee of safety.

The Yosemite Falls is always in sight, and El Capitan dominated the valley as usual. The trail grew steeper and more terrific, and after a time, by suggestion, most of the party dismounted, making the rest of the way on foot, the guides leading the horses. The path wound and doubled, always ascending for about a quarter of a mile, then led through pine-woods for a space, and finally ended upon Glacier Point itself, a rocky summit, 6,000 feet above the sea level.

A little foot-trail through the chaparral led to a smooth over-hanging rock, and here, for those who have the nerve to stand, or the moral courage to creep on hands and knees, lies the Mecca of their morning's pilgrimage. Again words fail to give any idea of the view to be gained from this eyrie, the more especially as all painters, photographers, and draughtsmen fail in giving the idea of profound depths uncontrasted with heights, and here all is depth, except, to be sure, the crests of the Sierras upon the horizon, and the splendid South Dome, North Dome, Cloud's Rest, Cap of Liberty, Mount Star King, and the other summits, whose level, or near it, has been attained ; but below are to be seen great trees two hundred feet in height, dwarfed to shrubs, houses like peas, a bright speck like a diamond, which is Mirror Lake, a thread, which is the Merced River, and small checker-board squares of verdure, which are the orchards and gardens of Lamar's and Hutching's claims.

Opposite lay the Mountain of the Royal Arches, or as the Indians more significantly called it, To-coy-ae, the Baby-Basket-Shade, for the silvery-gray face of the rock is cut in regular sweeping curves, just like the top of a Piute baby-basket. A little house has just been completed here, where one may dine, or, if one chooses, spend the night. An additional climb, on horseback, of a thousand feet brings one to Sentinel Dome ; this is the hardest part of the ride, as there is hardly any trail, but the horses pick their way, in some places very steep, among the stones strewing the dome-like summit, until a circle is reached of deep snow, and a gnarled and twisted old tree which marks the crest.

The view here takes in the entire valley from El Capitan to Vernal Falls, with South Dome, and Star King, and Cloud's Rest, and all the great still peaks, upon whose eternal silence and seclusion it seems so impertinent for chattering, staring, lunch-eating humanity to intrude. From here also is to be had the real idea of the formation of the valley, and it may be seen that it is not a level shut in by mountains rising on either hand, but a cleft in the immense plateau of the Sierras, and one may look down and down into its blue depths as one would look into the centre of the earth were it to open at one's feet.

The guide rolled an immense rock down the steep

incline, and it was fourteen seconds before a low tinkling sound told that it had struck below.

Mirror Lake is about three miles from the hotel, and the pictures impressed on its placid surface are best to be seen in the early morning. On its one side rises South Dome, and on the other Washington Column and North Dome, and the little lake is all shut in by the great chiselled walls of stone, carved as richly as any cathedral, Gothic or Norman, or as the old rock temples of the Egyptian kings.

Some great white scars upon North Dome, we were told, were caused by avalanches, or slides of rock, which take place almost every winter, under the influence of frost and sun and melting snows. But perhaps as fine a sight as Mirror Lake is to be found by following the Merced River down the valley until one reaches the pool it forms at the feet of El Capitan, and as one gazes upon the picture of the great monarch, it seems the grandest shadow of this world of shades.

But to catalogue the sights and wonders of the Yosemite Valley would be at once a thankless and unsatisfactory task ; each pair of eyes must see, each heart must open to receive, each memory must reproduce for itself the marvel of the great mountains, the bright, brilliant beauty of the falls, the loveliness of coloring, the unique charm and fascination of the whole. What use, for instance, to say that the Bridal Veil Cataract is six hundred and thirty feet in height? Does that fact give an idea of its undulating, gauzy, and ever-varying folds of most impalpable vapor and mist, now condensing into water, now etherealized into clouds? Or how can one, in words, convey an idea of the marvel and the delight to be gathered in a whole day devoted to the Nevada and Vernal Falls, whose foaming and rushing majesty of waters deign at last to be gathered into the rock-bound channel of the Merced River, scarcely ten feet in width in most places.

This excursion first, on horseback if you choose, or on foot if you are wise and physically strong, to the top of Vernal falls, and after dining and resting, still higher to the top of the Nevada Falls, is perhaps the finest of all that can be made in the Yosemite, although it seems basest ingratitude to rank anything lower than best, when all are so charming, and so far beyond the best of anywhere else, perhaps in the world. So, waiving all further attempts at description, we simply say, provide yourselves with good, plain, weather-proof clothes and boots; put money in your purse, and a cheerful and unexacting spirit in your temper, for the Yosemite is no paradise of creature comforts; arrange if you can a party large enough to fill a coach chartered for your private use, and then go your way, prepared to spend a week, if possible, in this wonderful place, whose remembrance will be a delight to you as long as you live.

An excursion we did not make, but what is said amply to repay the added fatigue, expense, and time, is the tour of the rim of the Valley. This can be made in four or five days, camping out at night with guides, tents, and animals to carry about those cumbersome appliances of civilization without which most of us find it so uncomfortable to exist for even a day.

11

CHAPTER XXVII.

THE MARIPOSA "BIG TREES."

WE left the valley about eleven o'clock one morning, looking our last, as we hurried past, at one object after another already grown familiar and beloved, and at Inspiration Point paused for one long, last, comprehensive gaze at everything from El Capitan to Vernal Falls, to gaze, to wipe the parting tear—and to lunch! Poor human nature, to whom crackers, sardines, and Pomery Sec. are still a necessity, let the South Dome glitter never so grandly, El Capitan look down serene and inscrutable as all Egypt, and the Bridal Veil float and glisten, and waver, as if it hid capricious Undine herself within its folds.

The day was hot and dusty, the reaction from intense delight and fatigue was upon us, everybody was silent and drowsy, and nothing appeared very cheerful until about sunset we came upon a herdsman's camp on Otter Creek, and saw the wild and picturesque-looking fellows lying or standing around their great fire, some merely posing, like Salvator Rosa's people, some preparing a supper of lamb, spitted for roasting, bread, ready kneaded for baking, and tin pots of coffee. Great flocks of sheep were grazing about, and all along the sides of the cañon fires had been kindled to keep away the panthers and bears which infest these woods.

The scene recalled an old German fairy story of the Charcoal Burners, in the Hartz Mountains, and one idly wondered if Rübezahl were not behind this or that great pine tree, ready to offer to some of us that wonderful bargain of all that this world holds, in exchange for what we hope in another, which some mortals would be so glad to make, if they had the chance, and some have already made, and some are sure they would never make, simply because they have never had the chance of making it.

About seven we reached Big Tree Station, dined, and wandered about in search of our detached bed-rooms, and then passed a pleasant evening beside the huge, blazing wood-fire in the cheerful parlor, listening to the diverse accounts and impressions of those who had made the journey to *the* trees which we were to visit on the morrow.

Directly after breakfast next morning the horses were selected and the party started for the excursion to the Big Tree Grove. The trail was an easy and safe one, winding along the hill-sides without sharp turns, but always rising through pine-woods for about five miles. The sugar-pines in this region grow to an enormous size, and happily but few of them have been burned, an operation which has nearly ruined the beauty of many fine tracts of woodland here. The dog-wood also grows into quite tall trees, and bears a larger flower than we ever see at the East. The party was followed part of the way by two Indians going out to fish, and we must say, with all deference to Mr. Cooper, that the "noble savage" is generally a very disgusting animal.

The first view of the Sequoias is rather disappointing; they are huge trees, no doubt, but so much has been said and written of them, and one's ideas become so romantically and vaguely raised, that probably no reality could have satisfied them; besides, we had already seen the Sonoma red-wood grove, and a first love, if not so worthy as the subsequent ones, is always *the first;* nor is the average (female) mind mathematical enough to admire the works of nature in exact ratio with their size, a very big tree usually exciting as much satisfaction as one a little bigger.

A stop was made beside the Fallen Monarch, lying two hundred feet or more along the ground, its white and polished sides completely stripped of bark to where the branches began, and above that thatched with slippery, shaggy, red scales. The bark of these trees is one of their most noticeable features, reaching sometimes the thickness of two feet, and averaging one foot; it is of a beautiful, light bronzed-brown color, and gnarled and twisted into the most fantastic curves and shapes.

Climbing a ladder leaned against this poor fallen monarch's side, one promenades up and down the trunk as in a dancing-hall, reminding one of the Liliputians swarming over prostrate Gulliver, until finally all wended their way to the Grizzly Giant, the next memorable tree. It is certainly a monstrous vegetable, measuring ninety-two feet in circumference, or thirty feet in diameter at

ASCENDING THE "FALLEN MONARCH." Page 244.

the ground, and throwing out great knotted claws of roots by which to grasp the soil. It has been sadly injured by fire, one side being quite burned away, and the height, altogether immense, seems disproportionate to the girth, the top, as with most of the Sequoias, being flat and unsymmetrical, as if they had been "headed in," and never recovered from it.

The Grizzly Giant is evidently immensely old, but the *savants* have not yet agreed if each ring signifies a year or only a few months' growth, and thus leaving one uncertain whether respectfully and with some degree of practicalness to imagine the Grizzly gaily flaunting its first suit of glossy leaves about the time when Alfred toasted the oak-cakes, or wildly to plunge back about ten thousand years into the dimmest sort of past, being some two or three thousand years before creation, if one is to follow the Biblical theory. At any rate, however, the poor old fellow will never see another thousand years, and as he stands there among the pines and dog-woods, which respectfully fall back to give him room, one feels the sort of awe and pity with which the Philistines may have regarded blind Samson, brought forth to make mirth for them.

Another mile very steep and rather tiring, and the main or upper grove was reached, where lunch awaited the party, and this being disposed of, it was found by wandering about that *the trees* are scattered around among sugar-pines, whose great cones strew the ground.

At the upper end of the grove lies Pluto's Chimney, a great tree burnt out black and smooth inside, with a flake of snow lodged in the gloomy tunnel. The horses were ridden through, the human heads bending a trifle on passing out at the upper end. A great burnt stump at the north side of the grove is said to indicate a tree larger than any now standing, but cannot be called, in its present state, a "thing of beauty," or "a joy forever."

The trees here are more in number and average larger in size than at the Calaveras Grove, but are not so tall. About five hundred years are required to bring a Sequoia to maturity, a fact militating against one's natural desire to carry home slips and seeds, and raise them, in mignonette boxes on one's window-sill!

A great deal of the pleasure of visiting these groves is destroyed by the ravages of fire, which has devastated them at different times, destroying many trees entirely, ruining the shape of others, and giving a general look of forlornness and smirch to the whole scene. Still, no one who can do so should omit to visit them, as they are certainly among the unique and marvellous works of Nature, of which California is justly proud.

CUTTING DOWN ONE OF THE BIG TREES.

CHAPTER XXVIII.

THE QUEEN OF THE ANGELS.

THE tedium of our return drive to Merced was en-
livened, apart from the internal resources of the
party, by the sight of several immense droves of sheep, and
one herd of the prettiest little white kids, capering about
among the chaparral so gracefully, that one profanely
wondered, if it might not be better, after all, to rank
as goat rather than sheep; after this came dinner at
Mariposa, and beyond Mariposa were some Chinese placer-
miners hard at work with shovel and pan; then we were
diverted by the struggles of some sheep in one of the
high bush fences, used to enclose them in this quarter,
and finally on the Merced Plains the series of entertainments concluded with a driving rain-storm accompanied
by a high warm wind.

Although disagreeable to us, the rain seemed to bring
delight to those residing in this locality, for the drought
had been so continued and severe that the sheep were
unable to find nourishment, and their owners were selling them at a couple of dollars each. All of a sudden
the storm cleared, the jack-rabbits and squirrels came out
in crowds to give us good-day, while at the mouth of
almost every burrow sat a solemn little gray owl, his
yellow eyes blinking in the sunshine which now broke

out. The great black thunder-clouds rolled off toward the north, the sky between them turned of a lovely turquoise blue, and we arrived at Merced in the full glory of a sunset brilliant enough to drive Turner mad.

We found the town excited over a fire which two nights before had burned down several blocks of warehouses, and everybody was on the alert to find the incendiary, who, being discovered, would, as Hiram, our driver, confidently averred, "tumble off a one-legged horse and break his neck, without troubling judge or jury."

Our hotel-car was to meet us at Merced, and did so, so that very night we settled down to the old life of sections and berths and the lullaby of iron wheels circling on iron rails, and felt that the homeward journey had begun, although our course was for the present southward.

The next day we passed over the famous Tehatchapi Loop, where the railway, after running through the Tehatchapi Mountain, loops around and crosses on itself by tunnel as the only possibility of getting over the tremendous grade between the two levels. The country now changed to a dry, desolate plain, dotted over with gray-green herbage-like sage-brush, and needle-palms with twisted branches studded with branches of sharp green spears. Nothing much drearier than this monotonous brown plain, shut in at the horizon by cone-like hills as bare and brown as itself, can be imagined, and it was a relief to arrive and get out for a few moments at Robber's Roost, a little beyond Mojave. It is named in honor of the famous robber, Vasquez, who had his principal stronghold here, and it was between this point and Santa Barbara that he was captured two or three years ago.

The principal feature of the place at present is a man-ufactory where paper is made from the fibrous wood of the needle-palm, which is cut into sections four inches thick, macerated in water, and afterwards treated precisely like other material. The result is a fine white and also a coarse light brown paper, both of them very satisfactory.

The rest of the way to Los Angeles was through the same arid plain and among broken hills dotted with cactus and needle-palms, hot, smoking, and tropical looking. We had appointed to meet Mr. Baldwin, of San Francisco, at Los Angeles, and to visit his ranch; but as he was not at the station on our arrival, we left our belongings in the car, and sallied forth to view the town.

It was quite different from any we had yet seen, having a distinctly Spanish and semi-tropical air, and making us feel more decidedly than we yet had done, that we were away from home and almost in a foreign land. The shops were most of them open to the street, and in the fruiterers' stalls hung great bunches and branches of oranges with the leaves on, as if just plucked. Besides the oranges, lemons, bananas and grapes, peaches and apricots were offered in great abundance, and all of most tempting size and beauty. In fact, one felt more as if promenading the hall of an Agricultural Fair than a public street, and found it hard to believe that just such fruits, or others as fine, besides an abundance of flowers, may be plucked at Los Angeles every day in the year.

In fact, this place seems the long-sought paradise for
11*

invalids and sybarites, and no doubt if poor Ponce de Leon had only come hither instead of going to sultry, boggy Florida, he would have found the Fountain of Perpetual Youth flowing into the San Gabriel River!

The stories told of the salubrity, the charm, and the equability of the climate are marvellous, and one thing not yet mentioned completes the list of attractions. One need not pass four anxious weeks in every year in considering one's spring, summer, autumn, and winter clothes, since where the thermometer never varies more than forty degrees through the year, and when Major Truman says he never changed his bed-coverings from January to December, surely there need not be a total revolution of costume four times during that period. We commend this consideration to the sex with whose cares and anxieties we are best acquainted, while to their lords we will simply say, "There are millions in it;" for let nations rise and fall, Turk or Russian beat, hard or soft money win the day, oranges will still be eaten, lemons will still be drunken, and grapes will be pressed into wine as they have been since the days of Noë, and of raising all these things there is no end here in the heart of semi-tropical California, and the wily heathen stands ready to labor for you well and cheaply.

The city itself, El Pueblo de la Reina de los Angeles, to give its full name, is "of a certain age," that is to say, an age difficult to determine, having originated in 1781, when Felipe de Nieve, then Spanish Governor of California, issued from his quarters at the Mission of St. Gabriel, nine miles distant, an order of a settlement bear-

ing the name popularly contracted in California to
" Angeles."

The town thus founded consisted of twelve invalided
soldiers with their families, and the horses, oxen, sheep,
goats, asses, and hoes, provided for them by a paternal
government quite alive to the fact that men cannot pay
taxes without the means of earning money. The village
thus constituted vegetated mildly for fifty years or so, and
in 1836, after the dear old Padres had been so unkindly
disturbed from their sleepy picturesque prosperity, and
their orange groves and olive gardens sold for the benefit
of the Mexican Government, Los Angeles was made into a
city, so called, and became the capital of Alta California.

Still it consisted of only one crooked street of adobe
houses, with a mission church at one end, an alcalde's
office, and no disagreeable agitation or novelty to show
that the nineteenth century had gotten hold of it, although
passing with the rest of California into possession of the
United States at the close of the Mexican war, until the
discovery of gold, and the consequent invasion of California by men who, with their lives in their hands, freely
offered to barter them for riches, brought this garden of
the State into notice. Capitalists, laborers, speculators
came, saw, and settled. The sleepy street of adobe
houses was relegated to the condition of a suburb, and
an American city was added to it somewhat in the style
that San Francisco was added to the Mission Dolores.

Churches, school-houses, banks, manufactories, hotels,
and newspaper offices have sprung up, some of them to a surprising size, English is spoken generally, railways connect

the city with every point north, south, east, and west that
any one would wish to visit, and some, like Fort Yuma,
that no one wishes to visit; in fact, Los Angeles has,
within ten years, become a "live" American city, and
might in one sense date its existence from about that time,
although in another claiming a century's growth. At any
rate, like some other creatures of an uncertain age, Los
Angeles is more charming on acquaintance than at first
sight, and one well believes that residents become sincere-
ly attached to the quaint, mild-tempered, uneventful little
city, with its legends and lingering flavor of Spanish and
monastic dominion, its fruit and flowers, and sweet and
fragrant atmosphere.

Even on that first day we found ourselves well pleased,
as we strolled up the wide street beneath the awnings
spread from every shop, and looked in at the open stalls.
In one stood rows of great red jars for water-coolers, reminding one of Ali Baba and the forty thieves, and gay
stuffs for dresses and mantles and scarfs, such as these
half-tropical women love to wear.

Now and then we met a Mexican woman, the head
muffled in her mantilla, and the sun glaring on her yellow
skin, and plenty of Chinese, cool, sleek, and comfortable.
Near the Pico House we passed a Spanish hostelry of
some sort, with a shadowy green court-yard in front, a
piano playing within doors, and a brown señora with some
pretty children strolling under the trees. We stopped to
dine at a French café called the Commercial Restaurant,
built around two square courts, upon the larger of which
the dining-room opened, so that sitting at table we looked

out upon the wide, sunshiny extent with a gallery running around it, and some orange trees in odorous bloom. Opposite our windows were those of the kitchen, with the white-capped *chef* giving his orders within, and a group of Chinese and French servants obeying them.

The dinner was delicious, and the shade and rest refreshing, but in a little while all were ready for further explorations, and began with a photographer's rooms, in one corner of whose salon was a dentist's office curtained off, and we were curious to discover whether the period just before or just after the dental operations is considered by the Angelites most favorable to sitting for a picture.

Here also was a large reading-room, well supplied with books and periodicals. After glancing at these we continued our explorations, and presently found ourselves in a square of little one-story buildings, whose red and gilt door-plates would have betrayed the presence of our Mongolian guests, even without the blue-clad, cork-soled, umbrella-hatted, and cunning-eyed figures, standing or squatting around, and the oddly coiffed woman stooping to relight one of the joss-sticks at her door. There were a few Chinese shops, but too small and dirty to be attractive, and in fact one's taste becomes in Los Angeles too distinctively Spanish to care for other flavors, so we soon drove back to the older part of the town, to gaze admiringly at the long low white walls and flat tiled roofs of the adobe houses, and the picturesque figures of their inmates, and the glowing sunlight which only shines in Spanish countries, and all of which recalled the pleasant days of Peruvian memory.

CHAPTER XXIX.

BALDWIN'S RANCH OF SANTA ANITA.

RETURNING to the station, we met Mr. Baldwin, our kind San Franciscan friend, who had volunteered to meet us here at Los Angeles, and show us his ranch and orange groves, and we now found him awaiting us with a six-in-hand carriage and a buggy.

We started just as the great white moon rose above the hills, and soon were out upon the open plain, flying over the hard, dry sod, which rang like iron beneath the horses' hoofs; the air was warm and balmy, the moonlight brilliant, the rapid motion exhilarating, and the whole drive delightful, except perhaps the moment when the leaders of the six-horse team suddenly gave a plunge which snapped the harness connecting them with the rest, fortunately entirely, and galloped away into the distance, leaving their comrades very much astonished, their driver very much discomforted, and ourselves not a little startled. The horses were found next day, one with a broken leg which could only be cured with a rifle ball, and the other safe in the barn of a neighboring ranch, where he had taken refuge.

The twelve miles' drive was speedily accomplished, and suddenly rounding the corner of a great unfenced field of barley, we drove through Mr. Baldwin's orange orchard, whose merits were then only to be judged by olfactory evidence, and presently arrived at the house, an old Spanish ranch recently purchased by its present owner and retaining the name of Santa Anita.

Like most of this class of house, it is a long, low building, surrounded by a wide piazza, and completely buried in evergreens, tree-ferns and climbing vines. A great Chinese lantern hung in the piazza, and a pretty, demure little housekeeper, with Spanish eyes and an English tongue, stood ready to welcome us and take us to our rooms, all opening into each other and out upon the piazza—charming rooms, large, cool, and with deep window-seats in the two-feet thickness of the walls.

Directly after breakfast the next morning, we sallied forth to see the wine-houses and other features of the plantation. Passing through the garden just behind the house, and by the pretty little lake, we crossed a wide open space among prickly pears and mock-orange vines, with tarantula holes under foot, and the wonderfully beautiful San Gabriel Mountains rising in purple cones just beyond the arid brown plain, mountain and moor all shimmering in the tropical sunshine, which seemed to rain down upon our unaccustomed heads, so that we were glad to get inside the great, cool, shady wine-houses.

In the first were the huge vats where the grape pressing takes place; in the second, great tuns of wine, sherry, claret, and angelica, all of which were tapped and offered for our inspection; and in the third were stills for converting wines into brandies.

Coming out of the wine-houses we found the carriage

awaiting us, and drove to the stables to see Mr. Baldwin's racers. The road lay through hilly fields hedged with willow and pepper trees, the latter a very ornamental shrub, and past some Mexican huts, delightfully pictu-resque of aspect, being constructed wholly of thatch, with sail-cloth tents adjoining just high enough to stand up-right in; half-naked children frisked in and out of these burrows, and hordes of dogs rushed yelping after us. The men work upon the estate, and the women do nothing, un-less taking care of hordes of babes may be considered em-ployment; a little cluster of huts farther on was devoted to the Chinese laborers, whom Mr. Baldwin highly approves.

At the stables were rows of windows, through nearly every one of which a horse's head protruded in the most sociable manner, and every head handsome enough for a picture. In the centre of the stables is the head groom's sitting-room, cosy and bright, and hung round with pic-tures of famous horses, principally racers, diversified with a few actresses, a rack of whips and some bright spurs, while gray rugs and horse-clothing lay neatly folded on shelves or in boxes, and altogether the place looked quite a little paradise for a person of equine propensities. We were introduced to Grimstead, who was at the Saratoga races last year, and to several unnamed beauties with their grace-ful heads, delicate limbs, and coats shining like satin.

Leaving the stables, we drove to Sunny Slope, Mr. Rose's famous ranch, 1,200 acres in extent. We recrossed much of the dry brown plains we had traversed on the pre-vious night, startling the little ground-squirrels, who scur-ried to their burrows and disappeared at our approach.

The green mock-orange vines with their globes scattered far apart were the only green things to be seen, until we turned into Mr. Rose's grounds and found ourselves in a grove of orange trees, extending in every direction to an indefinite distance. The trees were tall, thick, and sturdy, laden with heavy golden fruit hiding beneath the glossy leaves, and enough blossoms to load the air with the perfume of a thousand weddings; the trees are planted in regular lines, each one in a shallow basin formed in the earth around its roots, and trenches running between every five trees, which at certain intervals are filled with water, which is carried to every tree.

Farther on was a grove of lemons, the trees not so pretty in shape or foliage as the oranges, but laden with perfectly enormous fruit; then there were rows of fig-trees, and clumps of olive with their masses of dusky foliage, and here and there banana trees, although this fruit seems not so much at home here as the fig, orange, olive, and lemon. The irrigating trenches pervade all these plantations, and everything looks green and flourishing.

From here we visited the Mile Ranch, owned by Col. Kewen, who coming to this part of the country more than fifteen years ago, found on the spot selected for his future abode the roofless walls of an old stone building, built a hundred and one years before, by the San Francisco monks of the Mission San Gabriel, as a grist-mill and granary. Only the walls remained, but they were five feet thick and flanked at each corner by heavy buttresses, adding both to the strength and picturesqueness of the building.

Colonel Kewen restored and improved and added to

this ruin with artistic taste and a generous hand, so that it stands to-day one of the loveliest homes in California, the gray and brown stones of the old ruin enclosing every comfort of a modern American home, and surrounded by a perfect wilderness of flowers and greenery.

No walls or fences limit the view, and the satisfied eye roams over masses of heliotrope six feet high, roses of every shade, banks of honeysuckle, lilies heavy with perfume, azaleas, passion-flowers and pomegranates all on fire, cactii and aloes, and some grand old willows sweeping the ground with their slender finger-tips.

But with all the beauty of its surroundings El Rancho del Molino is uninhabitable—being haunted, so the Spaniards will tell you, by the spirit of the mill, a legacy bequeathed by the old monks, who may have walled up some recreant nun or heretical priest in one of the great corner buttresses.

At any rate no Spaniard will live at the Rancho del Molino, although Colonel Kewen and his family manage to exist very pleasantly, the ghost not troubling them half so much as the still smouldering enmity in the breasts of the native Spanish population, who regard the Saxons as interlopers and fraudulent possessors of land that should be theirs, as it was their fathers'.

Mrs. K. told us that when she first came here the country was overrun by herds of wild cattle—a beast for every blade of grass, she said, and it was impossible for her to ride any distance without a guard of fifteen or twenty *vaqueros* with their lassoes to protect her.

CHAPTER XXX.

A VERY OLD WOMAN AND A VERY OLD CHURCH.

WHILE in San Francisco we had been shown the photograph of Eulalia Perrez, of Los Angeles—the oldest woman in the world—and now finding ourselves in the close vicinity we resolved on paying her a visit. Mr. Baldwin accordingly drove us to her house, a quaint old brown adobe structure, with a projecting roof sloping steeply from the centre, and two or three old wine-vats built against the walls.

We mounted to a piazza, where we were met by a very pretty and very typical Spanish girl, wearing a high comb and speaking English with a very charming accent.

She showed us into a sitting-room, and having sent to call the old lady, entertained us to the best of her ability, informing us that she was Señora Eulalia's great-grand-daughter, her grandmother, the youngest grandchild, being sixty-five years old; her own father is an American, named Michel White; her great-grandmother's age, she said was about 140, " but old as she is, she cannot speak a word of English," added she, with conscious pride in her own proficiency. She said the old lady was always cheerful and sweet-tempered, although growing a trifle childish.

Presently she went out and returned with her great-

grandmother upon her arm, a short, shrunken figure, dressed in a dark calico shirt and sacque, with a gray shawl and
gay carpet-slippers, her head queerly covered by a close-
fitting black merino hood with a white kerchief inside,
and no hair visible even upon the forehead; her skin was
almost dark as a mulatto's, and seamed with a million fine
wrinkles. Her eyes were shrunken to such a degree as to
give the impression of having disappeared altogether, leaving only two narrow loopholes, red as fire, and uncanny to
look upon, but she presently gave a proof that the power
of discriminating sight remained, for after having talked
with me for some time she inquired if I were married,
and being answered in the affirmative, demanded to *which*
of the gentlemen present.

The Chief stood at the further end of the room, speaking with a friend in the party, and indicating him, I said,
"The gentleman with gray hair." "Yes," replied Eulalia
quickly, "but there are two gentlemen with gray hair,
which is yours?"

Then surveying first the one, and then the other, she
exclaimed rather impatiently, "Well, I should not think
you need have married a man with white hair," and
added some comments upon my appearance, which
showed that at least her sight was perfect, whatever may
be thought of her taste and judgment.

She seemed quite delighted at my speaking to her in
Spanish, and kept up the conversation in an eager and
animated manner, and with a strength of voice and quick-
ness of hearing quite extraordinary, accompanying her
words with marked gesticulations.

THE OLDEST WOMAN IN THE WORLD. Page 259.

She wore a brown rosary about her neck, and on my referring to her being a good Catholic said, that by the crucifix she had learned the lesson of how to live, and she hoped how to die.

She had been married twice, and said that in her youth she had many lovers, but could not decide which of them to marry until the padre interfered and insisted that she must make a choice, which she accordingly did, but was left a widow, and again she made a selection, and one based on maturer judgment, and she had been even happier in her second nuptials than in her first.

When asked her age, she counted on her fingers ten, twenty, thirty, and so on, up to 140, and it is certain, and on record, that when the present church of the Mission of San Gabriel was built, in 1771, she was a married woman with three children.

She has three daughters and two sons alive, and grandchildren eighty years old, all settled around the mission, and she lives with all of them alternately, going to church regularly every Sunday.

Two years ago she executed a piece of fine embroidery for sale at a fair, and still uses her needle constantly. It was proposed to take her to the Centennial Exposition in Philadelphia, and she actually went as far as the cars, when some of her relatives, to whom she is a revenue, interfered, and brought her home again.

Perhaps it was as well, for she has never been in all her long life farther than eight miles from Loretto, her birthplace, and the fatigue and excitement would, no doubt, have been a risk.

By the time she had told all this, we feared that the dear old lady, who, by the way, was most exquisitely neat, might be tired, although she gave no signs of fatigue, and so rose to take our leave.

She appeared really sorry to have us go, and followed us quite out to the carriage, bidding the spokeswoman an especial good-by with a prettily-turned Spanish compliment, not only upon my appearance, but what she called my amiability in visiting and talking to, and cheering a poor old woman. Pressing my hand in a firm, almost virile manner, she gently uttered in sweet, pure Spanish the blessing which comes with such authority and sanctity from aged lips, and we parted with mutual regret.

As a suitable pendant to this visit, we drove to the old mission, in whose shelter Eulalia Perez was born, has lived, and will doubtless be buried. The church stands in a little purely Spanish settlement of adobe houses, some roofed with thatch, some with fluted red tiles, bound together with thongs of raw hide. Some little shops hung out Spanish signs, but everything was old and falling to decay, except the chocolate-colored children, the dirtiest and prettiest creatures imaginable, who swarmed in and out of the uneven doorways.

The church itself is old and crumbling to decay, with a sort of sunburned and weary look to it, as if the century of exposure to this fierce heat and the downfall of the padres had disheartened and demoralized it.

Not far distant lay the mission gardens, surrounded by an adobe wall, and from it stretched a long cactus hedge, planted by the old monks to define their possessions. On the outside wall of the church, high out of reach, are the empty niches of forgotten saints, and in a queer gable-like belfry hung, each in its own niche, the old bells, cast in Spain more than a century ago, for a church in the city of Mexico, and containing no small quantity of silver and gold, cast into the cauldron of seething metal by men, women, and children, whose fervent piety had been wrought to this pitch by the preaching of the Jesuits about to sail upon the mission, whence they had only returned to ask for aid. The bells were subsequently brought to San Gabriel, with great trouble and expense, on the backs of mules and oxen, the cost of transportation being a hide for each pound of metal.

The day of their arrival was made a great *fiesta* in the colony, the Indians coming from far and near with their offerings, and showing as much pride and delight in their church's new power and dignity as the padres themselves.

The old doors also, oaken and curiously clamped and embossed with iron, were brought from Spain, as were some of the pictures, and other altar ornaments, communion plate, etc.

The keys were brought and we went in, the interior was dusky and venerable, but poor; the windows were high up, small and dusty, the roof unornamented, the floor uneven and decaying; a few bare pews—a modern innovation—and some prie-dieux afforded accommodation for such worshippers as objected to the floor.

Upon the pillars near the door hung tin placards, whose rudely lettered English inscription called a blush of shame to my cheek, by its suggestion of what conduct on the part of my countrymen must have necessitated them; these were:

"Take off your hats," and "Behave yourself."

The walls were crumbling and cracked, with great red weather-stains, and the aspect of everything mournful and neglected.

Near the chancel were two confessionals, and one smiled to fancy the *chronique scandaleuse* their hundred years' experience would furnish, could the brown old gratings repeat the secrets whispered through them.

The altar had been in its day rich and handsome, with a great altar-piece in six compartments behind it, and six great wax candles upon it, besides plenty of flowers, vases, and silk and lace hangings. An adoring cherub in plaster knelt upon a pedestal at either end, and the chancel was decked in the usual style.

We next went to visit the old orchards, still well stocked with the fruits and vines the Sybaritish fathers brought to such perfection, but, like the church and the mission, going slowly and inevitably to decay.

An adobe hut with a red-tiled roof stood just inside, and as we entered, a Mexican woman, with bright blue eyes and a pleasant face, came out to meet us, followed by a padre, with a broad bland face, smoking a cigarette. Besides these, the hut seemed to contain an indefinite number of children, dogs, and fowls who swarmed in and out during our brief stay.

The padre was from old Spain, and his sixteen years' exile in California had reduced him to an apathetic condition, from which he found it hard to rouse himself. He seemed to take it for granted that I was a compatriot and daughter in the faith, addressing me as *hija* and making fatherly inquiries into, my temporal rather than spiritual concerns.

" Was I married? Yes. To a Spaniard? No, to an Anglo-Saxon. Well, perhaps I had done wisely; he had heard they were generally rich, and kind to their wives, and although they were not of the true faith—yes, perhaps it was as well on the whole."

Having thus satisfied his conscience and curiosity, the padre turned his attention to hospitality and led us round the orchard, followed by the Mexican woman with the lovely blue eyes, who made up for his apathetic reserve by the most amiable and chirrupy volubility imaginable, loading us with oranges and sweet lemons in abundance. The padre at parting plucking us each a branch of the latter, and an especially fine one for his new-found daughter.

After we were seated in the carriage the Mexican lady's husband came out bringing a sack of oranges for us, and waved off the silver offered to him with true Castilian scorn.

From the Mission we had a short drive back to Santa Anita, and arrived just in time for a hasty toilet before dinner, which was as sumptuous as it was cheerful and home-like. Indeed nothing could exceed the hospitality and kindness extended to our large party by the courteous master of Santa Anita; from the moment of our arrival, when he surrendered his own elegant apartment

12

to our use, to that of our parting in Los Angeles, there was no possible attention or courtesy that was not offered, and the two days passed beneath his roof are one of our pleasant reminiscences of California.

One seldom hears Mr. Baldwin's name spoken in the land of his adoption—for he is an Ohioan by birth—without the prefix of " Lucky," and certainly his story would show him to be one of those rare individuals whose touch converts everything into gold. Perhaps, however, in all such histories one may discern the foundations of " luck " in shrewdness, clear-sightedness, courage, a wise prudence alternating with a wise audacity, and a resolute will. All these qualities I fancied myself able to read in our host's penetrating eyes and reticent lips, and I think, knowing nothing of him or his career, I should have said, " There is a man who will have the oyster out of this world's shell, let it be closed never so resolutely against him ! "

But I would rather after all call him Tasteful than Lucky Baldwin ; for an inspection of his hotel, his theatre, and his ranch, must prove him to deserve this title even more distinctly than the other.

After dinner we strolled out for a walk, and straying up the hill, came upon the Chinese huts, outside of which the men were sitting eating bacon and rice with chopsticks. They were not so clean as those we had been accustomed to see, and the peculiar odor of the Oriental was more pronounced, but they all looked very jolly and comfortable.

Passing on we arrived at the Mexican cabins, and paused for a little conversation, the men speaking broken

English, but the women only Spanish. The huts are the queerest little burrows imaginable, compounded of mud thatch and sail-cloth, and hardly larger than a rabbit-hutch.

A stately woman, with a black mantilla wound round her head, invited us, with quite an air of condescension, to come in and sit down, and we accepted so far as to step inside the door and look around. In one corner of the mud floor some hens were peacefully burrowing, a small fire burned in a hole about the centre, the stars peeped through the ragged thatch, and in a dark corner was a dim horror which may have been a bed. The whole house was as large as a small chamber, and not high enough for a tall man to stand upright; but it was the home of a large family—father, mother, and children.

Outside another house stood its mistress, the prettiest possible Spanish girl with two little children, Juanito and Tomasita—the former a boy four years old, clothed upon with a filthy little shirt reaching to his waist, and opened from the throat, whence it was confined by a providential button. Tomasita was a thin, brown baby, wearing earrings and a white petticoat, and clinging to her mother's neck.

A great many dark-bearded, grinning men clustered around us as we stood here; but all polite and amiable as the Chinese themselves.

Returning we stopped at the little lake, literally in front of Mr. Baldwin's door, and we were rowed out in his pretty little boat upon its moonlit waters. The shores were lined with little coves in which the herons and cranes were rustling about, and a chorus of frogs came in like a hailstorm of castanets.

The next morning, as we sat upon the varanda, a fiery little mustang dashed up the avenue and his rider dismounted at the steps—a handsome man, picturesquely dressed in buckskin, wearing a sombrero, high boots, and great cruel spurs. This was Fragnani, the artist, who has been living for two years near the Mission, painting local pictures and making studies for future works.

He came to call upon the Chief, and invited us to stop upon our way to Los Angeles at his studio. The carriages came around and we set forth, Fragnani's fierce little horse cantering along beside us, sometimes dashing far ahead, and returning, and occasionally bucking and curveting as if to give scope for his rider's perfect horsemanship.

Our last sight of the Mission remains an indelible picture in the memory. The dry, arid plain with the cone-shaped purple Mission Hills closing the horizon, the lonely, antique church, still, silent and crumbling to decay, the mossy old orchard with its adobe wall, the single hedge of cactus, the cluster of little thatched and tiled huts, with two tall palms standing gaunt and dry in the fierce sunshine, a dark grove of orange trees beyond the village, and for all sign of life the artist spurring his diabolical little horse across the plain, or pausing to let us examine the saddle and big stirrups—flaps of stamped leather, and the head-stall, bridle, and whip all in one piece of braided and tasselled raw-hide.

On parting with us at Los Angeles, Mr. Fragnani presented me with a fine specimen of the horned-toad, peculiar to Southern California. They are said to become so tame as to answer to a name, and are certainly very economical pets, as they live entirely upon flies. Our toad, for whom a rat-trap was purchased as a domicile, bore the journey Northward admirably, the only young, unmarried lady of the party constituting herself the toad-godmother, and the gentlemen developing wonderful zeal and industry in catering for him; but soon after his arrival at his new home he sickened, declined the daintiest of flies, emaciated painfully, seemed to collapse, and finally became extinct.

A still more tragic fate awaited a pair of prairie dogs, which with much care and solicitude we brought home from their native heath. They are not pleasant pets, having sharp teeth which they use on the hand that feeds them whenever they get the chance, and exhaling a rank and acrid odor. They behaved like saints and martyrs upon the journey, however, eating grass, and never once breaking bounds; but no sooner were they placed upon the ground in Saratoga than they gnawed their way out of their wooden cage and were immediately pursued and killed by the gardener, who took them for another kind of pretty and odorous little beast.

From Mr. Fragnani's and the Mission San Gabriel we drove directly into town, and at the station bade good-by to Mr. Baldwin and the artist, and from thence took train for Santa Monica, the Long Branch of California.

CHAPTER XXXI.

SANTA MONICA.

THE railway between Los Angeles and Santa Monica is a new one, without connection, but has already, in its two years' existence, paid the cost of its construction. It is a pretty route, running along by the San Gabriel and Santa Monica mountains, straight down to the sea, where it ends in a pier nearly a mile long running out into the Pacific Ocean.

We passed through estates belonging to a Mexican widow, who is said to own more land than any woman in America. Buying land is very difficult here on account of the numerous claims in the old Spanish families, who make an infinitude of trouble among American settlers.

We reached Santa Monica about four o'clock. On the right stands the hotel—two large two-storied buildings, connected by covered piazzas, and containing, spacious, neat, and well-furnished rooms, similar to, and quite equal to the same class of accommodations in our best hotels at Long Branch. At a short distance is a pavilion containing fine bowling alleys, ball-room, rink for skating, etc.

No sooner had we reached the hotel then we left it again, and descending several flights of wooden steps—again reminding us of the famous New Jersey watering-place—made our way to the beach. These cliffs have the appearance of crumbling, brown earth, but in reality are composed of a very rocky sort of rock, as one member of our party discovered in attempting to run down a steep incline, striking his heel into what he supposed earth, and finding himself so repelled by the strong substance, that he was compelled to roll and pitch down any way, and arrived at the foot sorely bumped and bruised.

The beach is soft white sand, without pebbles or shells, but strewn with sea-weed of various colors and kinds. The sea was calm and blue as a sapphire, and the brown cliffs curved gracefully down to meet it, forming the little Bay of Santa Monica, certainly one of the very prettiest watering-places on any coast. We wandered up and down the beach until tea-time, and the younger and more romantic portion of the party returned to enjoy it by the light of the just risen full moon.

At the end of the long pier was a little house occupied by a very polite young man, who offered his spy-glass with which to see the buoys far out to sea, upon which the seals do love to congregate. After a little effort we were able to make out the restless buoys, and the writhing black creatures might have been seals or kelpies for anything we could determine.

Last year a very big seal climbed up the cliffs to the hotel, and tried to enter the parlor; he was driven back to the sea with some difficulty, and renewed the attempt on another night, leaving no doubt in any reasonable mind that he was the victim of enchantment, some Tannhauser of the sea, perhaps!

Next morning we drove out over some newly constructed roads, and some not constructed at all, but only staked out—for Santa Monica is essentially a new place—and after winding through thickets of chaparral and sumach, emerged in a little cañon between two mountains, and here, in a clearing, stood a new little wooden house, surrounded by rows of beehives, children, dogs, and a pet lamb. This was a famous bee-ranch, recently built by a celebrated bee-raiser, who had lately been obliged to leave his old ranch on account of its desertion by the bees, who are very capricious little creatures.

A dark, fresh-looking Mexican woman came out to show us the hives, among which we walked quite unharmed by the bees, although some of the more timid of the party accepted a queer transparent covering for the head and face by way of protection from their possible stings.

The hives are boxes, two-stories high, each box fitted up with frames in which the comb is made, and when filled with honey, the frames are taken out and placed in a machine, where they are whirled violently round and the honey thrown out by centrifugal force. We saw one hive of a small variety and of a bright yellow which are considered very choice. Among the hives stood barrels of water covered with thin coarse cloth, upon which the bees settle and draw the water through the meshes of the cloth. We saw no flowers growing near, and could not imagine upon what the bees subsisted, but was told that they will travel miles to find their favorite food.

Time pressing we did not visit any more of the bee-ranches, of which there is an infinite number in this vicinity, but drove back to the hotel and were soon on our return trip to Los Angeles, traveling in the private palace car belonging to Senator Jones, and which is a perfect little *bijou*.

Arrived at Los Angeles we re-embarked on our own car, and began our northward journey. We reached the Tehachape Pass about dusk, and had an admirable moonlight view of the wild mountain scenery through which the road curves and twists and doubles in a perfectly marvellous manner.

We reached Stockton, the old capital of California in her mining days, in time for breakfast, and as we were to remain about three hours, we took a carriage and drove about the place. It stands on a flat and sandy plain, and is itself flat and sandy and straggling, with wide streets paved in wood, and fewer handsome houses than in most California towns of its size; almost every house, however, possesses a croquet ground, with an awning over it, and a boarding about six inches high around it to keep the bales within bounds.

We also noticed a great profusion of clipped cedar, and arbor-vitæ trees, and in the suburbs we came across one of the prettiest public gardens we have seen anywhere, laid out with nicely gravelled walks, tall hedges of pinks and lavender, and great colored masses of brilliantly colored flowers. Trellises covered with passion flower, and other vines, were artfully placed to conceal the boundary walls, and there were tubs for watering fed by whirring windmills close by the little green-house where the plants are started.

Stockton is the location of the State Lunatic Asylum,
12*

which is one of the finest of this melancholy nature in the country.

Returning to our car, laden with fruits and flowers, we resumed our journey, and about four o'clock reached Sacramento, stopping at the Arcade House, a pleasant hotel with a homelike parlor hung with pictures, and not so stereotyped as most public sitting-rooms. We went out for a little walk, and explored all the principal streets, which are quite fine, and the one long Chinese shop as good as any we had previously seen. The houses are all low, on account of the often recurring "shakes," whose effect may be seen in many quarters. One corner of our hotel had settled considerably, and the window ledges were cracked and sunken in consequence of one of these shakes.

The custom of building iron braces into the walls is a very good safeguard against serious damage, however, and the Arcade is well protected in this manner.

At nine o'clock we were again in our car, and we passed Cape Horn and American Cañon, with all its magnificent scenery, in the dead hours of the night, waking to find California already become a memory, and our delightful sojourn there a thing of the past.

One last glimpse of its beauties was taken as we dashed past Donner Lake, a beautiful, still, oval sheet of water, bedded deep in the dark, steep hills; then we plunged into a snow-shed, and slid down the steeps of memory into a profound sleep, which made recollection once more reality.

Our next view of the outer world was at Carson, where

the train stopped for breakfast, and we took a cursory view of the new, bare, comfortless place, whose only attraction lay in the streams of bright water running through stone channels along the streets, and a fountain set in a little square of greenery close to the station.

Some Indians, dirty and squalid, were lounging about, and the squaws begged vociferously, as usual, while the men stood ready to share or monopolize the plunder.

There is a rise of 1,700 feet from Carson to Virginia City, whither we were bound, and the train winds heavily up between mountain walls of dust-brown rock, whereon grows neither tree, shrub, herb, nor blade of grass, nothing with life or motion in it, except the brawling Carson River, which plunges down between these mountains on even a steeper grade than the road winds up.

All along the hills were little burrowed holes, with heaps of powdery, gray earth beside them, where was, or had been a man prospecting for gold, and nearly all the country was marked out with stakes, showing the claims of the different miners or companies.

In a hollow by the river we passed a quartz mill, and saw what is called the "tailing" process going on, in which the refuse washings of the ore are passed over a stretched blanket, to which the particles of gold adhere and are saved.

The twistings, and curvings, and tunnellings, and climbings of the road grew more and more pronounced, until one looked at last for some such arrangement as that at Mount Washington, where the car wheels are fitted with cogs to grasp each inch of the rail, and the traveller feels more like a fly walking up a wall than a rational traveller upon a pleasure excursion.

The distance in a straight line from Carson to Virginia City is about fifteen miles, but by the windings of the road this is more than triplicated.

CUTTING BARK AND CONES AS MEMENTOES OF THE MARIPOSA GROVE.
Page 245.

CHAPTER XXXII.

VIRGINIA CITY AND THE BIG BONANZA.

TO call a place dreary, desolate, homeless, uncomfortable, and wicked is a good deal, but to call it
God-forsaken is a good deal more, and in a tolerably large
experience of this world's wonders, we never found a
place better deserving the title than Virginia City.

To commence with, the conditions of its being are
highly disagreeable, for it is a town hooked on, as it were,
to the precipitous side of a barren and rocky mountain,
and one is always apprehensive that the adhesive power
may become exhausted, and the whole place go sliding
down to the depths of the valley below.

The streets are mere narrow terraces built along the
face of this precipice, like the vineyards along the Rhine,
or the steps of the Pyramids, whose arid and dusty desolation they also imitate, without the grandeur and mys-
tery which make one forget the rest.

Leaving the station we climbed a steep and long flight
of wooden steps to the street above, where stood the hotel,
a very good one, by the way, and flanked by some substantial stone and brick buildings, but this block is the
exception in the way of architecture, the rule being frame
houses, as loosely and carelessly put together as a child's
card house. The style may be inferred perhaps from the

fact that about two years ago the whole town burned down one night, and was rebuilt as good as ever in six days.

Nowhere does one find a level, the streets are all parallel, with the exception of one, leading up the mountain from the depot, and standing in any of them, one looks off as if from a belfry, across the tops of the houses below, and over the chimneys of quartz mills and mining works still lower down, until vision loses itself among the crowding brown peaks and waving mountain ranges, never coming to any resting point of level or of greenery, before the horizon line closes the dreary scene.

The Prince of the Power of Air reigns supreme in this region, and the fierce cold wind sweeps through the narrow streets with force enough to take one off one's feet. Very little rain falls here, but plenty of snow, coming early and remaining late, indeed possible in any month of the year, and sometimes lying there three feet deep in May, in which jocund month we were there.

Virginia City boasts of forty-nine gambling saloons and one church, open the day we were there for a funeral, an event of frequent occurrence in the lawless little city. The population is largely masculine, very few women, except of the worst class, and as few children.

Chinese are rare, not being in favor with the miners, who have a horror of their cheap labor, and show their dislike in very vigorous fashion when the opportunity occurs.

The hotel has been running only a few months, but is very comfortable, with a pretty parlor and handsome dining-room, where we enjoyed one of the best breakfasts since leaving San Francisco. A carriage was in waiting as we came out of the dining hall and took us to the Bonanza Mines, zigzagging from one steep and narrow street to another, like a magnified Yosemite trail with all the attractiveness left out, until at length we dismounted at the great building over the shaft of the California or Bonanza Mine.

Here we were received by Mr. Taylor, the Superintendent, and one of the most courteous and attentive of men, who invited us first to his own charming bachelor apartments in the mill building, and then took us all over the works and showed us the entire process of this sort of gold and silver mining; first, the cages running night and day hauling up the masses of quartz rock, which the miners, far below, have picked and shovelled out of its natural bed; then the crushing of the quartz, and its agglomeration with water in the great vats, into a dingy lead-colored pudding; then the amalgam mixed with quicksilver pouring out into iron vessels, in which it is taken to the crucibles, the quicksilver eliminated, and recondensed for farther service, the residuum of metal—gold and silver ore—run into bars and stamped.

We saw machinery enough to drive one crazy, and were almost suffocated with its hot, oily smell and steam, besides being deafened by the stamping and banging and crashing of the quartz-crushing machines which keep that whole section of the building in a state of jar and quiver, like an impending earthquake.

In another portion of the edifice we saw the pumps

which are always at work taking the water out of the
mine, and looked down the shaft used by the miners, two
square black holes, close together, with a cloud of hot,
white steam always floating up from them, product of the
heat and damp below, and each provided with an elevator worked by broad bands of wrought and woven wire,
immensely strong.

Postponing any farther investigations until the morrow, we left the mills and drove about the city, seeing little
more, however, than has already been described, returned
to the hotel for dinner, and after a while strolled out to
see what changes might have been wrought by night and
moonlight.

The changes were noticeable but not beautifying, and
the two policemen, who followed close at our heels, were
by no means a guard of ceremony but a most necessary
protection.   Every other house was a drinking or gambling
saloon, and we passed a great many brilliantly lighted
windows, where sat audacious looking women who freely
chatted with passers-by or entertained guests within.

Cheyenne did not seem to us to deserve its mournful
sobriquet, and Virginia City equally did seem to deserve,
although it has not received it.

The next morning we walked to the assaying office, to
see the gold and silver taken from the crucibles in which
they are finally purified, and we subsequently returned to
the Bonanza or California Mine, the chief and some others
of the party having resolved to explore its depths.

This mine is principally owned by Messrs. Flood &
O'Brien, and Mr. Fair.   The two former kept a small

drinking saloon in San Francisco, and were on intimate terms with some of their miner customers, one of whom, waxing confidential and good-humored in his cups, informed them of a wonderful "lode" just discovered and not yet known. With wise audacity they sold all that they possessed and invested every cent in the quarter indicated, managed to get control of the whole mine, worked it wisely and fortunately, and to-day are said to be worth fifteen millions each.

Mr. Fair, although equally rich, resides on the spot, and passes three hours daily down in the mine, personally superintending its operations. The receipts for this mine during fifteen months, were $24,850,524.85—and for over a year it has divided a million monthly, with no signs of exhaustion.

Mr. Fair took us first to the large long room where the miners change their clothes, and which was hung closely all around from the roof with miners' shirts and trousers, while on a long frame down the middle of the place stood their big, heavy shoes or brogans.

The men are divided into gangs, each working eight hours, and each gang having its division of this room, and every man his own especial hook, where he keeps his mining suit not in wear, it being necessary to change thoroughly every time they come out of the mine.

The men are mostly Cornish—no Irish and no Chinese allowed. The owners would like to employ the latter, but the Miners' Union is too strong for them, dictating eight hours a day as the period for labor, wages of four dollars per diem, and no competition.

The miners embrace every class of men, socially speaking, from the lowest grade of laborer to the ex-United States Senator, or man of title, obliged to resort to manual labor, and too proud to perform it in open daylight, preferring to pass his existence in digging living graves 1,700 feet below the surface of the earth.

Returning to the shaft, we encountered a party of miners just dressed to go down, having changed their clothes in the little office near the mouth of the pit. They looked very wild and strange in their great solid hats, like roofs, stiff enough to protect the head from falling bits of rock, their uncouth clothes and great brogans, each man carrying a lantern in his hand.

Nine men crowd upon the elevator at once, and at a given signal go dashing down into the hot, white steam, disappearing in a moment, absolutely swallowed up in the earth. The place swarmed with miners waiting their turn to go down, the elevator making its trip in about fifteen minutes.

A set came up while we stood looking after those who had gone down the other shaft, and such a set of ghosts one never saw : pale, exhausted, dripping with water and perspiration, some with their shirts torn off and naked to the waist, all of them haggard and dazed with the long darkness and toil. The heat in the shaft is fearful, and although the galleries are cooler, it is still so warm that the men are obliged to work half naked, sometimes wholly so, and word is always sent down when ladies are about to visit the mine.

Presently the chief, with the " forlorn hope," who had

volunteered to accompany him underground, retired to the dressing-room, and soon returned so queerly metamorphosed that it was hard to recognize them, and various complimentary remarks and quizzical comparisons accompanied them as they somewhat gingerly stepped upon the elevator and began their descent.

A sudden thrill of vague horror, however, superseded all disposition to laughter as the car swiftly and suddenly took our friends from our very midst, leaving only the black shaft with its ghostly clouds of hot, white steam to show where they had been. It was too much like that other dark and mysterious pit into which most of us have watched our friends go down to return no more, and I for one turned away shuddering and afeard.

The party remained below two hours, and returned tired, excited, delighted, and loquacious, to find us comfortably settled in Mr. Taylor's room, dispelling our anxiety as best we might by selections from our host's numberless volumes of our favorite poets.

So soon as our friends had bathed—for the directors have a private bath and dressing-room, which had been placed at the disposal of our party—and resumed their usual attire, and we had bidden good-by to our courteous hosts of the Big Bonanza Mine, we returned to the hotel, dined, and then drove to our car in the midst of a drenching rain, almost an unknown phenomenon in Virginia City, and looked our last upon the bare, brown hills and the city in the air through vertical sheets of drifting waters.

CHAPTER XXXIII.

HOMEWARD BOUND.

AT Ogden we resumed our Pullman car and settled ourselves in most luxurious manner just in time for breakfast. The rain still fell, but less furiously, and finally departed just in time to allow us to enjoy the glories of Weber's Cañon.

At Green River we stopped for twenty minutes, and got out to see some newly-caught California lions, romping and snarling in their cages on the platform.

An editorial party from Nebraska were on board with a small press, on which they printed the daily journal of their travels. We went forward to return their visits, and in order to do so had to pass through two or three sleeping-cars closely packed, and an emigrant-car where, by the dull light, we could see the poor creatures curled and huddled up in heaps for the night, with no possibility of lying down comfortably; but men, women, bundles, baskets, and babies, in one promiscuous heap.

During the darkness of the night we recrossed the Rockies, missing all the magnificent scenery we had so enjoyed on the outward trip. We made a little reconnaissance of Cheyenne, but found it this time quite deserted; not a scout nor an emigrant to be seen.

There was a beautiful red sunset as we passed the buttes

THE CALIFORNIA OR MOUNTAIN LIONS AT GREEN RIVER STATION.

near Sydney, and dusk was just coming on as we stopped at the town. The conductor strongly advised against any exploration of this place, at least by the ladies, and so of course we all assumed our bonnets and started forth, visiting first the tent of a photographer who said that the town was unusually quiet just now, but that fights and murders were of common occurrence, and that the inhabitants thought nothing of shooting a man who happened to hold different opinions from themselves, emphasizing his remarks by pointing to the graveyard and declaring that " pretty near every man there died with his boots on!"

The next day and the next we travelled without stopping, passing through Omaha and Chicago, and on the following we reached Detroit, pausing for a day to look about the fine city and see our old friend Senator Chandler, who took us to drive behind his superb span of horses, and to visit his elegant yacht—a fine sea-going craft. We passed a portion of the evening at his magnificent and tasteful home, and the day following found ourselves back in Gotham—a couple of months older than when we left it for the Golden Gate, and years older and incalculably richer in novel and charming experiences and grateful memories of the hospitality and courtesy extended to us, and the new friends who had treated us as old friends, and had gained in our recollection a place which time will never obliterate,

As *l'envoi*, I can say no more and no less than this to all the dear public who year by year wander up and down the earth seeking and not always finding delight, and expending money, which by no means always brings its *pro quid* of enjoyment. To them, I say, Go West, my friends, Go West! Within the Golden Gate lies all that you desire. Go West!

THE END.

FAITHFUL FOLLETTE.

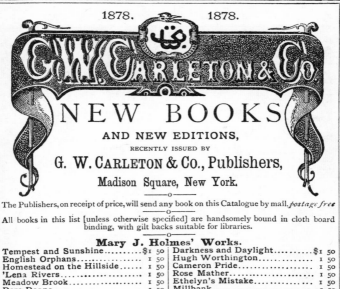

May Agnes Fleming's Novels.

Guy Earlscourt's Wife..........$1 75	A Wonderful Woman...........$1 75
A Terrible Secret................ 1 75	A Mad Marriage................. 1 75
Norine's Revenge............... 1 75	One Night's Mystery............ 1 75
Silent and True—(New)	Kate Danton................. 1 75

M. Michelet's Works.

Love (L'Amour)—Translation....$1 50 | Woman (La Femme)—Translation $1 50

Miriam Coles Harris.

Rutledge................... 1 50	The Sutherlands.............$1 50
Frank Warrington............ 1 50	St. Philip's................. 1 50
Louie's Last Term, etc.......... 1 50	Round Hearts, for Children 1 50
Richard Vandermarck 1 50	A Perfect Adonis—(New)......... 1 50

Italian Novels.

Dr. Antonio—By Ruffini........$1 50 | Beatrice Cenci—By Guerrazzi.....$1 50

Julie P. Smith's Novels.

Widow Goldsmith's Daughter..$1 75	The Widower..............$1 75
Chris and Otho................ 1 75	The Married Belle............. 1 75
Ten Old Maids................. 1 75	Courting and Farming.......... 1 75
His Young Wife—(New)........... 1 75	

Victor Hugo.

Les Miserables—In English......$2 50 | Les Miserables—In Spanish......$5 00

Captain Mayne Reid.

The Scalp Hunters $1 50	The White Chief.................$1 50
The Rifle Rangers 1 50	The Tiger Hunter.............. 1 50
The War Trail................. 1 50	The Hunter's Feast............. 1 50
The Wood Rangers............. 1 50	Wild Life 1 50
The Wild Huntress............. 1 50	Osceola, the Seminole.......... 1 50

Artemus Ward.

Complete Comic Writings—With Biography, Portrait, and 50 Illustrations....$2 00

A. S. Roe's Select Stories.

True to the Last.................$1 50	A Long Look Ahead $1 50
The Star and the Cloud......... 1 50	I've Been Thinking............. 1 50
How Could He Help It ?........ 1 50	To Love and to be Loved........ 1 50

Charles Dickens.

Child's History of England—Carleton's New "*School Edition*." Illustrated.$1 25

Paper Covers, 50 Cents—Cloth, $1.00.

Tom's Wife—By G. D. Tallman.......	Solomon Isaacs—By B. L. Farjeon....
That Comic Primer—By Frank Bellew.	That Horrid Girl...................
That Awful Boy......................	Me—July and August. By Mrs. S. C. Coe.
That Bridget of Ours................	He and I—Sarah B. Stebbins..........
Our Artist in Cuba, etc. G. W. Carleton.	Annals of a Baby— do..............
Why Wife and I Quarreled..........	That Charming Evening—Bellew.....

Mrs. Hill's Cook Book.

Mrs. A. P. Hill's New Southern Cookery Book, and domestic receipts........$2 00

Hand-Books of Society.

The Habits of Good Society—The nice points of taste and good manners.....$2 00	
The Art of Conversation—For those who wish to be agreeable talkers......... 1 50	
The Arts of Writing, Reading, and Speaking—For self-improvement....... 1 50	
New Diamond Edition—Small size, elegantly bound, 3 volumes in a box....... 3 00	

Carleton's Popular Quotations.

Carleton's New Hand-Book—Familiar quotations, with their authorship......$1 50

Famous Books—"Carleton's Edition."

Robinson Crusoe—Griset's Illus..$1 00	Don Quixote—Dore's Illus........$1 00
Arabian Nights—Demoraine Illus.. 1 00	Swiss Family Robinson—Marcel 1 00

Josh Billings.

His Complete Writings—With Biography, steel portrait, and 100 illustrations.$2 00	
Trump Cards—Illustrated..... ... 25	Farmer's Alminax—Illustrated.... 25